D0375410

DATE DUE

JOURNAL & LETTERS
OF PHILIP VICKERS FITHIAN

Journal & Letters of
Philip Vickers Fithian
1773-1774:
A Plantation Tutor of the
Old Dominion

EDITED, WITH AN INTRODUCTION, BY
HUNTER DICKINSON FARISH;
ILLUSTRATED BY FRITZ KREDEL

The University Press of Virginia
Charlottesville

Library of Congress Catalogue Card Number 57-13498

The University Press of Virginia
First printing for Dominion Books
October 1968

Fourth printing 1990

PRINTED IN THE UNITED STATES OF AMERICA

Preface

ONCE in a great while historians find a firsthand account that provides striking insight into a past era. Only rarely is such a document written with the perception and charm that make its readers feel as if they had participated in the incidents described and shared the experiences related. The journal and relevant correspondence of Philip Fithian constitute this kind of source.

Fithian was reared in New Jersey and attended the College of New Jersey in Princeton, receiving his degree in 1772. Before entering the Presbyterian ministry, he followed the advice of President Witherspoon of Princeton and became a tutor in the family of Robert Carter at "Nomini Hall" plantation on the Northern Neck of Virginia. The reactions of the somewhat austere young man to the rich, warm life of a Virginia plantation are always instructive and often amusing. The Carters and their seven children were a fascinating family, liberal in their sentiments and deeply interested in books and music. Fithian sets forth truthfully, yet with lively touches, the family's assessments of the society in which it moved, the institution of slavery, and the dispute developing with the mother country. Throughout his experiences Fithian remained true to his "fair Laura"—Elizabeth Beatty in far off New Jersey.

The journal, with certain of the letters, was first published in 1900, in somewhat abbreviated form, by the Princeton Historical Association. Dr. Hunter Dickinson Farish, in his edition of *The Journal and Letters of Philip Vickers Fithian* (Williamsburg Restoration Historical Studies, III; Williamsburg, Va., 1943), included the complete journal, added other relevant letters as well as Fithian's catalogue of Carter's library, and supplied a thoughtful Introduction.

Dr. Farish was Director of Research at Colonial Williamsburg from 1937 until ill health forced him to retire in 1944. He broadened the program there by bringing young research associates to the staff, making grants-in-aid to scholars in the field of early American history, and establishing and editing the Williamsburg Restoration Historical Series. He also taught at the College of William and Mary and helped to work out the organizational plans for the Institute of Early American History and Culture, which since 1943 has been jointly sponsored by Colonial Williamsburg and the College of William and Mary.

Dr. Farish's edition of the *Journal* had been out of print for a few years when, in 1957, Colonial Williamsburg reissued it, with pen and ink illustrations by Fritz Kredel designed to interest new readers. The present edition by the University Press of Virginia reproduces the 1957 one, but in convenient paperback form. Young Fithian's revealing picture of Virginia plantation life will always be a key source for the historian and an absorbing human document for the general reader.

EDWARD P. ALEXANDER
Director of Interpretation

Colonial Williamsburg
September 1967

Contents

CHAPTER ONE

Virginia During The Golden Age

IN the "Golden Age," or half-century immediately preceding
the American Revolution, a remarkable civilization reached its
zenith in the broad coastal plain of eastern Virginia. Gradually,
during a century of colonization and expansion, the heavily wooded
tidewater had been converted into a land of settled order and accu-
mulated wealth. Vast estates had been carved out of the wilderness
and large plantations were everywhere the rule.

Embraced by numerous arms of the Chesapeake and covered by
a network of wide rivers and creeks, this sylvan Venice abounded in
safe and convenient water routes. Pressing through the mouths of
the deep estuaries, the ocean tides reached the "fall-line," beyond
which the streams were inaccessible to shipping owing to the rapids.
Ocean vessels could penetrate to the plantations in every part of the
lowlands and carry cargoes thence straight to the wharves of London
and the outports. Despite the distance and rigors of the voyage, the
colonists of the Tidewater had maintained a constant intercourse
with the mother country from the time of their earliest settlement.

The hope had long persisted that this coastal plain might yield the
ores, timber, ship stores and other products England needed, and
for which she then largely depended on foreign potentates. Lacking
an ample supply of cheap labor, however, colonial industries could

not compete with well-established ones of the Old World. For well over a century tobacco proved the one commodity which the colony could profitably produce for the home market in large quantities.

A notable result of the method of tobacco cultivation was a rapid depletion of the soil. Intent only upon reaping quick returns, men customarily neglected the most ordinary precautions to preserve fertility. Since the tobacco plant required the richest loam to produce the leaf in its perfection, fields were usually abandoned after three or more crops had been harvested, and "new grounds" were cleared. Thus there developed an ever recurring need for fresh lands.

Under so wasteful a system, Virginians had soon realized the necessity of acquiring many times the quantity of land they could cultivate at any one time. Farseeing men, realizing a day would come when fertile soil could no longer be had for a song, wished also to provide sufficient elbow room for their children at a future day. The appreciation in land values in a new country provided a further incentive to the accumulation of large holdings. As a result, enterprising persons everywhere competed to secure the best tracts.

Towards the close of the seventeenth century the practice of engrossing lands gained increased momentum. African slavery was rapidly superseding white indentured servitude as the principal source of labor supply. The price of tobacco had steadily declined owing to overproduction, the burdens of the Navigation Acts, and the effects of European wars. As a result of these conditions, the margin of profit from the leaf had so decreased that the cheaper labor of slaves and large-scale production had now become virtually essential to economic survival. After he had served his indentureship, the white servant could no longer establish himself as an independent farmer as he had once done, and the small yeoman now usually felt obliged to sell his lands to his wealthier neighbor and either become his tenant or migrate to some other section or colony. Political developments likewise favored the accumulation of large estates. Through repeated intermarriage certain families had acquired a very extensive influence. Members of these families were active in the Governor's Council or the House of Burgesses and held other high offices as a matter of course. Their official position often aided them as private individuals in acquiring lands. Through the presentation of "head right" certificates, compensation for military services, purchase from private proprietors, and other ways they obtained domains comprising thousands of acres. Some carved out what resembled small principalities. William Fitzhugh of Stafford County owned over 50,000 acres, and by 1732 Robert or "King" Carter of Lancaster County held some 333,000 acres.

The estates of such men, far from consisting of one compact property, generally comprised many separate and sometimes widely scattered tracts, perhaps in half a dozen or more counties. They ranged in size from a few hundred to thousands of acres. The individual owner acquired his holdings over a period of years, in what often appeared a haphazard manner. Not infrequently, a planter, foreseeing the depletion of his Tidewater lands, engrossed large tracts in the Piedmont and Valley sections.[1]

Life in the Tidewater during the Golden Age was dominated, to a remarkable extent, by families possessing vast estates. Not everyone, it is true, owned such princely domains as the Carters or Fitzhughs, but men in their station were imbued with a deep sense of their obligation to society. They sat as justices in the county courts, served as sheriffs and as colonels of the militia in their counties, and acted as vestrymen and church wardens in their parishes. They accepted seriously their duty to preserve the peace and watch over the less fortunate classes. Because of their wealth and position, their education, resourcefulness and keen sense of public responsibility, they were able to influence and to impress their ideals and tastes upon the community in a measure rarely equalled by a similar aristocracy.

The great landed proprietors operated their estates in either of two ways or a combination of the two. They might take full responsibility themselves, planting tobacco and secondary crops; they could lease tracts to others to cultivate; or they might do both. Sometimes a man leased more of his arable lands than he reserved for his own use. Though disturbed conditions in Europe and the burdens imposed by the British regulatory system led to repeated attempts to develop other staples for export, tobacco continued to be the mainstay. Aside from money crops, however, the great landowners had to supply numerous foodstuffs and other commodities needed on their plantations.

A proprietor customarily resided on what was generally known as the "manor plantation."[2] This seat usually served as the nerve center of the activities of his entire estate, with the other units subordinate to it. Not infrequently some of the outlying properties were devoted to producing commodities needed by the manor plantation and by such other plantations as were engaged in raising tobacco and other marketable staples. Overseers or stewards managed the units over which the owner found it difficult to exercise personal supervision. These men reported to him at regular intervals to receive instructions and give an account of their stewardship.

Though the basis of life was agricultural, the great landowners discharged a wide variety of other economic functions. They served as factors for their neighbors, buying their crops, selling them supplies, and providing them with credit facilities. Many sent vessels regularly up and down the Chesapeake and the Virginia rivers, purchasing the produce of others for later marketing. In like fashion they brought manufactured goods from overseas for sale in the plantation stores. When European conditions interfered with the import trade, enterprising men frequently set up grist mills, textile factories, foundries, and other manufactories on their plantations, to supply their own and their neighbors' needs.

The great Tidewater proprietors of the Golden Age were, then, no perfumed courtiers spending their days in idleness and diversion and consciously seeking to avoid all "taint of trade." In a very real sense they were capitalists, acute men of business, seriously concerned with managing their estates, tilling their lands and disposing of their produce, and eager to reap a profit through trading with their neighbors. Their ledgers and their correspondence reveal their energy, shrewdness, and enterprise. In a similar way the constant stream of letters they wrote the factors who served them in London, Bristol, and other ports of the mother country show their vital interest in conditions in the world market.

The planters' preoccupation with such matters does not signify that they lacked grace of living, nor that they were deficient in aristocratic ideals. They were determined they should not revert to barbarism in the wilderness. At no time did they allow themselves to forget that they were inheritors of British civilization.[3] Taking the English gentry as their model, they tried, insofar as colonial conditions would allow, to follow the ways of the country gentlemen of the homeland. On that pattern they fashioned their manners, their homes, their diversions; and with a similar aim they sought to acquire, and instruct their sons in, every branch of knowledge useful to a gentleman.

That it was a constant concern of these planter-businessmen to see that their children should acquire "polite" accomplishments is clearly revealed in their papers. In a letter in 1718 Nathaniel Burwell of "Carter's Grove" deplored his son's inattention to his studies, not only because an ignorance of arithmetic would hamper him in "the management of his own affairs," but also because, lacking a broad basis of knowledge, he would be "unfit for any gentleman's conversation and therefore a scandalous person and a shame to his relations, not having one single qualification to recommend him."[4] In a like spirit William Fitzhugh of "Bedford" in Stafford County asserted in 1687 that his children had "better be never born than illbred."[5]

Though a parent sometimes specified that his sons be taught languages, philosophy, dancing, fencing, and other such "polite" subjects, practical studies were not neglected. Such subjects as mathematics, surveying, and law prepared a youth for managing the estate he would one day inherit and for discharging the obligations to society imposed by his position. The goal was not professional specialization, but, rather, an education which would develop fully every side of a gentleman's character. George Washington expressed this ideal in referring to plans for the education of his ward, young "Jacky" Custis, in 1771. Admitting that "a knowledge of books is the basis upon which other knowledge is to be built," he explained that he did not think "becoming a mere scholar is a desirable education for a gentleman."[6] Thus, also, Robert Beverley, father of Harry Beverley of "Hazelwood" in Caroline County, directed in his will that his son's guardians should continue the boy's education until he should be taught "everything necessary for a gentleman to learn."[7]

Books provided a ready means of transmitting English standards of life to the colony. The carefully selected volumes in the manor houses clearly reveal their owners' aspiration to become "compleat gentlemen." It was not unusual for the collection of a prosperous planter to number as many as one or two thousand. Works providing guidance in the mode of life they admired greatly predominated, though works of literature were not absent. English "courtesy" and "conduct" books were on every gentleman's shelves. Richard Allestree's *A Gentleman's Calling* and Henry Peacham's *The Compleat Gentleman*, and other works which portrayed fortitude, prudence, temperance, justice, liberality, and courtesy as cardinal virtues appear again and again in the inventories of the period, along with the writings of Castiglione and other Italians of an earlier day from whom English authors had derived ideas of courtly conduct.

Most numerous were works stressing a gentleman's religious obligations. Duty to God and Church was set forth in devotional works of various kinds, collections of sermons, and theological treatises. Then came books on historical subjects which offered actual examples of men of great deeds. There were also many volumes on politics and statecraft and military manuals, all of them useful in teaching the larger obligations which a man of wealth owed to society. Guidance in the practical duties of a great estate was furnished in treatises on various phases of farming and gardening, manuals of medicine and surgery, books on surveying and engineering, commentaries on law and legal procedure and handbooks of architecture.[8]

Naturally, the character of the schooling provided for the growing generation greatly concerned the Virginia gentlemen. Many, eager to give their children direct contact with the traditional learning and culture of the mother country, sent them for a period of years to English schools.[9] Not infrequently, mere infants were placed under the protection of relatives and friends in the mother country. As early as 1683 William Byrd II, then nine years old, and his sister Susan, about six, were being watched over in English schools by their Horsmanden grandparents, and plans were making to send over their little sister, Ursula, aged four. Each of the great "King" Carter's five boys was sent overseas at an early age. In 1762 John Baylor of Caroline County, who had received his own education at Putney Grammar School and Caius College, Cambridge, sent his twelve-year-old son to Putney, and about the same time put his four young daughters at a boarding school at Croyden in Kent.[10]

The high value placed upon schooling in England is well illustrated in the attitude of Robert Beverley of "Blandfield" when he prepared to send his young son, William, abroad in 1773. Confiding the lad for a season to a tutor in the home of his father-in-law, Landon Carter of "Sabine Hall," he carefully explained his purpose. "I would recommend to Mr. Menzies the Latin Lillies Grammar," he wrote Carter, "because, as no other rudiments are used in any Schools of Eminence, when he goes to England, he may in part have gotten over the Drudgery of Education. All I wish to learn him in Virginia is, to read, write, & cypher, & do as much with his Grammar, as the Time will admit of. . . ."[11] Planters frequently provided in their wills that their young sons and daughters be educated abroad. It is likely that an even larger number of small children would have been sent "home," as the planters fondly called the mother country, had their parents not feared the dangers of an ocean voyage and the mortal effects of the small-pox which was raging in England during the eighteenth century.

As an alternative to sending children overseas, the traditional learning of the English schools could be brought to Virginia by English-trained tutors and governesses. Well-to-do planters customarily engaged such persons to instruct their children at home, even when it was planned to send the youngsters abroad later. They also employed dancing and music masters to visit their households at regular intervals. A building near the mansion was generally set aside as a schoolroom. There the master's children and perhaps those of some neighboring planters were taught. The young men and women who came overseas to teach the children of Virginia were honored members of the households in which they lived. Great care was taken in selecting them. After a number of young Scotchmen had come to the colony as tutors during the eighteenth century, it was feared they would "teach the children the Scotch dialect which they can never wear off."[12] Throughout the period one finds frequent mention of the need of suitable instructors in the letters of the planters to their factors in the mother country. After the middle of the century, tutors were sometimes secured from Princeton and other American colleges.[13]

A goodly number of the youths sent to the English schools enrolled later at the colleges of Oxford and Cambridge, and others who had been educated by private tutors were also sent there. Certain families sent generation after generation of sons to these universities. At intervals from the time that Ralph Wormeley, the second of that name, had matriculated at Oriel College, Oxford, in 1665, until the outbreak of the Revolution, his kinsmen were found in English colleges. Not a few young Virginians attended the Inns of Court.

In his domestic establishment the planter sought to reproduce as nearly as he conveniently could the residence of the English gentry with its gardens, lawns, and parks. Plans of English homes and gardens, which intelligent workmen or even a layman might adapt, were accessible in the handbooks of architecture and gardening found in many of the planters' libraries. In some instances the striking similarity of detail leaves little doubt that the plans for a planter's residence derived directly from plates in these books. All the forms common to the English country architecture of the period were employed in the plantation residences. Sometimes English master builders and gardeners were imported to supervise the construction of the residences and the planting of the grounds.

The vogue for formality in English architecture and landscaping was mirrored in the arrangement of the Virginia estates. The mansions were generally placed according to carefully preconceived plans in a formal setting which nonetheless managed to achieve an air of ease and naturalness. Balance and symmetry were observed everywhere, with the buildings, gardens, and extensive lawns forming component parts of one composition. Walks of brick or oyster shell crossed the grounds in geometric pattern. If a bowling green or formal garden flanked one side of the mansion, an orangery or perhaps a park stocked with deer flanked the other.

English box and other ornamental plants were used with fine effect. Terraces, elaborate parterres, sunken panels, canals, and dramatic vistas gave variety to the scene. "Falling gardens" were popular at the residences situated on high eminences overlooking the great rivers and marshes.[14] Not infrequently, as at "Blandfield," a ha-ha provided a note of pleasant surprise for one walking on the lawns.[15] Graceful garden houses, dovecots, and other miniature structures, carefully placed, sometimes imparted a fanciful atmosphere to the whole. Every estate had its orchard, the fruit of which surpassed the choicest specimens of the homeland. Wildernesses or preserves of transplanted trees might be found at some distance from the residence, and sometimes serpentine drives and walks invited one to explore hidden retreats.

Situated amidst such attractive surroundings, the residences appeared to fine advantage. Their architectural arrangement contributed much to their impressiveness. At the same time it was admirably suited to the peculiar needs of plantation life. The mansion or "great house" was but the central unit, about which, at carefully spaced intervals, stood numerous smaller structures, all subsidiary to it. Spoken of indiscriminately as "offices," these dependent buildings all served some useful purpose or function in the domestic economy.

The mansion was usually a substantial two-story, rectangular building of brick, though sometimes it was built of stone or wood. The rather low-pitched roofs were generally shingled with cypress or slate. Since many of the activities of the household were carried on in offices under separate roofs, a central structure approximately seventy-five feet long and forty-two feet wide was usually regarded as commodious. The exteriors of these houses were often characterized by an elegant simplicity achieved through perfection of line and proportion. The severity of a facade might be relieved by a handsome wooden cornice, a pedimented hood over the doorway, a string-course and water table of molded brick, and window and door facings of rubbed brick. Sometimes pilasters of finely molded brick framed the doorways.

Not infrequently the principal offices, set in advance or in the rear of the mansion, served as foils to impart greater dignity to it. Sometimes, as at "Blandfield" and "Mount Airy," the major offices were connected with the central building by straight or curved lateral passages. The great house and its dependent structures were generally placed in such a relation as to form one or more rectangular courts.[16] The principal offices were often large and contained a number of rooms.

To one unfamiliar with plantation life, the number and diversity of the offices about the manor house occasioned astonishment. A Huguenot exile who visited "Rosegill," the home of Ralph Wormeley, as early as 1686, recorded that the master's residence comprised at least twenty structures. "When I reached his place," this Frenchman wrote, "I thought I was entering a rather large village, but later on was told that all of it belonged to him."[17]

Offices near the great house were utilized as counting-rooms, schoolrooms, and sleeping quarters for the sons of the family as well as for a variety of other purposes. The kitchen, wash-house, dairy, smoke-house, and other offices intimately connected with the processes of housekeeping were usually set farther away in order to keep the mansion cool in summer and free it of the noise and odors of cooking.[18]

Within the manor house the lower floors were usually devoted entirely to social purposes. Halls and chambers were generally finely panelled in native pine or walnut, and the symmetry of the paneling, the deeply recessed windows, and the excellent proportion of the doors and mantels imparted dignity and beauty to the rooms. Frequently the effect was heightened by fine carving, and occasionally the pink or orange tones of mantels of sienna marble lent a pleasing touch of color.

In many of the apartments there were fine cornices, modillions, and dentils. Delicately fluted pilasters often flanked windows and doors. Elaborately carved cornice and mantel friezes and frets represented the most skilled craftsmanship of the period. Sometimes, as at "Carter's Grove," the miniature carving of the friezes was of exquisite beauty. Motifs such as the egg and dart, the Wall of Troy, and the Tudor rose were employed with fine effect.

In the halls ornamentation was frequently given freer scope than elsewhere. The wide passageways which extended through the houses were customarily broken midway by arches of fine proportions. The usual focal point of interest in the hallways, however, was the stairs, the sweep of which was often majestic. Carved and hidden newel posts were common, and sometimes the pattern of the posts reappeared in elaborate friezes below the landing. Twist-carved balusters were placed on the steps, and running floral and foliated carving decorated the risers or step-ends of many of the stairs.

For these homes the Virginia aristocrats imported furniture, china, plate, and other furnishings from England and France. Their letters to factors in the homeland were filled with descriptions of the articles wanted, and frequently specified that items must be in the latest London fashion. Choice pieces of walnut and mahogany, expensive mirrors, and carpets and hangings of the best quality graced their drawing rooms. Harpsichords, spinets, and other fine instruments stood in many homes, and portraits of members of the family, some by the best artists of the day, hung on their walls. In the dining rooms, fine crystal and plate emblazoned with the family crest gleamed on polished sideboards and tables.

Though they sometimes maintained residences at Williamsburg for the court season, the Virginia great were rarely absentee landlords in the sense that planters in other colonies were. Rather, they were country gentlemen residing on their manor plantations, and, as we have seen, seriously interested in improving their homes and domains. A family was customarily identified by reference to its seat. "Epping Forest," "Marmion," "Berkeley," "Chelsea," "Elsing Green," and the other musical names by which the homes were called, impart a romantic and picturesque flavor to the literature of the region, and reveal the strong hold retained over men's affections by the mother country.

Since no land in the Tidewater was cleared until it was to be utilized for tobacco culture, and since discarded fields were allowed to grow up in thickets, the plantation establishments were generally located at a considerable distance from one another and separated by heavily wooded tracts.[19]

Set in a land abounding in excellent house sites, the planters' homes generally stood near the bank of one of the great rivers or upon some natural eminence. In the former case these houses had two fronts, a land and a water entrance. The approach from the public highway generally led through a wide avenue of trees, perhaps a mile or more in length, or the house might be shielded from the public gaze by a park of stately beeches or poplars. Since overland routes often presented serious difficulties, the Virginians made highroads of their rivers and creeks, and the side of the mansion facing the water generally constituted its true front. This is evidenced by the fact that one usually ascended the stairs from the water side. Isolated as the homes were, the Virginians were able to enjoy the seclusion so greatly prized by the gentry of the mother country, and they developed to a high degree the hospitable and generous traits and the love of outdoor sports that have usually characterized country squires.[20]

The constant activity that centered about the great house is clearly reflected in the journals, letters, and account books of the day. Through their pages may be seen the great planter-businessmen, the members of their families, the overseers and stewards, the free white artisans, the Negro slaves, and the indentured servants moving about their daily tasks. The master of the plantation in a counting room near his mansion balances accounts, writes letters to his factors in England, or converses with the overseers and stewards from his other plantations who have come for instructions regarding their work. The children of the household and their tutor pass to and from the office used as a schoolroom. A ship from the homeland touches at the plantation landing and its captain comes ashore to bring letters and the latest news from the mother country, and perchance to dine at the planter's table. Visitors from neighboring plantations or from adjoining counties arrive in sloops or in coaches or sedans. Rooms reserved for guests are rarely empty and almost any event serves as the excuse for a celebration. A peripatetic dancing master arrives, the children of the neighborhood gather, and an informal dance is held after they have been singly instructed. Even passing strangers are accorded hospitable entertainment and treated as welcome guests. The planter and his family frequently ride out in a coach or chair for "an airing" or to call upon neighbors or relatives. On Sunday, if the weather be good, he takes his family by water to attend services at the parish church. Not infrequently a neighbor's servant arrives bearing venison or some other delicacy for the master's table.

Countless articles are bought or taken from the plantation stores. In the smith's shop nails and other articles are forged for plantation use, and the chair of a neighbor is mended or his plows pointed. Provisions are sent to the outlying plantations and supplies needed for the home place brought from them. In buildings near the mansion, tobacco is cured and prized. Hogsheads are rolled to the wharf to be shipped.

Such was the nature of the world about "Nomini Hall," the manor house of Robert Carter III in Westmoreland County, to which Philip Vickers Fithian, a young Princeton-bred theological student, went as a tutor to the children of the household in 1773.

CHAPTER TWO

Philip Fithian And The Carter Family

DURING his residence at "Nomini Hall" from October, 1773, to October, 1774, Philip Fithian recorded his impressions of the life about him in a daily journal and in letters to relatives and friends. These impressions constitute a detailed and illuminating account. The civilization he described differed in many respects from that he had known in New Jersey. His austere Presbyterian training caused him to look with disfavor or misgiving upon many of the gay diversions and other social customs of Virginia. Yet he was open-minded to an unusual degree and not unsympathetic to the people among whom he lived. His freshness of viewpoint led him to comment upon various features of Virginia civilization which would doubtless have escaped the attention of one more familiar with them. He admired many aspects of Southern life and for the members of the Carter household Fithian developed a genuine and lasting fondness. The account possesses both vivacity and charm.

At "Nomini Hall" Philip Fithian found himself in an excellent observation post. Robert Carter, its owner, was the scion of one of the wealthiest and most influential Tidewater families. His great-grandfather, John Carter, had emigrated to Virginia from England in 1649. Acquiring some 13,500 acres in the Northern Neck, the fertile region between the Rappahannock and Potomac rivers, John Carter had established his home "Corotoman" on the Rappahannock in Lancaster County. Becoming ere long a successful planter and businessman, Carter served first as a Burgess and then as a member of the governor's Council.

Robert or "King" Carter, son of the emigrant, so eclipsed his father that he has usually been regarded as founder of the family in Virginia. Bold, capable, and acquisitive, "King" Carter strove ceaselessly to expand the family fortunes. By strict attention to business and a close regard for his prerogatives as agent of the Fairfaxes, the proprietors of the Northern Neck, he ultimately became the richest and perhaps the most powerful man of his day in Virginia.[1] First as a Burgess and then as a member and President of the Council, he exerted a political influence that contributed greatly to the management of his private affairs. Realizing earlier than most the need future generations would have for fresh lands, he obtained for his progeny altogether some 333,000 acres.

Under the custom of primogeniture, Carter arranged that the bulk of his lands, including "Corotoman," should go to his eldest son, John Carter II. He, nonetheless, saw to it that his other sons, Robert, Landon, Charles, and George should have ample estates. Robert Carter II, however, died a few months before his father, leaving a young son, Robert III, and a daughter, Elizabeth. A short time after "King" Carter's death his surviving sons procured a special legislative enactment investing the share of the estate intended for the dead son in the young grandson. When Robert Carter III reached his majority, therefore, he would become master of more than seventy thousand acres.

The young boy's uncles, John, Landon, and Charles Carter, acted as his guardians. As a result of his mother's early second marriage to Colonel John Lewis, he lived at the latter's manor plantation, "Warner Hall" in Gloucester County. When the lad was nine, he was sent to the College of William and Mary. Nothing further is definitely known of how his youth was spent.

On reaching twenty-one Robert at once began preparations for a trip to England where he remained two years. The purpose of this visit is not known. It is probable, however, that he was following the example of his grandfather, his father, and the other sons of "King" Carter who had all completed their education in the mother country. Indeed the records of the Inner Temple reveal that he was admitted to the privileges and assumed the agreeable duties of a member of that august legal society a few months after he arrived there.[2] Whatever his motives, though, it is unlikely that a spirited young man, possessed of ample means and free of parental restraint, would bury himself entirely within musty college walls. Reports at home had it that he spent his time in idleness and gay diversions. A portrait painted at this time by a fashionable artist, probably in the studio of Sir Joshua Reynolds, shows him arrayed in a fine doublet of silk and a high lace collar, with a mask in one hand as if to indicate he was about to hasten away to some masquerade.

Whatever his youthful follies may have been, Robert Carter possessed a gentle and thoughtful nature. As he matured, he became increasingly a serious man of business and of scholarly and cultivated tastes. Returning to Virginia in 1751, he soon married and settled down to the life of a country squire at "Nomini Hall," the manor house his father had built in Westmoreland County.

On a visit to Maryland, Carter had met Frances Anne Tasker, the sixteen-year-old daughter of one of the foremost citizens of that colony. Struck by the beauty, good sense, and fortune of the young girl, he had secured her consent to become his wife. Frances Tasker Carter was an uncommon person. Notwithstanding the numerous children she had already borne her husband when Philip Fithian entered her household, she was still beautiful, elegant, and youthful looking. She was also well-informed and frequently surprised Fithian with the breadth of her interests. Ever cheerful and agreeable, she managed the household with fine success and carefully trained her seventeen children.

Besides a handsome dowry, Frances Tasker brought her husband a family influence that proved of great assistance in both his public and private career. Benjamin Tasker, her father, who had wide commercial connections, had served for thirty-two years as a member and President of the Council of Maryland, and for a period as acting-Governor. Her mother, Anne Bladen Tasker, was the daughter of William Bladen who had been successfully Secretary and Attorney-General of that colony. Thomas Bladen, her mother's brother, a former governor of Maryland, had removed to England and become a member of Parliament for Old Sarum, where he was now in an excellent position to promote the interests of his American relatives.[3]

Robert Carter led a busy life at "Nomini Hall." To utilize profitably the resources of an estate of seventy thousand acres was a task that demanded foresight and planning. He customarily cultivated as many as a dozen large plantations at once, and it was necessary that the operations on the several units be carefully integrated. Though tobacco constituted the crop of first importance on his estate, entire plantations were sometimes devoted to producing grain stuffs and supplies needed at "Nomini Hall" and on the other plantations. From time to time, too, Carter sought to develop other money crops which might supplement the constantly dwindling profits from tobacco. The preparation of new grounds to replace discarded fields constituted a laborious task that had to be coped with at intervals. He set up and equipped so many plantations that he resorted at one time to the signs of the zodiac for names for them.

Apart from the lands he himself cultivated, Carter rented or leased a large proportion of his estate to others. He developed an elaborate system of tenancy reminiscent in its principal features of the modern lien system and "share cropping." Lands were leased for varying periods under specific agreements as to the uses to be made of them, the provision of tools and other supplies by the landlord, and the proportion of the crops to be paid as rent. Other tracts were leased for a fixed money rental.

To Carter's interests as a planter and a landlord he added those of a manufacturer. When conditions made it economical or necessary to furnish his own supplies, he operated textile factories, salt works, grain mills, and bakeries to fill his own and his neighbors' needs. In his smiths's shops the simple farm implements of the time were forged and repaired, and work was also done for near-by planters. Through his wife's relations he received a one-fifth share in the Baltimore Iron Works. As part owner of this firm he produced bar and pig iron in large quantities on a commercial basis, and incidentally supplied raw materials needed on his plantations. He also carried on extensive operations as a merchant and factor. From his stores at "Nomini Hall," European manufactures and merchandise of every sort were dispensed. He owned a number of vessels which regularly carried supplies to the landings of other planters on the Virginia rivers and the Chesapeake and took their produce off their hands. Sometimes he provided these men with banking and credit facilities.

The scope of Carter's activities is indicated by the fact that at one time his slaves numbered over 500. In addition, he employed numerous white stewards, overseers, clerks, skilled craftsmen, and artisans. In a labor force so numerous and diversified the most careful adjustments in human relationships were necessary. In a very real sense Carter acted as a protector, father, physician, and court of last resort for all his people. No complaint was too insignificant to receive the master's consideration.

As part of the obligations of his station, the master of "Nomini Hall" served as a vestryman and a warden of his church in Cople Parish and performed other public duties. At the age of twenty-eight he was made a member of the governor's Council. His large estate made him eligible and his wife's uncle, Thomas Bladen, supplied the influence in England necessary to secure his appointment to this highest governing body in the colony. By virtue of belonging to the Council he also served as a colonel in the militia. As was customary, he was henceforth known as Colonel or Councillor Carter. In the latter capacity, he went twice a year to Williamsburg to advise the royal governor and to sit as a member of the General Court. For a decade after 1762 he found it pleasant and convenient to live at the Capital the greater part of the time. He acquired a residence in the town and established his wife and children there. With the outbreak of the disturbances which led to the Revolution, however, he returned with his family to "Nomini Hall" where he lived during the remainder of his active years, devoting his time to the development of his estate and the promotion of his commercial interests, the rearing of his family, and the quiet enjoyment of his scholarly and cultivated tastes. Despite his many duties, he spent much time in reading and in scientific investigation. An accomplished musician, he practiced daily on some of the numerous instruments at his home.

The social life of the family at "Nomini Hall" was of the most agreeable sort. Situated on a hill overlooking the Potomac and Nomini rivers, the mansion was admirably suited to the hospitable tradition of the region. A large rectangular structure of brick, covered with stucco, the great house was surrounded by more than thirty dependent structures or offices and presented an attractive and imposing appearance. The four principal offices were set off at a distance of one hundred yards from the corners of the house, and within the rectangle formed by these buildings was a long bowling green. Extensive and well-tended gardens provided agreeable promenades for members of the family and guests. One approached the mansion from the public highway through a wide avenue of poplars which terminated in a circle about the house. Viewed through this avenue from a distance, Fithian asserted, "Nomini Hall" appeared "most romantic, at the same time it does truly elegant."

The lower floor of the great house contained the master's library, a dining room, used also as a sitting room, a dining hall for the children, a ballroom thirty feet long, and a hallway with a fine stairway of black walnut. The upper rooms were used as sleeping quarters for members of the family and for guests. The older boys and their tutor slept above-stairs in one of the large offices that was also used as a schoolhouse. During the time Fithian was there Carter arranged to convert one of the lower rooms of this office into a concert or music room. Here he proposed to place the harpsichord, harmonica, forte-piano, guitar, violin, and German flutes which were in the great house, and to bring up for that purpose from his Williamburg residence, the organ which had been built for him in London according to his own specifications.

Seven of the nine surviving Carter children[4] and the Councillor's nephew, Harry Willis, were placed under Fithian's care. Benjamin, the eldest son, was a quiet, studious boy of eighteen. Robert Bladen, two years younger, loved the out-of-doors and cared little for learning. John Tasker, only four, was too young for instruction. Priscilla, the eldest daughter, was an attractive girl of fifteen. Anne Tasker, called Nancy, and Frances or Fanny, whom Fithian thought the "Flower of the Family," were thirteen and eleven respectively. Betty Landon was ten, and Harriot Lucy, a "bold, fearless, merry girl," was seven. Sarah Fairfax, the baby, was only a few months old at the time Fithian arrived.

Apart from the members of the family, the tutor, and the numerous domestics, various other persons maintained a more or less permanent connection with the household. Among these were Miss Sally Stanhope, the housekeeper, Mr. Randolph, who served as clerk and steward for Carter, Mr. Christian, a peripatetic dancing master who visited most of the great manor houses of the Northern Neck, Mr. Stadley, music master to the children, and Mrs. Oakley, who had nursed several of them at Williamsburg.

In no section of the colony were the great planters more numerous than in the Northern Neck; in none did they dominate society more completely. The families on the manor plantations associated on terms of intimacy. Gay assemblies, dances, balls, and banquets brought them together frequently. Dancing masters held their classes in rotation at the great plantation houses. At these homes their pupils assembled in turn, frequently accompanied by parents and friends. After the master had instructed the young men and women on these occasions, an informal dance was generally held. These families customarily congregated about the parish church before and after services to enjoy social exchanges. Attendance at county court provided another regular opportunity for commingling. Boat races, barbecues, "Fish-feasts," and horse races brought friends together at intervals. Sometimes elaborate private entertainments were given at which music, feasting, and dancing continued for several days. Rarely a day passed but found some guest at the Councillor's table. Members of the Carter household constantly exchanged visits with the plantation families of their neighborhood and with relatives and friends in adjoining counties. They dined frequently with the Turbervilles at "Hickory Hill," the Washingtons at "Bushfield," the Lees at "Chantilly" and "Stratford," and with the more distant Tayloes at "Mount Airy."

With all these persons the young Princeton tutor was familiar. He accompanied the Carters frequently when they dined at their friends' tables, he attended banquets and balls with them, conversed with the people of the vicinity at the parish churches, met them at races, and observed their conduct as guests at "Nomini Hall." The sprightly interest with which Fithian comments upon these men and women and their way of life makes them seem as real today as then.

For more than a century the manuscript of Fithian's journal and the letters he wrote home remained unpublished. During that time, some years apparently after Philip's death, his brother, Enoch, assembled the letters and papers and the various sections of the journal kept over a period of years and copied them in several bound volumes from the loose and various-sized sheets upon which they were written. It is from this transcript that the journal is known today, and the irregularities in punctuation, spelling, and capitalization in the form in which it has been preserved are doubtless due largely to this fact.

The journal kept at "Nomini Hall" and a group of letters written by Fithian during his residence there were finally published in 1900 by the Princeton University Library, into whose custody had come seven manuscript volumes of Fithian's papers in Enoch Fithian's hand. This publication was edited by John Rogers Williams, a member of the Princeton Historical Association.[5] A small part of the journal and certain letters which the editor regarded as "of too intimate and personal or too trivial a character" were omitted, his object being "in general to present such as have some bearing on historic places and personages, together with representative ones showing" Fithian's "character and circumstances."[6] The editor, moreover, was interested in Fithian's manuscripts primarily from the standpoint of the tutor's association with Princeton.

In the present edition the manuscripts have been treated with special reference to the light they throw on life in the Old Dominion. The journal kept at "Nomini Hall" and all the letters written by Fithian from Virginia are given in their entirety. Several letters written after his departure from "Nomini Hall," but which relate to matters and persons in Virginia, are now printed for the first time.

The journal and letters of Philip Fithian are so revealing of his personality that one inevitably becomes attached to the young tutor, and the reader today may well be curious to know his subsequent career. Having prepared himself for the Presbyterian ministry, Fithian left the Carter household late in 1774 despite the strong ties of friendship and gratitude which now bound him to the family. His decision to return to New Jersey was influenced both by a sense of duty and his growing attachment for Elizabeth Beatty, the "fair Laura" of his journal. In December, 1774, he was licensed to preach by the Presbytery of Philadelphia. That winter he filled vacancies in West Jersey and the following summer served as a Presbyterian missionary in the Valley of Virginia and Pennsylvania. He married Elizabeth Beatty in October, 1775. Early in 1776 he enlisted as a chaplain in the Revolutionary forces. Shortly after the battle of White Plains he died as the result of an attack of dysentery and exposure in camp. Though his promise to visit the family at "Nomini Hall" again was never fulfilled, the letters he wrote to members of the Carter household after his departure reveal the tender regard in which all were held.

JOURNAL & LETTERS
OF PHILIP VICKERS FITHIAN

JOURNAL & LETTERS

OF

Philip Vickers Fithian

[ANDREW HUNTER,[1] JR., TO PHILIP VICKERS FITHIAN]

Nassau-Hall June 26th 1773.

SIR.

I expected notwithstanding your small offence you would have let me know before this time whether you had made any determination different from what you designed when I left you. If you design teaching before you get into business, there are now several considerable offers made to young men who are willing to go to Virginia by some of the first gentlemen in the colony; one particularly who will give as good as 60 £, the best accomodations, a room to study in and the advantage of a library, a horse kept and a servant to wait upon you.

Dr Witherspoon[2] is very fond of getting a person to send him. I make no kind of doubt but if you were to write to the doctor but he would engage it to you, the terms are exactly as I write you as I have informed myself that I might let you know—

There are a number of our friends and class-mates getting into business as fast as possible, whether they are called or not I cannot pretend to judge, this much I would say that I think it is not any ones duty to run too fast. No less than four Debow, Reese, McCorkle, Allen, under trials by a presbytery, and Bryan[3] trying to get license to plead law in some of the best courts on the continent, if infamy were law or lies were Gospel he might get license either to plead or preach.

3

We have had the pleasure of Laura's[4] company here for some weeks past, I hope you will not envy us considering that continual pleasure is too much for such mortals as we to bear.

I beg that you may no longer refrain from writing, as I should be very glad to hear many things from you and other of my friends in Cohansie which you can relate with little trouble. If you have been trying with me who could keep from writing longest, I own fairly beat. The number of our students are considerably increased, and our school consists of thirty-nine—I have heard there are some disagreeable stories going through your country I wish you would let me know something about them. Doctr Ward spent part of yesterday with me in his return.

My love to Mr and Mrs Green.

  I am, Sir,
     Your very friend,
          ANDW HUNTER.

[JOURNAL]

July 1. [*1773*]

Rose at five. Read in the greek Testament, the third Chapter of the Acts. Breakfasted at seven. Busy the greater part of this Day in coppying off some loose miscellanous Pieces. P. M. Read the Spectator in my Course. Received in the Evening, by the Stage, a Letter from Mr and: Hunter jur In which he invites me to remove, & accept a School, of very considerable Consequence, in Virginia. He also informs me that four of our Class-Mates, are on Trial, under a Presbytery, for Preachers; & one has applied for Licence to plead Law in Maryland; Poor Boys! hard they push to be in the midst of Tumult, & Labour.

[PHILIP V. FITHIAN TO ANDREW HUNTER, JR.]

            Deerfield July 3. 1773.

SIR

I am sorry you impute neglect of writing in me to so wrong a cause, as an old trivial offense, I confess that I am to blame, and am willing to stand reproved by you, for having been so long silent. If I should offer any thing in excuse it would be great hurry arising

from the duty of my station, on which account I have wrote only two
or three letters since you left us. The school in town, which I had
in view, as I make no doubt you know, is now occupied by Mr
Lynn. And the terms of the school at *Blandensburg* are I think too
low, to divert me from the course of my business. I would not however forego a good offer in a school abroad, for some short time.
What you write concerning the offer of a Gentleman in Virginia, is,
I think of considerable consequence, provided the conditions of
teaching are not over burdensome; I should speedily agree to go and
apply for the place, were I made satisfied as to this.

I shall however, beg the assistance of your friendship, to enquire
in what county the school is; what number and degrees of scholars
there are; and if you think the place suitable, and if the Docter shall
think proper to appoint me to it, I am not unwilling to remove and
accept it. Please to mention this to the Docter; and if he has not engaged a teacher, and is pleased to accept me, I hope you will acquaint
me as speedily as may be, with what you can learn as to the time
of beginning, the custom of the school, &c. You mentioned four in
your last, who have applied to Presbytery, and are on tryal, I can
tell you another, Mr Heith; he applied to the Philadelphia Presbytery; but came to town, I understood so late, that before he made application the Presbytery was dissolved, some of the Members however, being still in town, at his request, gave him sundry pieces of
exercise, which it is expected the Presbytery will acknowledge, so
that he is the fifth out of our class who is designing soon to appear in
public!

I am Sir yours, &c.

PHILIP. V. FITHIAN

[JOURNAL]

Fryday july 30.

Rose pretty early. Breakfasted with Mrs *Buck.* Wrote a Note, after
Breakfast to Holinshead. Soon after which, I set out for Home, & by
the favour of a young man who lodges at Mr Bucks I rode to the
Ferry, & was home by eleven.

Received several Letters by the Stage to Day; One especially from
Mr Hunter, in which I am pressed to accept the proposal by the
Gentleman in Virginia. The Offer is very proffitable; Colonel *Carter*

has four Sons. To a private Tutor for which he proposes to give sixty-five Pounds pr Year; find him all Accomodations; Allow him a Room for his own Study; And the Use of an eligant Library of Books; A Horse to ride; & a Servant to Wait. I am inclined to go, but dont meet with much Encouragement from those who have the Direction of my Studies.

We had Company in the Afternoon; & expected Miss *Grimes*, & Miss Ewing, til Evening, but they never came.

Saturday july 31.

Rose early. After Breakfast rode to Deerfeild, & consulted with Mr Green⁵ but he gives only his usual Indifference; Dined at Mr *Nathan Leeks*, the Day excessive hot; Drank Tea at Mrs *Pecks*.⁶ & returned in the Evening to Greenwich.

Sunday. August 1:

Rose pretty early. Attended the Funeral of Mr *Hugh Stethern*. who died yesterday morning. Many are now ill of what is called the *Fall Fever*.

Mr *Hunter*⁷ preached both Parts of the Day.

Monday August 2.

Concluded, this Day, with the Concurrence of Mr *Hunter*, to set of for Princeton, & know of Dr Witherspoon something more particular concerning the Proposal for my going to *Virginia*. Busy all the Afternoon in preparing to go.—Evening very hot. Went on foot to the Stage.—Drank a Bowl of Punch with Mr *Richard* Howel, & to bed by ten.

Monday August 9

Waited on Dr Witherspoon, about nine o Clock, to hear his Proposal for my going to *Virginia*—He read me a Letter which he receivd from Col: Carter, & proposed the following Terms—To teach his Children, five Daughters, & three Sons, who are from five to seventeen years Old—The young Ladies are to be taught the English Language. And the Boys are to study the English Language carefully; & to be instructed in the Latin, & Greek—And he proposes to give thirty five Pounds Sterling, which is about Sixty Pounds cur-

rency; Provide all Accommodations; Allow him the undisturbed Use of a Room; And the Use of his own Library; find Provender for a Horse; & a Servant to Wait—

—By the Advice of the Dr & his Recommendation of the Gentleman, & the Place, I accepted the Offer, & agreed to go in the Fall into *Virginia* —

I took this morning, from Dr Wiggins, a Balsam that has removed the Pain wholly from my Breast; he called it the Balsam of *Cappewee*. Probably I spell it Wrong.

Teusday August 17.

Rose at seven—Very much fatigued with yesterdays Ride—Found the Students well; & the Seniors in particular In high Spirits on their Expectation of speedy Liberty—I begin to grow sick of my Virginia Voyage; But sick or sorry I must away—I waited on the Dr, But he has yet received no Intelligence.

After Evening-Prayrs, by particular Requests, I attended in the respectful Whigg-Society[8]—The Members are Orderly—Their Ex-

ercises are well chosen—And generally well-conducted; & as to
speaking, & Composition well-performed—
They conferrd Degrees formally on Six who are to be graduated in
the College the ensuing Commencement. The Moderator for the
Time being confers the Degree; The Formula is short & eligant, &
pronounced in latin—They give also Diploma's, in Latin likewise,
which are plain & full.

Expence of this Day.
For the Hire of our Carriage 10s.
For a Bowl of Punch 1s/6d
For a Glass of Bitters 4d   Sum 11s 10d.

·   ·   ·   ·   ·   ·

[LETTER OF PHILIP V. FITHIAN TO ELIZABETH BEATTY]

Prince-ton. August 17th: 1773.

To LAURA.

If I could only tell you the Incidents of Yesterday, you would
laugh as loud & as cordially as ever—Smith did all the Oddities of
Miss Cateness.

I was, & for my Life, could not avoid, being dumpish & melancholy,
in the midst of Humour & Pleasantry—Smith[9] was in great Distress
on Account of his approaching Examination; He is in the Senior-
Class, & that Class is to be examined for their Degree tomorrow, so
that he too was sour all Day.—Directly opposite to both was your
Brother; he was noisy, & troublesome; We dined at Mr Irwin's. Your
Brother kindly rode with us to the Ferry, where we parted; he for
Mr McConkey's; We for Princeton. I am to day happy as Amusements & good-Company, in this lovely Habitation of the Muses, can
render me.

There is yet, among my Acquaintances, a young Lady; & She is
also, I firmly believe, one of your most agreeable Intimates, whose
Friendship I think so valuable, & whose Manner every Way, is so
peculiarly engaging, that if you should soon see her, whom you have
sometimes heard me call Laura, give my Duty, my Love to her, &
acquaint her with what I have often told you of her, that She is, in
my undisguised Oppinion, "A Pattern for Female Excellence."

Tell her also, that a singular, & very important Occurrence, which has lately presented itself to me, seems to make it necessary, if it be any how agreeable to her, She should in some Way, chosen by Herself, signify to you that I may thereby know, whether She favours or dislikes what I have told her.

I assure you, Madam, so strong is the Esteem I have for that dear Girl, which certainly I shall ever retain, that neither, Place, nor Time, nor any Alteration in my Condition of Life, will blot it out.

This, however, I intrust only to you, & put so great Confidence in the many Expressions of your Friendship for me, that I hope you will use your Influence to persuade her that what I write is Truth.

I expect to leave Deerfield[10] & go Home next Week; But I am not determined yet upon going to Virginia. Dr Witherspoon desires & advises me to go—My Directors here seem backward, & rather unwilling.—I myself Am yet in doubt—But, on the Whole, it is probable I shall go down in October. But whether I do the one or the other I am always

Yours,

PHILIP. V FITHIAN.

[JOURNAL]

Monday August 30.

Rose by half after six—Wrote a Letter to Dr Witherspoon concerning my going to Virginia—I hear that many of my Friends in this Place are unwilling I should go—I am indeed in a Dilimma—But I have agreed—Well, I must away—And I hope in the Kindness of him who was my Fathers God, & has been the Guide of my Youth, that he will save me from being corrupted, or carried away with the Vices which prevail in that Country—Wrote a Letter to And: Hunter— In the Evening, rode with my Letters, to the Stage—Saw there by Chance, the famous Miss *Betsy Elmore:* famous for *Wit*, Extensive Knowledge, but especially for *Volubility of Tongue*—

[LETTER OF PHILIP V. FITHIAN TO DR. WITHERSPOON]

Greenwich august 30th 1773.

Revd Sir.

I am sorry that I may inform you of the dissattisfaction which my friends in general since my return home seem to discover, with my intention of going this fall to *Virginia*. However willing I am myself to accept the proposal and go, it will not be easy to break through the entreaties of those who are my neares[t] relations, and who have all along, with the warmest friendship interested themselves to procure my welfare. I do not intend by any means, abruptly to decline the fulfilling my agreement, but only desire to know, if there are not some to be found among the late Seniors who would willingly discharge me by accepting the offer themselves. If not I have only further to beg, that you would be pleased, Revd Sir, to favour me with the proposal of the gentleman; and so soon as there is a return from him, I shall be glad to know the time when I must leave home;

> I am Revd Sir,
>
> with great respect
>
> your humble Servt
>
> PHILIP V. FITHIAN

P. S. Letters come safe sent by the princeton stage, and directed to me at Greenwich.

[PHILIP V. FITHIAN TO ELIZABETH BEATTY]

Princeton. August 31. 1773.

To LAURA.

As an old Sinner, who has been long accustomed to Mishief, cannot bear to think of quitting his much-loved Practice; so I, from Time to Time, with few Returns, am intruding my Epistles upon you.

I have just been reading Yorrick's celebrated Letters to Eliza: They are familiar—They are plain—They are beautiful. I love Eliza, from the admirable Description he has given of her: But possibly he has been wholly romantic; & only painted the Woman he could love; or, if has given his own candid Sentiments, & described that Woman in Truth; There is in America an Eliza I would venture, from Yorricks own Picture, to set against it; & let Yorrick himself be Judge, should I venture never so largely, I am sure I should succeed—

I was, yesterday, at Deerfield, & heard News enough—I was told that a civil, good looking Gentleman; who had been lately from N—n, told them he saw me there with you—That I was wild, & noisy

—He thinks I shall make a damn'd droll Figure in a Pulpit, with Powdered-Hair; a long Cue; & deep Ruffles!—I fancy myself it would appear odd!—I was told there also every Circumstance of our Ride from Princeton to N—n. Of my being with your Brother in Philadelphia as I went up, & returned—Of almost the whole of my Company & Conduct while in Town.

It is something curious, tho' by no Means troublesome, that every part of my Behaviour, is in whatever Place I go, so circumstantially inspected.—I shall suppress all I heard of you, only that you are soon to be married, & I should not have mentioned this, but that I might let you know it was told in Triumph to dash me!—Yet if it had wounded my Soul I would have sustained & concealed the Pain, to outbrave such Insolence! I cannot help, however, when I am alone in my Chamber, reflecting on the Danger of the Impropriety I may possibly be guilty of in thus continuing my Intimacy with you.

But I turn it all off with a Smile, &, if the Report be true, with a Wish, in the Language of the Poet Walter to a Lady of his Acquaintance "That you may possess all your Wishes, as to earthly Happiness & Comfort, in the Society of him whom you have preferr'd to the rest of Men; & that you may feel as much for him, of that Anxiety which arises from Esteem, as others have felt for you"—I am going, next Month to Virginia, unless the Remonstrances of my Relations prevail with me to decline it.

But on I go little thinking how much I may incur your Censure by writing so freely, & so long—O Laura, I wish most ardently, that I could with Propriety, from the present Moment, spend all my hours near your Person.—They would then, with their purple Wings, fly along through the Sorrows, & Tumults of Life, wholly unnoticed.

Laura, yours

PHILIP. V. FITHIAN.

[ANDREW HUNTER TO PHILIP FITHIAN]

Nassau Hall Septr 6th 1773

DR SIR.

I am very sorry that I cannot answer your letter so much to your satisfaction as I could desire. Doctor Witherspoon is gone to New-England to the convention and is not expected home 'till the latter end of this week—he received no account from Virginia before he went from home. You may trust that I will let you know when ever I can hear any thing related to your prospect of going to the southward.

Mr Imlay[11] is gone from College and is not expected back 'till near commencement, however I have talked with some of his acquaintances, and they say he expects to go.

I would have the spelling of your name corrected, but the catalogue is sent off, and I suppose by this time is in the press. I must thank you for the good news you give me concerning the young lady's health.

I was very uneasy about the account we heard before you left princeton.

We go on pretty well in College, but I hope we shall have two or three of the *possessed swine* turned off when the Doctor comes home.

Do write me every week and give what news you can.

I am, Sir,

Your friend.

ANDW HUNTER.

[JOURNAL]

Wednesday Sept: 8.

Received a Letter from Mr Hunter—No News from Princeton— Nor Virginia—Evening Mr Paterson came home with Uncle.[12]

. . . .

[LETTER OF PHILIP V. FITHIAN TO ELIZABETH BEATTY]

Greenwich. Sept: 10th: 1773.

To LAURA.

I hope the World is using you very well, & that you enjoy yourself in Contentment; & the Society of your Friends with Pleasure. The Reason of my saying this, is, because many People here are often enquiring about you; Where you live? How you do? When you will return? The Cause of your Absence?—And forty other things that none knows, or ought to speak of, but yourself.

You inform me that you propose to be at the approaching Commencement: It will not be in my Power, with any Convenience, to go—I can, however, give you a Caution; Let not Pity so much affect you, nor Fear so much alarm you, as again, (you remember last Fall) to excite Tears in your Eyes, or one sorrowful Ake in your Breast, if any of Nassau's bold Sons shall attempt once more, to support their Right by suppressing Impertinence & Violence.

There are many going from Philada &, I am told, some Ladies of Note & Eminence—There are many expected from the Southern Colonies—And, because of the Connexions, many from York, & the New-England Goverments. The Assembly, no Doubt, will be large, & splendid—And I hope the Exercises may be worthy their Attention & Approbation. Nothing hinders my being there but only my Purpose of going soon to the Southward.

I may not omitt telling you that—Smith as we were returning Home, pitied you from his Heart; An agreeable, & sensible young Lady, separated from genteel Society, & prisoned in a Room in the Woods, in the Midst of an unpleasant Country, like a penitent Virgin conscious of her Sins, voluntarily retiring to a lonely Monastary!—But he forgot, Laura, that infelt Peace, makes us always happy, even tho' our Circumstances be apparently distressful.

I am, Eliza,

yours   PHILIP. V. FITHIAN.

[JOURNAL]

Wednesday. Sept: 15.

Rose at seven; slept but little for I was affraid—Breakfasted on Oysters, at the Ferry-Mans, with John Holmes, Esq:—Had an Hours Conversation with him, on Lotteries—Whether they are just & lawful—He thinks not—At ten we came up to his Brother Benjamin Holmes's Esq:—They mentioned to me an Intention they have to erect, & establish a School, among them, that their Children may be taught, Latin, Greek, & the Practical Branches in Mathematicks—They desired to know if it would be convenient, & agreeable for me to undertake with them, to prosecute their Plan. But I must, with Doubt, away to *Virginia*—It would be a laudable undertaking if such a School could be founded in this Part of our Province; & I think ought to be duely encouraged—

I left Mr Holmes's about twelve, & came to Mr Hunters about four, seventeen Miles—Evening walked Home. Expence 2s/o.

Sunday. Sept: 19.

Rose half after six—Read some in Pictete—Walked to Sermon by ten; Smith Rode in order to go home with Mr Hunter after Sermon —Dr Ward seems very low, confined commonly to his Bed; the Disorder it is to be feared is a Consumption, & increases in malignity almost daily—How much will Cohansie feel his Death if by this Illness he is soon taken of, or by the Violence of it wholly disabled to practice among us, who has been so long successful in his Work! Received a Letter late last Night from Mr Hunter at College, and He informs me that the Dr insists on my Going to Virginia—

. . . .

[WILLIAM R. SMITH TO PHILIP FITHIAN]

Philadelphia Octr 3d 1773.

FUTURUS PEDEGOG'ISSIMUS.

Fe-O-whiraw, whiraw, hi, fal, lal fal, lal de lal dal a fine song— commencement is over whiraw I say again whiraw, whiraw.

And what is more never was there such a commencement at princeton before and most likely never will be again. The galeries were cracking every now and then all day—every mouse hole in the church was cram'd full—The stage covered with Gentlemen and ladies amongst whom was the Governor and his lady; and that he might not appear singular Lee[13] was stiff with lace, gold-lace—

A band of music from Philadelphia assisted to make all agreeable and to crown the whole the eloquence of Demosthenes was heared in almost every mans mouth, so that the person who spoke last was always the hero of the tale—O murder! what shall I do I want to say a great deal to you but cannot for the girls who are almost distracting my heart—O murder! murder, murder I say what will become of me, murder, murder—I shall go distracted—I saw Dr Beaty[14] and Betsy—I gave your love to them—and indeed to tell you the truth I could not for my life help leaving my own heart, and love, and all with Besy—she is realy a sweet soul. I wish ten millions and she were mine, I should be a happy creature, happy indeed to the last degree—. I got cleverly up from cohansie early in the evening—My love ten thousand times and ten thousand kisses to all the girls of my acquaintance.

I cannot quit but must

WILLM R. SMITH.

[JOURNAL]

Wednesday. Octob. 6.

Walked with *Paterson*, after Breakfast to Mr *Hunters*, where we met with Mr *Smith*, & Mr *Irwin* two young Clergimen, & Mr Hunter Junr. They came down yesterday, & inform that the Commencement was the most splendid, & honoured with the greatest Number of Strangers of any one, perhaps, since it was founded, May it still increase, & long flourish!—Immediately after Dinner *Smith* & *Irwin* set off for *Cape-May*—Andrew brings me Word that I must by the twentieth of this Month meet Mr *Imlay* in New-Castle, who is going down into Virginia. And I must at last, away—The thought is indeed hard!

Thursday Octob: 7.

Slept but little last Night; my Mind seems troubled and involuntarily disturbs me! Rose early—After Breakfast rode to Deerfield. Settled all my Affairs, & took a formal, final Leave of my Friends, & Relations there! Rode home in the Evening. By the State I received a Letter from Mr *McCalla*,[15] with a Suit of *Cloths*. Cost £ 6/16/6.

Expence in the Evening for a Bowl of *Punch* 1/6—

Fryday Octob: 8.

To Day is the Fast before our Sacrament—O that the mighty God would teach me true Humiliation for my many Sin's, & give me Grace that shall enable me to hate & forsake them!—Grace to keep me right in the Path of Life, & to guide me to his heavenly Kingdom.—Mr Hunter preached two useful Sermons, describing worthy, & unworthy Communicants—

Saturday October 9.

Rode to the *Bridge*, & bought a Saddle, Bridle, Spurrs, &c. for my intended Journey—Returned before Evening, & of Saml Dennis bought a Pr of Sadle-Bags.—

Monday Octob: 11.

By Six up—Busy in Preparing for my Journey—Agreed with Uncle for his Horse; I am to give him 25 £.—The Money to be paid in May next.

Teusday October 12.

Rose early; very busy—Had my Boots altered & mended—Was measured for a Surtout-Coat—Drew up a Form to settle my Affairs before I leave Home—Afternoon Mrs Peck, Mrs Hoshel, Johnny Peck, Stephen Ranney, Miss Abby Peck call to see me & take a final Adieu for the present—The Thought of Leaving Home haunts me at Times!

Wednesday Octob: 13.

Dismissed Study, & begin to take Leave of Relations & Friends!—

Dined at Mrs Brewsters, and at two went to Mr Danl Mashells; & from thence to Mr John Gibbon's, At all which Places I gave them my last *Farewel*—

Thursday Octob: 14.

Rose early—Busy in making Preparations—Had my Horse shod, Did sundry Pieces of Writing—This Eveng Mr *Irwin*, & Smith returned from Cape-May.

Friday Octob: 15.

Rose early—Did sundry Pieces of Writing—At twelve Mr Irwin gave us a Sermon, on Felix's trembling before Paul preaching—He preached without Notes; His Sermon was easy, well-digested, plain, yet pathetic, short, and in general much admired—

Mr Smith & Mr Hunter junr dined with me—In the Evening of this Day I had a severe Fit of the Fever & Ague—Violent Pains in my Head, & Back!

Saturday. Octob: 16.

Rose at seven; feel bewildered, & unesy—Finished some necessary Writings, & begin before noon to grow better.

Sunday Octob: 17.

Rose early—Not well—Attended Sermon; Mr Smith preached—Before the last Sermon was done I was obliged to come Home with my second fit of the Fever & Ague. It kept on me violently while about seven in the Evening; then went off in a gentle Sweat!—

Monday Octob: 18.

My Fit is well gone off, & I feel bravely—Finished & executed some Writings to Joel Fithian[16] for the Securing the Several Porttions to the Children—Took my Leave of Mr *Wallings*, & Mr Ewings Families. Mr Paterson in to see me in the Evening—In the Night we had a fine Shower—I have through this Day taken the Peruvian Bark, to try if by any Means I can break my Fits.

Teusday Octob: 19

Early went to Mr Hunters; took my Leave & left them by eleven—Rode & took Leave of all my Relations—How hard is it at last? My Heart misgives, is reluctant, in spite of me; But I must away!

Protect me, merciful Heaven, & keep me under the Wing of thy over-ruling Providence—Make me know myself, & my constant, & necessary Dependance on thee!

The Continuation of my Journal, &c.

Wednesday October 20th 1773.

Left Greenwich by six in the Morning. Rode to Michael Hoshels 8 Miles. Thence Mr Hoshel, & John Peck along, rode to Quintons-Bridge 8 Miles. Expence there 1s/: Rode thence to Penn's-Neck Ferry by two oClock 10 Miles. Expence at Toll-Bridge /2. Ferriage over Delaware 4s/6d. Oats & Cordial in New-Castle 1s/2d. Rode thence to Mr Achans Tavern 12 Miles. Whole Distance 38 Miles. Whole Expence 6/10.

Octob: 21.

Expence at Mr Achans 3s/4d. Rode thence to North-East 12 Miles. Breakfast 1s/6d. Thence to Sesquehannah 10 Miles. Ferriage 1s/: Oats /9d. At Bush-Town by 4 o Clock 12 Miles. Whole Distance 34 Miles. Whole Expence 6s/7d.

Fryday 22d

Expence at Bush-Town 4/2. Rode thence to a small, mean Tavern to Breakfast, 13 Miles—Expence 1/6. Thence to Baltimore by one O-Clock 13 Miles. Whole distance 26 Miles—Whole Expence 5/8.

Saturday 23d

Expence at Baltimore *15/3.* Rode and forded Petapsko[17] to a small Tavern 15 Miles. Expence *1/11.* Rode thence to Blandensburg 23 Miles. Whole distance 38 Miles. Whole Expence *17/2.*

Sunday 24.

Expence at Blandensburg *5/7.*[18] Rode thence to Georgetown[19] 8 *Miles.* Expence *1/6.* Ferriage */6.*—From thence we rode by *Alexandria,*[20] 9 Miles—Thence to Colchester[21] 18 Miles—Dined—Expence *3/9.* Ferriage */6.* Rode thence to Dumfries 10 Miles.[22] Whole distance 45 Miles. Whole Expence *11/4.*

Monday 25.

Expence at Dumfries 4/5. Rode thence to Aquia 10 Miles.[23] Expence 2/4—Rode thence to Stafford-Court-House 12 Miles.[24] Whole Distance 22 Miles. Whole Expence 6/6.

Teusday 26.

Expence at Stafford 5/. Stopped at Colonel Thomas Lees,[25] only a few Rods from Stafford Tavern. Continued there all day, and the following Night. Expence to Day 5/.

Wednesday 27.

Expence to boy 1/. Rode from Mr Lees to a small poor Ordinary 13 Miles—Expence /8 for Oats—Rode thence, without feeding to Captain Cheltons.[26] on the Potowmack 32 Miles—Whole Distance 45 Miles. Whole Expence 1/9.

Thursday 28.

Rode after Breakfast to the Honorable Rob: Carters the End of my Journey; 12 Miles, by two o-Clock in the Afternoon. Both Myself, and my Horse seem neither tired nor Dispirited—Occasional Expences on the Road. In Baltimore for some *Buff-Ball*, 1/6. In Blandensburg for having straps put to my Saddle-Bags 3/. In Colchester for Shaving and Dressing 1/3. The whole 5/9. So that my whole Distance appears to be *260 Miles*, perform'd in seven Days. And my whole Expence appears to be 3 £ 6s 6d.

Fryday 29.

Settled myself in the Room appointed me—and adjusted my Affairs after my Ride.

Saturday 30.

Rode with Mr Carters eldest Son[27] to a Store, about seven Miles—Bought half a Box of Wafers for 1/—And a quire of paper for 1/6. Dined at three—And rode into Richmond Parish 15 Miles to Mr Fantleroys[28]—Was introduced to Mr Fantleroy—two of his Sons—Mr Christian[29] a dancing a dancing-Master—

Sunday 31.

Rode to Church six Miles[30]—Heard Mr Gibbern[31] preach on Felixes trembling at Pauls Sermon.

Monday Novemr 1st

We began School—The School consists of eight—Two of Mr Carters Sons—One Nephew—And five Daughters—The endest Son[32] is reading Salust; Gramatical Exercises, and latin Grammer—The second Son[33] is reading english Grammar Reading English: Writing, and Cyphering in Subtraction—The Nephew[34] is Reading and Writing as above; and Cyphering in Reduction—The eldest daughter[35] is Reading the Spectator; Writing; & beginning to Cypher—The second[36] is reading next out of the Spelling-Book, and begining to write—The next[37] is reading in the Spelling-Book—The fourth[38] is Spelling in the beginning of the Spelling-Book—And the last[39] is beginning her letters—

Teusday 2.

Busy in School—begun to read Pictete[40]—

[Letter of Philip V. Fithian to the Reverend Enoch Green]

Westmoreland. Novr 2d 1773.

Revd Sir.

According as I appointed I take this early oppertunity of acquainting you that I am arrived safe; and I am to assure you that I find the place fully equal to my highest expectations—I am situated in the *Northern-Neck*, in a most delightful Country; in a civil, polite neighbourhood; and in a family remarkable for regularity, and oeconomy, tho' confessedly of the highest quality and greatest worth of any in *Virginia*. I teach only Mr Carters children, and only one of them is to learn Languages, and he is reading Salust and the Greek grammer, is seventeen years old, and seems to be a Boy of Genius—the other two learn writing and Arithmetic—But he has four Daughters, young Misses that are at times to be taught writing and English —I have the terms as I expected, and find the place wholly agreeable —and am strongly solicited to stay many years—But money nor conveniency shall detain me long from my most important connections at home—You may expect me in may at the *Synod*. Please to have my compliments to Mrs Green, to Miss Betsy if at Deerfield, and to my acquaintances that shall enquire and accept to yourself the

   Respect of your humble Servt

PHILIP V FITHIAN

[JOURNAL]

Wednesday 3.

Busy in School—

Thursday 4.

Busy in School—To day the two eldest Daughters, and second Son attended the Dancing School.[41]

Fryday 5.

Busy in School—

Saturday 6.

Catechised in School til twelve—the Children. And dismiss'd them.
Afternoon rode with Ben Carter to the Bank of Potowmack[42]—8
Miles—Returned in the evening—Expence Ferriage *1/.*

Sunday 7.

Rode to Ucomico Church[43]—8 Miles—Heard Parson Smith.[44] He
shewed to us the uncertainty of Riches, and their Insufficiency to
make us happy—Dined at Captain Walkers;[45] With Parson Smith,
his Wife; her Sister, a young Lady; &c—Returned in the Evening.

Monday 8.

Busy in School—Finished reading the first, and begun to read the
Second Book of Pictetes Theology. Expence to Boy */4.*

Teusday 9.

Busy in School—

Wednesday 10.

Busy in School—The eldest Daughter taken off by her Teacher in
Music; Mr Stadley[46] who is learning her to play the *Forte-piano*—

Thursday 11.

Rose by seven—Busy in School—Miss Carter still absent—

Fryday 12.

Rose by Seven—Ben begun his Greek Grammer—Three in the Afternoon Mr Carter returned from *Williamsburg.*[47] He seems to be
agreeable, discreet, and sensible—He informed me more particularly
concerning his desire as to the Instruction of his Children—

Saturday 13.

Catechised the Children and dismissed them about Eleven—Read
in Pictete—and proceeded in writing my Sermon for the Presbytery[48]—Expence for my Horse *1/3.*

Sunday 14.

Rode to Nominy Church about six Miles—the day Cold—Parson Smith preached—"What shall a man be profited" &c. Rode home after Sermon—Dined at Mr Carters to day Mrs Turbuville,[49] Miss Jenny Corbin,[50] and Mr Cunningham[51] a young Merchant.

Monday 15.

Busy in School—Wrote in the Evening at my Sermon.

Teusday 16.

In School—Writing at my Sermon.

Wednesday 17.

Busy in School—

Thursday 18.

Busy in School—

Fryday 19.

Busy in School—

Saturday 20.

Rode to Mr Fishers[52] dined with Mr Cunningham at 3 o-Clock—Rode in the evening to Mr Lancelot Lees,[53] a young Gentleman, who has lately come from England; sup'd on Oysters—Rode home about nine o-Clock he along—

Sunday 21.

Rode to Church—Mr Smith preached on the Parable of the rich Man. Dined at home—Mr Lee dined with us—Reading in Pictete—Feel very home-Sick—Saw two Brothers quarrel—Doleful Sight.—

Monday 22.

Busy in School—Mr Lee gave us his Company in the morning in School, and was very chearful—he left us about twelve o-Clock—

Teusday 23.

Busy in School—Miss Carter rode out with her Dady and Mama to the County Court[54]—Writing at my Sermons.

[Poem Inserted in Journal]

Who knows what heaven may have in view?
What yet remains for me to do?
But knowlege here might give me grief.
Instead of pleasure and relief;
I therefore yield and peaceful wait
On Providence to rule my fate;
Nor if it long 'til' I must fly
Unbodied to my judge on high
Why need I then disturb my mind?
Why not lye humble and resign'd?—
Yet tho' 'tis wrong for me to try
Into these mysteries to pry
Sure I may sit and simply sing
(I dare not strike a lofty string)
The various scenes through which I've past
I may be now acting my last;
Here in Virginia, far from friends
Except those Heaven in pity sends!

Novr 23d 1773.

Wednesday 24.

Busy in School.

Thursday 25.

Rode this morning to Richmond Court-house,[55] where two Horses run for a purse of 500 Pounds; besides small Betts almost enumerable.

One of the Horses belonged to Colonel John Taylor,[56] and is called *Yorick*—The other to Dr. Flood,[57] and is called *Gift*—The Assembly was remarkably numerous; beyond my expectation and exceeding polite in general.

The Horses started precisely at five minutes after three; the Course was one Mile in Circumference, they performed the first Round in two minutes, third in two minutes & a-half, *Yorick* came out the

fifth time round about 40 Rod before *Gift* they were both, when the
Riders dismounted very lame; they run five Miles, and Carried 180
lb—Rode home in the Evening—Expence to the Boy 7½ d—

Fryday 26.

Busy in School—Robin, & Nancy at dancing-School.

Saturday 27.

Robin and Nancy yet at Dancing-School—Mr Harry Fantleroy
call'd after dinner to see us. In the Evening Ben & I rode with him to
his fathers; I was introduced to one Mr Walker a Scotch Gentleman,
lately a School-master but has quit, and is going in the Spring for
the Gown to England.[58]

Sunday 28.

Rode to Church—the Parson was absent; it is indeed a little cold!
The Clerk read prayers for us—We rode home—Found at Home
two young Ladies, Miss Corbin, and Miss Turburville and Mr George
Lee, brother to the Gentleman here last Sunday, & has lately returned
from England—I was introduced by Mr Carter to the two latter—

Monday 29.

All our Scholars present—Mr Carter has put into my hands; Tyre's
Dictionary, & the pronouncing Dictionary, to improve his Sons in
Grammar classically, both Latin and English. and he has given me
Fenning in Arrithmetic.

Teusday 30.

Busy in School—I was solicited the other Day at the Race by one
Mr *Gordon*,[59] to take and instruct two of his Sons, Saturday also I
was again solicited by Mr Fantleroy to take two of his Sons—But
I must decline it—

Wednesday Decemr 1st 1773.

Busy in School—Wrote home by the Post, to Mr Green & *Johnny
Peck*. Afternoon Vacant.

[LETTER OF PHILIP V. FITHIAN TO THE REVEREND ENOCH GREEN]

Decemr 1st 1773.

REVD SIR.

As you desired I may not omit to inform you, so far as I can by a letter, of the business in which I am now engaged, it would indeed be vastly agreeable to me if it was in my power to give you particular intelligence concerning the state and plan of my employment here.

I set out from home the 20th of Octr and arrived at the Hon: Robert Carters, of Nominy, in Westmorland County, the 28th I began to teach his children the first of November. He has two sons, and one Nephew; the oldest Son is turned of seventeen, and is reading Salust and the greek grammer; the others are about fourteen, and in english grammer, and Arithmetic. He has besides five daughters which I am to teach english, the eldest is turned of fifteen, and is reading the spectator; she is employed two days in every week in learning to play the Forte-Piana, and Harpsicord—The others are smaller, and learning to read and spell. Mr Carter is one of the Councellors in the general court at Williamsburg, and possest of as great, perhaps the clearest fortune according to the estimation of people here, of any man in Virginia: He seems to be a good scholar, even in classical learning, and is remarkable one in english grammar; and notwithstanding his rank, which in general seems to countenance indulgence to children, both himself and Mrs Carter have a manner of instructing and dealing with children far superior, I may say it with confidence, to any I have ever seen, in any place, or in any family. They keep them in perfect subjection to themselves, and never pass over an occasion of reproof; and I blush for many of my acquaintances when I say that the children are more kind and complaisant to the servants who constantly attend them than we are to our superiors in age and condition. Mr Carter has an over-grown library of Books of which he allows me the free use. It consists of a general collection of law books, all the Latin and Greek Classicks, vast number of Books on Divinity chiefly by writers who are of the established Religion; he has the works of almost all the late famous writers, as Locke, Addison, Young, Pope, Swift, Dryden, &c. in Short, Sir, to speak moderately, he has more than eight times your number[60]—His eldest Son, who seems to be a Boy of Genius and application is to be sent to Cambridge University, but I believe will go through a course either in Philadelphia or Princeton College first. As to what is commonly said concerning Virginia that it is difficult to avoid being corrupted with the manners of the people, I believe it is founded wholly in a mistaken notion that persons must, when here frequent all promiscuous assemblies; but this is so far from truth that any one who does practise it, tho' he is accused of no crime, loses at once his character; so that either the manners have been lately changed, or the report is false, for he seems now to be best esteemed and most applauded who attends to his business, whatever it be, with the greatest diligence. I believe the virginians have of late altered their manner very much, for they begin to find that their estates by even small extravagance, decline, and grow involved with debt, this seems to be the spring which induces the People of fortune who are the pattern of all behaviour here, to be frugal, and moderate. You may expect me at home by the permission of Providence the latter end of april next, or the beginning of May; and as I proposed I shall present my exercises for the examination of the Presbytery; and if they think proper I shall gladly accept of a licence in the fall: I must beg your favour to mention me to such of my acquaintances in Deerfield as you think proper, but especially to Mrs Green, Miss *Betsy*, your family, and Mrs Pecks—I must also beg you to transmit so much of this intelligence to Mr Hunter as that my relations in Greenwich may know that I am through the mercy of heaven in good health. I beg, Sir, you will not fail to write, and let it be known to Mr Hunter, that a letter will come as secure by the Post as from Cohansie to Philadelphia; the Letters are to be directed to me thus, To Mr Philip V. Fithian at Mr *Carters* of Nominy, to be left at Hobes Hole[61]

I am, Sir, yours

PHILIP V FITHIAN

[JOURNAL]

Thursday 2.

Busy in School.

Fryday 3.

Busy in School. Expence to Boy for trimming my Horse half a Bit. Evening after School walked in the fields with Mrs *Carter*, Miss Carter, and Miss Nancy.

Saturday 4.

About Eleven Ben and I rode to Mr Lees walked over a Part of his Farm; from his House we see the Potowmack, and a fine River putting from it. We returned in the Evening, found Mr Fantleroy, and Mr Walker at Home; at Supper I had the pleasure to toast in my turn Miss Corbin—But I meant the absent *Laura!*

Sunday 5.

Rode to Richmond upper Church, a Polite Assembly; Mr Gibbern gave us a Sermon on, O Death I will be thy Plague &c., a warm discourse Dined at Home.

Monday 6.

Mr Walker left us after Breakfast. Busy in School.

Teusday 7.

Mr *Stadley* Miss Priscilla's Music Master arrived this morning—He performed several peices on the Violin.
Expence for an Orange half a Bit.

Wednesday 8.

Miss Priscilla with her Music Master, they performed together to day—

Thursday 9.

Mr Stadley left us. Busy in School.

Fryday 10.

Miss Nancy is beginning on the *Guitar*. Ben finished reading Salusts Cataline Conspiracy.

Saturday 11.

Rode and Dined with Captain Walker—Saw and dined with Miss *Simpson* & Mr Warden.[62]

Sunday 12.

Rode to Nominy-Church, parson Smith preached 15 minutes—
Advertisement at the Church door dated Sunday Decemr 12th Pork
to be sold to-morrow at 20/. per Hundred—dined with us to day
Captain Walker. Colonel Richd Lee,[63] & Mr Lanclot Lee. sat after
Dinner till Sunset, drank three Bottles of Medaira, two Bowls of
Toddy!—

Monday 13.

Mr Carter is preparing for a Voyage in his Schooner, the Hariot,[64]
to the Eastern Shore in Maryland, for Oysters: there are of the party,
Mr *Carter*, Captain *Walker* Colonel *Richd Lee*, & Mr *Lancelot Lee*.
With Sailors to work the vessel—I observe it is a general custom on
Sundays here, with Gentlemen to invite one another home to dine,
after Church; and to consult about, determine their common business,
either before or after Service—It is not the Custom for Gentlemen
to go into Church til Service is beginning, when they enter in a Body,
in the same manner as they come out; I have known the Clerk to
come out and call them in to prayers.—They stay also after the Service is over, usually as long, sometimes longer, than the Parson was
preaching—Almost every Lady wears a red Cloak; and when they
ride out they tye a white handkerchief over their Head and face, so
that when I first came into Virginia, I was distress'd whenever I saw
a Lady, for I thought She had the Tooth-Ach!—The People are extremely hospitable, and very polite both of which are most certainly
universal Characteristics of the Gentlemen in Virginia—some swear
bitterly, but the practise seems to be generally disapproved—I have
heard that this Country is notorious for Gaming, however this be, I
have not seen a Pack of *Cards*, nor a *Die*, since I left home, nor gaming
nor Betting of any kind except at the Richmond-Race. Almost every
Gentleman of Condition, keeps a Chariot and *Four;* many drive with
six Horses—I observe that all the Merchants & shopkeepers in the
Sphere of my acquaintance and I am told it is the case through the
Province, are young Scotch-Men; Several of whom I know, as *Cunningham, Jennings, Hamilton, Blain;*—And it has been the custom
heretofore to have all their Tutors, and Schoolmasters from Scotland,
tho' they begin to be willing to employ their own Countrymen—
Evening Ben Carter and myself had a long dispute on the practice of

fighting—He thinks it best for two persons who have any dispute to go out in good-humour & fight manfully, & says they will be sooner and longer friends than to brood and harbour malice—Mr *Carter* is practising this Evening on the *Guittar* He begins with the *Trumpet Minuet.* He has a good Ear for Music; a vastly delicate Taste: and keeps good Instruments, he has here at Home a *Harpsichord, Forte-Piano, Harmonica,*[65] *Guittar, Violin,* & *German Flutes,* & at Williamsburg, has a good *Organ,* he himself also is indefatigable in the Practice.

Teusday 14.

Busy in School—The Weather vastly fine! There has been no Rain of consequence, nor any stormy or disagreeable Weather, since about the 10th of last Month! From the Window, by which I write, I have a broad, a diversified, and an exceedingly beautiful Prospect of the high craggy Banks of the River *Nominy!* Some of those huge Hills are cover'd thick with *Cedar,* & Pine Shrubs; A vast quantity of which seems to be in almost every part of this Province—Others are naked, & when the Sun Shines look beautiful! At the Distance of

about 5 Miles is the River Potowmack over which I can see the smoky Woods of Maryland; At this window I often stand, and cast my Eyes homeward with peculiar pleasure! Between my window and the potowmack, is Nominy Church, it stands close on the Bank of the River Nominy, in a pleasant agreeable place, Mr Carters family go down often, so many as can with convenience in a Boat rowed by four Men, and generally arrive as soon as those who ride.

The mouth of Nominy River where it falls into Potowmack is about 25 miles above the mouth of Potowmack or where it falls into the Chessapeak-Bay. And about 12 Miles below the mouth of Nominy the River Ucomico[66] puts up into the country, near which River, and about three miles from the mouth stands the lower parish Church of Westmorland County call'd Ucomic Church.[67] The River Potowmack opposite to us the People say is 18 miles over, but I think it is not more than 8. Afternoon Captain *Grigg*,[68] who arrived last Sunday moning into the River Ucomico from *London* visited Mr Carter. Evening reading Picteete.

Wednesday 15.

Busy in School—To day Dined with us Mrs Turburville, & her Daughter Miss Letty[69] Miss Jenny Corbin, & Mr Blain. We dined at three. The manner here is different from our way of living in Cohansie—In the morning so soon as it is light a Boy knocks at my Door to make a fire; after the Fire is kindled, I rise which now in the winter is commonly by Seven, or a little after, By the time I am drest the Children commonly enter the School-Room, which is under the Room I sleep in; I hear them round one lesson, when the Bell rings for eight o-Clock (for Mr Carter has a large good Bell of upwards of 60 Lb. which may be heard some miles, & this is always rung at meal Times;) the Children then go out; and at half after eight the Bell rings for Breakfast, we then repair to the Dining-Room; after Breakfast, which is generally about half after nine, we go into School, and sit til twelve, when the Bell rings, & they go out for noon; the dinner-Bell rings commonly about half after two, often at three, but never before two.—After dinner is over, which in common, when we have no Company, is about half after three we go into School, & sit til the Bell rings at five, when they separate til the next morning; I have to myself in the Evening, a neat Chamber, a large Fire, Books, & Candle & my Liberty, either to continue in the school room, in my own

Room or to sit over at the great House with Mr & Mrs Carter—
We go into Supper commonly about half after eight or at nine & I
usually go to Bed between ten and Eleven. Altho the family in which
I live, is certainly under as good political Regulations, and every way
as suitable & agreeable as I can expect, or even could desire; & though
the Neighbourhood is polite, & the Country pleasant, yet I cannot
help reflecting on my situation last winter, which was near the lovely
Laura for whom I cannot but have the truest, and the warmest Esteem! possibly, If Heaven shall preserve my life, in some future time,
I may again enjoy her good society.

Mr Carter heard this Evening that Captain *Walker* cannot go to
Maryland, he is thus stop'd.

Thursday 16.

I can only to day write down my Misfortune; my poor Horse as he
was feeding in a miry Bottom, walked upon a sharp Stick, which
stuck into his Thigh on the under Side about four Inches below his
Flank!—The stick went in more than three Inches!—He is very lame,
but they tell me will recover, The Hostler, when we had lead him
to the Stable, applied Spirits of Turpentine to the part, and in the
Evening is to fill it with Comfrey Roots pounded Soft.

I had the pleasure of walking to Day at twelve o-Clock with Mrs
Carter; She shewed me her stock of *Fowls* & *Mutton* for the winter;
She observed, with great truth, that to live in the Country, and take
no pleasure at all in Groves, Fields, or Meadows; nor in Cattle,
Horses, & domestic Poultry, would be a manner of life too tedious to
endure; Dined at three.

Fryday 17.

I dismissed the children this morning til' monday on account of
Mr Christian's *Dance*, which, as it goes through his Scholars in Rotation, happens to be here to Day—and I myself also am unwell, so as
not to go out;—Mrs Carter sent me over Coffee for Breakfast; & soon
after some Spirits of *Hartshorn* for my Head—At twelve she sent the
waiting Man to know if I was better, & what I would choose for
Dinner. I thank'd her, & desired that She would give herself no trouble; She was careful, however, from her undistinguished kindness, to
send me before Dinner some hot *Barley Broth*,—*Ben Carter* before
Noon introduced into my Room, Mr *Billy Booth*,[70] a young Gentle-

man of Fortune, who is one of Mr Christians pupils—The two Master Fantleroys came in also to see me—There came to the dance three *Chariots*, two *Chairs*, & a number of Horses. Towards Evening I grew Better, & walked down, with a number of young Fellows to the River; after our return I was strongly solicited by the young Gentlemen to go in and dance I declined it, however, and went to my Room not without Wishes that it had been a part of my Education to learn what I think is an innocent and an ornamental, and most certainly, in this province is a necessary qualification for a person to appear even decent in Company!—

Mrs *Carter* in the Evening, sent me for Supper, a Bowl of hot Green Tea, & several *Tarts*. I expected that they would have danced til late in the Night, but intirely contrary to my Expectation, the Company were separated to their respective apartments before half after nine o*Clock*.

Saturday 18.

Rose by Seven, Sent for Mr Carters Barber and was drest for Breakfast—We went in to Breakfast at ten;—I confess I have been seldom more dash'd than when I entered the dining-Room, for I must of necessity be interrogated by Mr *Carter* before them all, about my indisposition, and if I was better.—I went through the several Ceremonies with as much resolution, and speed as possible, and soon mixed with the Company in promiscuous conversation. There were present of Grown persons Mr & Mrs. *Carter*, Mrs *Lee*, & Miss *Jenny Corbin*; young Misses about Eleven: & Seven young Fellows, including myself;—After Breakfast, we all retired into the Dancing-Room, & after the Scholars had their Lesson singly round Mr Christian, very politely, requested me to step a *Minuet*; I excused myself however, but signified my peculiar pleasure in the Accuracy of their performance—There were several Minuets danced with great ease and propriety; after which the whole company Joined in country-dances,[71] and it was indeed beautiful to admiration, to see such a number of young persons, set off by dress to the best Advantage, moving easily, to the sound of well performed Music, and with perfect regularity, tho' apparently in the utmost Disorder—The Dance continued til two, we dined at half after three—soon after Dinner we repaired to the Dancing-Room again; I observe in the course of the lessons, that Mr Christian is punctual, and rigid in his discipline, so strict indeed that he struck two of the young Misses for a fault in the course of their performance, even in the presence of the Mother of one of them! And he rebuked one of the young Fellows so highly as to tell him he must alter his manner, which he had observed through the Course of the Dance, to be insolent, and wanton, or absent himself from the School—I thought this a sharp reproof, to a young Gentleman of seventeen, before a large number of Ladies! —When it grew too dark to dance, the young Gentlemen walked over to my Room, we conversed til half after six; Nothing is now to be heard of in conversation, but the *Balls*, the *Fox-hunts*, the fine *entertainments*, and the *good fellowship*, which are to be exhibited at the approaching *Christmas*.—I almost think myself happy that my Horses lameness will be sufficient Excuse for my keeping at home on these Holidays.—Mr Goodlet[72] was barr'd out of his School last Monday by his Scholars, for the Christmas Holidays, which are to continue til twelfth-day; But my Scholars are of a more quiet nature, and have consented to have four or five Days now, and to have their full Holiday in May next, when I propose by the permission of Providence to go Home, where I hope to see the good and benevolent *Laura*.

When the candles were lighted we all repaired, for the last time, into the dancing Room; first each couple danced a Minuet; then all joined as before in the country Dances, these continued till half after Seven when Mr Christian retired; and at the proposal of several, (with Mr Carters approbation) we played *Button*, to get Pauns for Redemption; here I could join with them, and indeed it was carried on with sprightliness, and Decency; in the course of redeeming my Pauns, I had several Kisses of the Ladies!—Early in the Evening cam colonel Philip Lee,[73] in a travelling Chariot from Williamsburg— Half after eight we were rung in to Supper; The room looked luminous and splendid; four very large candles burning on the table where we supp'd, three others in different parts of the Room; a gay, sociable Assembly, & four well instructed waiters!—So soon as we rose from supper, the Company form'd into a semicircle round the fire, & Mr Lee, by the voice of the Company was chosen *Pope*, and Mr Carter, Mr Christian, Mrs *Carter*, Mrs *Lee*, and the rest of the company were appointed Friars, in the play call'd "break the Popes neck"—Here we had great Diversion in the respective Judgments upon offenders, but we were all dismiss'd by ten, and retired to our several Rooms.

Sunday 19.

Early this morning, I was awaked out of sleep by two youngsters, (for we are thronged with company, so that two slept in my Room) who were agreeing upon a Ride the Day after Christmas, (which will be Sunday) up to Fredricksburg, which lies upon the Rapahannock, fifty Miles higher up the country than where we live;—Breakfasted at nine, soon after which all our company dispersed; I had the offer of a Horse, & was strongly solicited to go to Church, but I declined it—My Horse is very lame, his Thigh, from the sore down to his knee is much swell'd!—It runs however, and the Hostler tells me it is mending. Dined at three; Miss Betsy Lee [74] dined with us—Writing to day my Sermon for the Presbitery. Sup'd on Oysters.
This is the first day I have missed Church.

Monday 20.

Rose at half after Seven; the Morning extremely cold—We had in School to Day as visitors Miss Betsy, and Miss Matilda Lee [75] Mr Carter gave me for his Daughter Nancy to Read, the "Compleat Letter-writer"—Also he put into my hands for the use of the School, "the British-Grammar."

Teusday 21.

Rose by Half after seven—the weather serene but sharp and cold. —To day, before Dinner called in and stayed a short time Mr *Blain* and Mr *Lee* who were going to one Mr Lanes [76] to a *Christning*, which I understand is one of the chief times for Diversion here—Miss *Carter*, this afternoon told me that her Mama thought of giving a small *Ball* at the approaching Christmas for select friends.

[PHILIP V. FITHIAN TO ELIZABETH BEATTY]

Nominy-Hall Virginia. Decem: 21. 1773.

To LAURA.

If these shall be so fortunate, as to come to your Hands, I beg leave to acquaint you that I am as agreeably settled as I can possibly be when so remote from the chief object of my Esteem on Earth—

And, that I am, & have been, since I left Home, through the Kindness of Heaven, in good Health.

You will be surprized if I tell you that I should have been now in Cohansie, had I never seen you, or had you been less uncertain of your future Purpose! That you may not be wholly without a Reason for what I say, I must tell you, that in your Absence last Summer I found it difficult to restrain myself from Writing frequently to you; And after I was compell'd, tho' unwilling, to believe that you would grant me no Return; lest I should be troublesome or impertinent, when I had an advantageous Offer from the Gentleman with whom I now reside, I determined to leave Home a few Months. So far I have jested—But to be serious, Laura, I hope to see you in the Spring as I propose to be at Home by the Beginning of May—Perhaps the fine Air; the sprightly Conversation; the sociable Balls; & various Pleasures so common here, will have made so very a "Coxcomb" of musty Philander, that you will blush to confess you ever knew him! Be not hasty to judge—Possibly, on the other Hand, Laura; even Laura, may appear so dull & unfashionable that Philander tho' a Coxcomb will look down & despise her—No Laura, for tho, we have fine Ladies; Gay Fellows, charming Music; rich & I may say luxurious Entertainment; to all which I am almost every Week strongly invited; Yet I find greater Pleasure at Home, where I have every genteel Accomodation I could wish, and a Family of lovely Children to instruct—You would envy me if I was able to tell you how kind, obedient, & beautiful the Children are which I teach!—I have three Boys the youngest of which is about the Age & Size of your Brother R—Also five Girls between five & fourteen years Old. The Girls all dress in White, & are remarkably genteel. They have been educated in the City Williamsburg in this Colony—The two eldest are now learning Music, one to play the Harpsichord; the other the Guittar, in the practice of which they spend three Days in the Week—I have only further to acquaint you that every one is now speaking of the approaching Christmas.—The young Ladies tell me we are to have a Ball, of selected Friends in this Family—But I, hard Lot, I have never learn'd to dance!

I am, however,

my dear Eliza, thine

PHI: V. FITHIAN.

[JOURNAL]

Wednesday 22.

Mr *Cunningham* came last Evening and staid the Night.—There is a Report that he is making suit to Miss *Jenny Corbin.*

To day I finished my Sermon for the Presbitery—I read *Pictete,* The *Spectator, Salust, History of England, English Grammar, Arithmetic,* and the *Magazines* by turns. Miss *Priscilla,* and Miss *Nancy* rode this morning in the Chariot over to Mr *Turburvills*—Bob, every day at twelve o-Clock, is down by the River Side with his Gun after Ducks, Gulls &c.—Ben is on his Horse a Riding, Harry, is either in the Kitchen, or at the Blacksmiths, or Carpenters Shop. They all find places of Rendesvous so soon as the Beell rings, and all seem to choose different Sports!—To day dined with us Mr Cox the Gentleman at whose House I breakfasted the Day after I came first.—Evening Mr Carter spent in playing on the Harmonica; It is the first time I have heard the Instrument. The music is charming! He play'd, Water parted from the Sea.[77]—The Notes are clear and inexpressibly Soft, they swell, and are inexpressibly grand; & either it is because the sounds are new, and therefore please me, or it is the most captivating Instrument I have Ever heard. The sounds very much resemble the human voice, and in my opinion they far exceed even the swelling Organ.

Thursday 23.

Rose at eight—Rains this morning, the weather is also warmer. Mr Carter has sent his son Ben to his head *Overseer,* to take notice and account of the measuring the Crop of Corn—For the Planters now have just gathered in their Summers Crop!—To Day I write a letter to *Laura:* Waft it, kind Oppertunity, soon to the dear Maid, and Make it easy, & desirable for her to make me a Return!—

At Dinner Mr & Mrs *Carter* gave their opinion concerning what they thought pleasing and agreeable in a person; Mrs Carter said she loved a sociable open, chatty person; that She could not bear Sullenness, and stupidity—Mr Carter, on the other-hand, observed that it is just which Solomon says, that there is a "time for all things under the Sun"; that it discovers great Judgment to laugh in Season, and that, on the whole, he is pleased with Taciturnity—pray which of the two should I suit?—It is a custom with our *Bob* whenever he can coax his *Dog* up stairs, to take him into his Bed, and make him a companion; I was much pleased this morning while he and *Harry* were reading in Course a Chapter in the Bible, that they read in the 27th Chapter of Deuteronomy the Curses threatened there for Crimes; Bob seldom, perhaps never before, read the verse, at last read that "Cursed be he that lyeth with any manner of Beast, and all the People shall say Amen." I was exceedingly Pleased, yet astonished at the Boy on two accounts.—1st At the end of every verse, befor he came to this, he would pronounce aloud, "Amen." But on Reading this verse he not only omitted the "Amen," but seem'd visibly struck with confusion!—2d And so soon as the Verse was read, to excuse himself, he said at once, Brother *Ben* slept all last winter with his Dog, and learn'd me!—Thus ready are Mankind always to evade Correction!—This Evening, after I had dismiss'd the Children, & was sitting in the School-Room cracking Nuts, none present but Mr *Carters Clerk*, a civil, inoffensive, agreeable young Man, who acts both in the character of a Clerk and Steward, when the Woman who makes my Bed, asked me for the key of my Room, and on seeing the young Man sitting with me, she told him that her Mistress had this afternoon given orders that their Allowance of Meat should be given out to them to-morrow.—She left us; I then asked the young man what their allowance is? He told me that excepting some favourites about the table, their weekly allowance is a peck of Corn, & a pound of Meat a Head!—And Mr Carter is allow'd by all, & from what I have already seen of others, I make no Doubt at all but he is, by far the most humane to his Slaves of any in these parts! Good God! are these Christians?—When I am on the Subject, I will relate further, what I heard Mr George Lees Overseer, one Morgan, say the other day that he himself had often done to Negroes, and found it useful; He said that whipping of any kind does them no good, for they will laugh at your greatest Severity; But he told us he had invented two things, and by several experiments had proved their success.—For Sulleness, Obstinacy, or Idleness, says he, Take a Negro, strip him, tie him fast to a post; take then a sharp Curry-Comb, & curry him severely til he is well scrap'd; & call a Boy with some dry Hay, and make the Boy rub him down for several Minutes, then salt him, & unlose him. He will attend to his Business, (said the inhuman Infidel) afterwards!—But savage Cruelty does not exceed His next diabolical Invention—To get a Secret from a Negro, says he, take the following Method—Lay upon your Floor a large thick plank, having a peg about eighteen Inches long, of hard wood, & very Sharp, on the upper end, fixed fast in the plank—then strip the Negro, tie the Cord to a staple in the Ceiling, so as that his foot may just rest on the sharpened Peg, then turn him briskly round, and you would laugh (said our informer) at the Dexterity of the Negro, while he was re-leiving his Feet on the sharpen'd Peg!—I need say nothing of these seeing there is a righteous God, who will take vengeance on such Inventions!—Miss *Priscilla* and *Nancy* returned in the evening.

Fryday 24.

Ben Rode off this morning before day to Mr Fantleroys, for Christmas I dismiss'd the children while next Wednesday. I was introduced by Mr Carter at Dinner, to Dr Jones[78] a practitioner in Richmond. I spent my Day in my Room alone as agreeably as I have done any since I have been in virginia coppying off my Sermon, & correcting it. Retirement is as pleasing, & desirable to me here as at *princeton*, or *Cohansie!* & by Gods blessing I hope to make it as profitable. In the Evening I read the two first Books of *popes Homer*. Dr Jones supped with us, & is to stay the Night. The conversation at supper was on Nursing Children; I find it is common here for people of Fortune to have their young Children suckled by the Negroes! Dr Jones told us his first and only Child is now with such a Nurse; & Mrs Carter said that Wenches have suckled several of hers—Mrs Carter has had thirteen Children She told us to night and she has nine now living; of which seven are with me. Guns are fired this Evening in the Neighbourhood, and the Negroes seem to be inspired with new Life.[79] The Day has been serene and mild, but the Evening is hazy.

Supp'd on Oysters.

Saturday 25.

I was waked this morning by Guns fired all round the House. The morning is stormy, the wind at South East rains hard Nelson the Boy who makes my Fire, blacks my shoes, does errands &c. was early in my Room, drest only in his shirt and Breeches! He made me a vast fire, blacked my Shoes, set my Room in order, and wish'd me a joyful Christmas, for which I gave him half a Bit.—Soon after he left the Room, and before I was Drest, the Fellow who makes the Fire in our School Room, drest very neatly in green, but almost drunk, entered my chamber with three or four profound Bows, & made me the same

salutation; I gave him a *Bit*, and dismissed him as soon as possible.—
Soon after my Cloths and Linen were sent in with a message for a
Christmas *Box*, as they call it; I sent the poor Slave a Bit, & my thanks.
—I was obliged for want of small change, to put off for some days
the Barber who shaves & dresses me.—I gave *Tom* the Coachman,
who Doctors my Horse, for his care two Bits, & am to give more
when the Horse is well.—I gave to *Dennis* the Boy who waits at Table
half a *Bit*—So that the sum of my Donations to the Servants, for this
Christmas appears to be five Bits, a Bit is a pisterene bisected; or an
English sixpence, & passes here for seven pence Halfpenny. the whole
is *3s 1½d.*—

At Breakfast, when Mr Carter entered the Room, he gave us the
compliments of the Season. He told me, very civily, that as my Horse
was Lame, his own riding Horse is at my Service to ride when &
where I Choose.

Mrs Carter was, as always, cheerful, chatty, & agreeable; She told
me after Breakfast several droll, merry Occurrences that happened
while she was in the City Williamsburg.—

This morning came from the Post-office at Hobbes-Hole, on the
Rappahannock, our News-papers. Mr Carter takes the Pennsylvania
Gazette, which seems vastly agreeable to me, for it is like having
something from home—But I have yet no answer to my Letter. We
dined at four o-Clock—Mr Carter kept in his Room, because he
breakfasted late, and on Oysters—There were at Table Mrs Carter
& her five Daughters that are at School with me—Miss *Priscilla,
Nancy, Fanny, Betsy,* and *Harriot,* five as beautiful delicate, well-
instructed Children as I have ever known!—*Ben* is abroad; *Bob* &
Harry are out; so there was no Man at Table but myself.—I must
carve—Drink the Health—and talk if I can! Our Dinner was no
otherwise than common, yet as elegant a *Christmas Dinner* as I ever
sat Down to—The table Discourse was Marriage; Mrs *Carter* observ'd
that was she a Widow, she should scruple to marry any man alive;
She gave a reason, that She did not think it probable a man could love
her grown old when the world is thronged with blooming, ripening
Virgins; but in fact Mrs Carter looks & would pass for a younger
Woman than some unmarried Ladies of my acquaintance, who
would willingly enough make us place them below twenty!—We
dined at four; when we rose from table it was growing dark—The
wind continues at South East & is stormy and muddy.

Mr *Randolph* the Clerk told me this Evening a Circumstance concerning *Bob* which tho it discovered stupidity, yet at the same time discovered great thoughtfulness.—It was about his sleeping with the *Dog;* Mr *Randolph* told me *Bob* asked him with great solemnity if he thought *God Almighty* knew it!—While we supped Mr *Carter* as he often does played on the *Forte-Piano*. He almost never sups. Last Night and to night I had large clear, & very elegant Spermaceti Candles sent into my Room;

Sunday 26.

I rose at eight—The morning is fair; all seem quiet—I went to the window before I was drest, having only a Gown thrown about me & enjoy'd a beautiful Prospect of the high Banks of the River Nomini gilded by the morning Sun—I could not help casting my Eyes with eagerness over the blue Potowmack and look homewards.—After having paid my morning secret Devotion to the King of Kings, I sat myself to the correcting and transcribing my Sermon—I had the pleasure to wait on Mrs *Carter* to Church She rode in the Chariot, & Miss Prissy and Nancy; Mr Carter chose to stay at Home—The Sacrament was to have been administred but there was so few people that he thought it improper, and put of til Sunday fortnight. He preach'd from Isaiah 9.6. For unto us a child is Born &c. his Sermon was fifteen Minutes long! very fashionable—He invited me very civilly to Dine & spend the Evening with him, but I could not leave the Ladies! He made me almost promise, however to call some Day this Week.

At the Church to day I heard an impious Expression from a young Scotch-Man,[80] Tutor in Mr Washingtons Family; he meant it for a Satire upon the neglect of the people in suffering their Grave Yard to lie common—He saw some Cattle & Hogs feeding & rooting in the yard; "Why, says he, if I was buried here it would grieve me to look up and see *Swine* feeding over me"!—But I understand only the lower sort of People are buried at the Church; for the Gentleman have private burying-Yards.

Monday 27.

At Breakfast Mrs Carter gave me an Invitation to wait on her to Parson *Smiths* Mr Carter offered Me his riding Horse, A beautiful grey, young, lively Colt; We sat out about ten, Mrs Carter, Miss

Prissy, Miss Fanny, & Miss Betsy, in the Chariot; Bob and I were on Horse back; Mrs Carter had three waiting Men; a Coachman. Driver & Postillion. We found the way muddy; got there a little after twelve; Mr Smith was out; I was introduced by Mrs Carter to Mrs Smith, and a young Lady her Sister who lives with them; At Dinner I was at Mr Smiths request to "say Grace" as they call it; which is always express'd by the People in the following words, "God bless us in what we are to receive"—& after Dinner, "God make us thankful for his mercies—As we were sitting down to Table Ben Carter rode up; when we had dined, the Ladies retired, leaving us a Bottle of Wine, & a Bowl of Toddy for companions—Ben came with a Message for me to go to a Ball, but poor fellow, I cant dance!—He prest me very much, but I was forced to decline it—We returned in the Evening; & found Mr Carter & Miss Nancy practising Music, one on the Forte-Piano, and the other on the Guitar. Mr Carter is Learning Bedford, Coles hill, and several other Church Tunes.

Teusday 28.

Last Night there fell a Snow, which is about half Shoe deep, the Air is sharp, the wind at North, & Snows yet by turns. I finished and laid by my Sermon for the Presbytery this morning—Breakfasted at ten: Ben staid last Night at Mr *Turbuville's* & got Home to day about twelve from his *Christmas Jaunt*.

Spent most of the Day at the great House hearing the various Instruments of Music. Evening, at Miss Prissy's Request I drew for her some Flowers on Linen which she is going to imbroider, for a various Counterpane.

Wednesday 29.

This Morning our School begins after the Holidays. Bob seems sorry that he must forsake the Marsh & River when he is daily fowling, & never kills any Game. At Dinner we had the Company of Dr Franks[81] who has been all along Mr Carters Clerk; but is now leaving Him. We had a large Pye cut to Day to signify the Conclusion of the Holidays. I drew, this afternoon more Flowers for Miss Prissy.

Thursday 30.

Dr Franks is moving. he has lived in the House adjoining our School. The morning is fine, I rose by eight, breakfasted at ten, Miss Prissy & Nancy are to-Day Practising Music one on the Forte Piano, the other on the Guitar. their Papa allows them for that purpose every Teusday, & Thursday. Ben is gone to the Quarter to see to the measuring the crop of Corn. On his return in the Evening, when we were sitting & chatting, among other things he told me that we must have a House-warming, seeing we have now got possession of the whole House—It is a custom here whenever any *person* or *Family* move into a *House*, or repair a house they have been living in before, they make a *Ball* & give a Supper—So we because we have gotten Possession of the whole House, are in compliance with Custom, to invite our Neighbours, and dance, and be merry—But poor me! I must hobble, or set quiet in the Corner!

Fryday 31.

I rose at eight. *Ben* gone again to the quarter—*Harriot* to Day for the first time said all her letters—
The Colonel shewed me after Dinner a new invention, which is to be sure his own, for tuning his *Harpischord* & *Forte-Piano:* it is a number of *Whistles*, of various Sizes so as to sound all the Notes in one Octave. At twelve o-Clock Mr *Carter* ordered his Boy to bring two Horses, and himself & Miss *Prissy* rode out for an airing as the Day is vastly fine—Assoon as the Bell rang & I had dismissed the Children I took a walk in the Garden; When I had gone round two or three Platts Mrs Carter entered and walked towards me, I then immediately turn'd and and met Her; I bowed—Remarked on the pleasantness of the Day—And began to ask her some questions upon a

Row of small slips—To all which she made polite and full answers;
As we walked along she would move the Ground at the Root of some
plant; or prop up with small sticks the bended *scions*—We took two
whole turns through all the several Walks, & had such conversation
as the *Place* and *Objects* naturally excited—And after Mrs Carter had
given some orders to the Gardiners (for there are two Negroes
Gardiners by Trade, who are constantly when the Weather will any
how permit working in it) we walked out into the *Area* viewed some
Plumb-Trees, when we saw Mr Carter and Miss Prissy returning—
We then repaired to the Slope before the front-Door where they dismounted—and we all went into the Dining Room. I shall in a proper
time describe the great-House, & the several smaller ones in its neighbourhood; the *Area, Poplar-Walk, Garden,* & *Pasture:* In the mean
time I shall only say, they discover a delicate and Just Tast, and are
the effect of great *Invention* & *Industry,* & *Expence.* At Dinner we
were conversing on the seasons of the Year, & giving our different
opinions of which of the Seasons we each thought most agreeable:
Mrs Carter chose the Months of October, November & December,
her reasons were, that we are always most sensible of pleasure when
it succeeds Axiety & Pain; therefore because these months immediately follow those in which there is usually Thunder & Lightning &
intense Heat, She thinks them most pleasant: The Colonel agreed
with her as to the Months but gave a different Reason; He supposes
that in these Months the Air is more uniform and settled than at any
other so long time in the year. I preferr'd May, June, and July, because our Bodies at that Season are generally sprightly, vigorous and
healthy, and the world around us is beautiful & growing to necessary
perfection. Miss Prissy & Miss Nancy were on my side.

Mrs Carter told the Colonel that he must not think her setled (for
they have been for a long time from this place in the City *Williamsburg*, and only left it about a year and a half ago) till he made her a
park and stock'd it; while these and many other things were saying,
I was surprized at a Remark which Miss *Prissy* made, "Why Mama
says she, you plan and talk of these things as tho' you should never
die"!

Saturday January 1. 1774.

Another Year is gone! Last New years Day I had not the most
remote expectation of being now here in *Virginia!* Perhaps by the

next I shall have made a longer and more important Remove, from this to the World of Spirits!

It is well worth the while, for the better improving of our time to come to recollect and reflect upon the Time which we have spent; The Season seems to require it; it will give entertainment at least, perhaps much substantial pleasure too, to be able to make with a considerable degree of certainty a review of the general course of our Actions in the course of a year. This shall be my employment, so far as I am able to recollect, when I shall have suitable time for the fixing & laying my thoughts together—

In the mean time I observe that the Day is most pleasant, the wind is West, not fresh; the air is void of clouds, but near the Earth is smoky; the Ground is clear of Frost and setled, what can be finer? Mr Carter Miss Prissy and myself were to have rode out for an Exercise at twelve, but we were prevented by the coming of a Gentleman, Dr *Fantleroy*,[82] to whom Mr Carter introduced me—

After Dinner was finished which was about four o-Clock, Miss Prissy & Myself, together with a Servant (for Mr Carter would not trust us alone he said) rode on Horse-Back to Mr Turbuvilles, about three quarters of a Mile distance; It is the first time I have been there, the House is near, & in Sight, and the families intimate. I rode my Horse for the first time since his misfortune. When we returned about Candlelight, we found Mrs Carter in the yard seeing to the Roosting of her Poultry; and the Colonel in the Parlour tuning his *Guitar*.

Sunday 2.

The weather warm and Damp—The Family rode to Church to-day and are to dine out. Mr Carter at my request, gave me the Keys of his Book-Cases and allowed me to spend the Day alone in his Library.

The place seems suitable for Study, & the Day ought to be spent in serious contemplation; therefore, as I proposed Yesterday, I shall collect together and write down what I have been doing in the last Year. But will my Life bear the review? Can I look upon my Actions and not Blush! And shall I be no less careful, or have no better Success, in the prosecution of my Duty the Year to come, if I shall be kept alive to the Close of it?—

In the Beginning of the last year I was in Deerfield, in Cumberland

County New-Jersey, with the Rev'd Mr Green; Under him I studied the Hebrew-Language and Divinity. I left the college the last of September 1772. After having setled my business at Home, I entered upon the Study of Divinity with the Rev'd Andrew Hunter; I was with him about a Month, and on the first of December I went to Mr *Green* with a design to acquaint myself with the Hebrew Tongue; he put me to the Grammar, which I learn'd through, and read some Chapters in the Psalter in the Course of the Winter: In Divinity, he advised me to read Ridgeleys body of Divinity for a System: And he gave me several separate treatisses on Repentance, Regeneration, Faith, &c, & towards spring gave me subjects to consider in the Sermon-Way. Yet how barren am I still? It is an arduous task to bring the Mind to close application; & still greater to lay up and retain useful Knowledge. I continued with Mr *Green* & pursued my studies, I hope with some Success till August 1773. when I was solicited by Dr *Witherspoon* to go into *Virginia* & teach in a Gentlemans Family—The Offer seem'd profitable; I was encouraged by the Dr and was to have his Recommendation—I had likewise myself a strong inclination to go—Yet I was in great Doubt, & Wholly undetermined for some Weeks, because many of my friends, and some of my near Relations opposed my leaving Home, and all seem'd utterly unwilling to advise to go—It is time, according to the Course of my Life they said that I was settling to some constant Employment, and they told me I ought especially to enter with as great speed as convenient into that plan of Life for which I have in particular had my Education—That Virginia is sickly—That the People there are profane, and exceeding wicked—That I shall read there no Calvinistic Books, nor hear any Presbyterian Sermons—That I must keep much Company, and therefore spend as much, very probably much more Money than my Salary—These considerations unsettled for a while my mind—On the other hand I proposed to myself the following advantages by going—A longer opportunity for Study than my friends would willingly allow me If I should remain at home—A more general acquaintance with the manners of Mankind; and a better Knowledge of the Soil, & Commerce of these neighbouring Provinces—And a more perfect acquaintance with the Doctrines, & method of Worship in the established Church in these Colonies, & especially with the Conduct of the Clergy of which there have been so many bad reports—All these however when I had laid them together, seem'd to overbear

the others, so that I determined at last to break through and go!—
Here now I am in a strange Province; But I am under no more nor
stronger temptations to any kind of vice, perhaps not so great as at
Cohansie,—unless sometimes when I am solicited to dance I am forc'd
to blush, for my Inability—I have the opportunity of living with
Credit perfectly retired—in a well regulated family—With a man
of Sense—May God help me to walk in his fear & Gloryfy his
Name!—

Monday 3d.

Last Evening, by Miss Prissy, I was complimented with an Invitation
from Mr *Turburville* to Dine with Him tomorrow—Squire *Lee*[83] is
as Miss Prissy told me, preparing to make a splendid *Ball*, which is to
last four or five Days; we are to be invited!—But I must stay at Home
and read *Salust*—Mr Carter is at Richmond-Court, which is held
monthly here in every County. In the Evening Mr Warden, a young
Scotch Lawyer came home with him. I spent the Evening in the
Parlour—After Supper when I was call'd upon for my Tost I mentioned with Pleasure Miss *Betsy Beaty*.

Teusday 4.

Rose by eight—Mr *Warden* breakfasted with us. Miss Prissy befor
Breakfast, as it is her practising Day, gave us sundry Tunes on the
Forte Piano. I kept the children while twelve then as we were to dine
out, I dismiss'd them till morning, and prepar'd to ride—Mrs Carter,
Miss Sylla, and Miss Betsy rode in the Chariot, and set off about half
after twelve with three waiting men—Mr Carter, Ben, and myself,
waited, & left Home by half after one, we rode on Horse back, and
waited on ourselves—It was two o-Clock when we got to Mr Turburvilles where we were to dine—We found there two Gentlemen, with
their Wives, and one of them had also a Son & Daughter Mr Booth
also came in a short time after us; So that there dined to day with
Mr Turburville to day besides his usual Family thirteen Persons.—
And if I mention the Waiting Men With the Carriages they were
twenty. We had an Elegant Dinner, but it did not in any thing
exceed what is every day at Mr *Carters* Table.
—We all returned Home before Dark—In the Evening the Colonel is
busy in transposing Music, I have not been at any house since I left

Home, which, from the appearance of its Situation, and the Economy
of the Family, or any other apparent Convenience, I would so soon
choose to reside in as a tutor, as the one in which it is my lot to be
placed—The Family is most agreeable! Mr Carter is sensible judi-
cious, much given to retirement & Study; his Company, & conversation are always profitable—His main Studies are *Law* & *Music*, the
latter of which seems to be his darling Amusement—It seems to
nourish, as well as entertain his mind! And to be sure he has a nice
well judging Ear, and has made great advances in the Theory. and
Practice of music—

Mrs *Carter* is prudent, always cheerful, never without Something
pleasant, a remarkable Economist, perfectly acquainted (in my Opinion) with the good-management of Children, intirely free from all
foolish and unnecessary fondness, and is also well acquainted (for
She has always been used) with the formality and Ceremony which
we find commonly in high Life—Ben, the eldest, is a youth of genius:
of a warm impetuous Disposition; desirous of acquiring Knowledge,
docile, vastly inquisitive & curious in mercantile, and mechanical
Matters, is very fond of Horsses, and takes great pleasure in exercising
them—Bob, the other Brother, is By no means destitute of capacity,
As Mr Marshal who was his last Tutor has asserted, & as many now
suppose: He is extremely volatile & unsettled in his temper, which
makes it almost wholly impossible to fix him for any time to the same
thing—On which account he has made but very little advancement
in any one Branch of Study, and this is attributed to Barrenness of
Genius—He is slovenly, clumsy, very fond of Shooting, of Dogs, of
Horses, But a very stiff untoward *Rider*, good natur'd, pleased with
the Society of persons much below his Family, and Estate, and tho'
quick and wrathful in his temper, yet he is soon moderated, & easily
subdued—Harry the Nephew, is rather stoical, sullen, or saturnine in
his make. He is obstinate, tho' Steady, and makes a slow uniform advance in his Learning, he is vastly kind to me, but in particular to my
Horse, of his health or Indisposition—Miss *Priscilla*, the eldest Daughter about 16, is steady, studious, docile, quick of apprehension, and
makes good progress in what She undertakes; If I could with propriety continue in the Family, I should require no stronger Induce-
ment than the Satisfaction I should receive by seeing this young Lady
become perfectly acquainted with any thing I propose so soon as I
communicate it to her, but the situation of my affairs makes it out of

my power to stay longer than a year; She is small of her age, has a mild winning Presence, a sweet obliging Temper, never swears, which is here a distinguished virtue, dances finely, plays well on key'd Instruments, and is upon the whole in the first Class of the female Sex.

Nancy the Second, is not without some few of those qualities which are by some (I think with great ill nature, and with little or no truth) said to belong intirely to the fair Sex. I mean great curiosity, Eagerness for superiority, Ardor in friend ship, But bitterness and rage where there is enmity—She is not constant in her disposition, nor diligent nor attentive to her business—But She has her excellencies, She is cheerful, tender in her Temper, easily managed by perswasion & is never without what seems to have been a common Gift of Heaven, to the *fair-Sex*, the "*Copia Verborum*," or readiness of Expression!—She is only beginning to play the *Guitar*, She understands the Notes well, & is a graceful Dancer.

Fanny next, is in her Person, according to my Judgment, the Flower in the Family—She has a strong resemblance of her *Mama* who is an elegant, beautiful Woman—Miss Fanny seems to have a remarkable Sedateness, & simplicity in her countenance, which is always rather chearful than melancholy; She has nothing with which we can find Fault in her Person, but has something in the Features of her Face which insensibly pleases us, & always when She is in Sight draws our Attention, & much the more because there seems to be for every agreeable Feature a correspondent Action which improves & adorns it. Betsy next is young, quiet, and obedient—Harriot is bold, fearless, noisy and lawless; always merry, almost never displeased; She seems to have a Heart easily moved by the force of Music; She has learned many Tunes & can strike any Note, or Succession of Notes perfectly with the Flute or Harpsichord, and is never wearied with the sound of Music either vocal or *Instrumental*.

These are the Persons who are at present under my direction, & whose general Character I have very imperfectly attempted to describe.

Wednesday 5.

Rose at Seven. The morning very stormy. *Bob* & *Nancy* before Breakfast had a quarrel—Bob called Nancy a Lyar; Nancy upbraided Bob, on the other Hand, with being often flog'd by their Pappa; often by the Masters in College; that he had stol'n Rum, & had got drunk; & that he used to run away &c—These Reproaches when they were set off with Miss Nancys truely feminine address, so violently exasperated *Bob* that he struck her in his Rage—I was at the time in my Chamber; when I enter'd the Room each began with loud and heavy complaints, I put them off however with sharp admonitions for better Behaviour.

The morning was so extremely stormy that I declin'd going to Breakfast—All the others went my Breakfast was sent over—Immediately after Breakfast Ben came over with a Message from Mr *Carter*, that he desired me to correct *Bob* severely immediately—Bob when I went into School sat quiet in the corner, & looked sullen, and penitent; I gave some orders to the Children, and went to my Room. —I sent for Bob—He came crying—I told him his Fathers Message; he confess'd himself guilty—I sent him to call up *Harry*—He came— I talked with them both a long Time recommended Diligence, & good Behaviour, but concluded by observing that I was obliged to comply with Mr Carter's request; I sent *Harry* therefore for some Whips.—*Bob* and poor I remained trembling in the chamber (for Bob was not more uneasy than I it being the first attempt of the kind I have ever made—The Whips came!—I ordered Bob to strip!—He desired me to whip Him in his hand in Tears—I told him no—He then patiently, & with great deliberation took of his Coat and laid it by—I took him by the hand and gave him four or five smart twigs; he cring'd, & bawld & promis'd—I repeated then about eight more, & demanded and got immediately his solemn promise for peace among the children, & Good Behaviour in general—I then sent him down— He conducts himself through this day with great Humility, & unusual diligence, it will be fine if it continues. At noon I went over to Dinner, but it was storming, & continues so bad that I choose rather to go without Supper than venture out in the Storm.

Thursday 6.

To Day about twelve *Bob* & *Prissy* & *Nancy* went in the Chariot to Stratford, to attend the Dancing-School—Mr Taylor,[84] the Colonels principal Overseer dined with us—After School in the Evening, I sat with *Betsy* & *Fanny* while they sung me many songs, When they had done I waited on them Home, & spent the Evening with Mr & Mrs *Carter*.

Fryday 7.

The morning cold, muddy and drisly—Our School seems still, and vacant. *Betsy* & *Fanny* at their Leisure are constantly knitting with small smoth stiff straws, in imitation of their Sister *Sylla*, who knits sometimes. The Colonel told me last Evening that he proposes to make the vacant End of our School-Room, Where Dr Frank lived a Concert-Room, to hold all his instruments of Music—As he proposes to bring up from *Williamsburg* his *Organ*, & to remove the *Harpsichord, Harmonica, Forte-piano, Guittar, Violin,* & *German-Flutes,* & make it a place for Practice, as well as Entertainment.

This afternoon *Dennis*, a Boy of about twelve Years old, one of the Waiters at Table, as he was standing in the front Door which is vastly huge & heavy; the Door flew up, and drew off the Skin & Flesh from his middle Finger caught between, took off the first Joint, and left the Bone of the greater part of the Rest of the Finger naked.

Saturday 8.

Catechised the Children, and dismiss'd them about ten. The morning pleasant—Rode before Dinner to Mr Blains Store—Was introduced to Dr *Thompson*,[85] Mr *Balantine*,[86] Mr *Carr* a young Scotch-Man Clerk, to Mr Blain; dined with Mr Blain. Parson *Smith*, his Wife, & her Sister were there —Colonel Washington, his Wife, & their Daughter Miss Jenny a young Lady of few words, a sanguine Countenance, and as to her Size, something below what Ladies call elegant; neat but not *flashy* in her Dress; Some of her Dress I admired because I have seen *Laura* in the like, yit strongly shewed me that it is not Dress alone I admire in Her. All these had been at a Widding in the country and were returning—In Dr *Thomsons* Room there was hanging against the Wall a Skeleton!—Balantine, either to shew himself a true full-blooded Buck, or out of mere wantonness & pastime turned the Bones (as they were fixed together with Wires) into many improper and indecent postures; but this officious industry met with such reception from the company as it Justly merited, and as I wish'd might happen; for they gave visible signs of their contempt of his Behaviour —About Six in the Evening the Chariot returned with *Bob*, Miss *Prissy* & *Nancy* from the Dance at *Stratford*—They brought News as follows: Miss Prissy told us, that they had an elegant Dance on the Whole; that Colonel Philip Lee, where they met to Dance, was on

Fryday, at the Wedding of which I made mention Just now; that Mr *Christian* the Master danced several Minuets, prodigiously beautiful; that Captain Grigg (Captain of an English Ship) danced a Minuet with her; that he hobled most dolefully, & that the whole Assembly laughed!—*Bob* told us that there was a Race between Mr —— And Colonels Horses—that they run a Mile, & that *Dottrell*[87] belonging to Mr —— won the Race;—*Bob* told me in private, after we were alone in my Room, that Colonel Lee took an Opportunity, & asked him in the Hearing of a large company at Supper, what sort of *Fellow* he is whom your *Papa* had provided for your *Tutor*—*Bob* told me that for answer he Informed him I was good and agreeable—That Miss Jenny Corbin, (a young Lady with whom I have had the greatest Opportunity of being acquainted, of any young Lady in Virginia) gave him so favourable an Account of my Behaviour, that he was pleased to say He should be glad to see me at his House, & of my company—But after having heard this much, I shall esteem myself pardonable, & shall always think it proper to refuse without thanks his warmest Invitations; & will plead for my excuse nothing else than mere inclination.

In the Evening about seven o-Clock it snowed exceeding fast til

Eight when it ceased, it being the second Snow we had this winter here, At Supper we had much conversation about the Dance.
Mrs Carter & myself, sat while ten and the Colonel read philosophy.

Sunday 9.

The Morning very cold—None from our Family went to church; *Bob* beg'd of me to let him go, I refused him; he then asked to go and dine with Mr Turburville, I gave him no liberty.—I wrote to-Day a letter to *Laura,* I wish it *speed* & *Success*—I wrote also a letter to Mr *Bryan* in Baltimore; Another to the Gentleman who keeps the "Fountain Inn" in *Baltimore;* & one to Dr *John Beaty*—Bob returned in the Evening after having stole away and spent the day at Mr *Turhurvill's* with a Note to his Papa from Squire *Lee,* in which Mr Carter & his Family are invited to the Ball at his House on Monday the 17th Instant But I must stay alone.

[LETTER OF PHILIP V. FITHIAN TO ELIZABETH BEATTY]

Nominy-Hall. Virginia. Jan: 9th: 1774.

To LAURA.

The long Distance there is between us, & Uncertainty of the Conveyance, makes it improper for me to write what I wish to tell you. I may not, however, neglect to acquaint you that you still possess the largest earthly Share of my Regard; & that my Fidelity towards you is unshaken & inviolable.

I continue this Winter, by the Kindness of Heaven, in perfect Health; & expect to return by the last of April next, if no Accident comes between, when I promise myself Madam, much Pleasure, much Peace in your Company.

The Family in which I live, is so kind, & suitable to my Wish, that I would gladly continue in it—Or, at least, provide some well-qualified Person to succeed me since I must by previous Agreement, shortly leave it, as I do not propose to let my coming here put off my entering on the Great-World.

If I shall be so happy as to meet with you in the Spring, I will tell you many curious Occurrences of this Winter; but none with greater Truth than that I have been your constant Admirer.

PHILIP. V. FITHIAN.

[JOURNAL]

Monday 10th

The Morning very cold—Dined with us to-day Mr *Sanford* a Captain of a Sloop which trades out of *Potowmack* to *Norfolk*—I wrote out some Exercises for *Bob* & *Harry*—In the Evening the Colonel began with a small Still to distill some Brandy from a Liquor made of Pisimmonds. I set Ben this Evening to writing. I likewise gave *Catalines* Speech in *Salust* to commit to memory in Latin, which he is to pronounce Extempore. In the Evening I borrowed of *Ben Carter* 15s.—I have plenty of Money with me, but it is in Bills of Philadelphia currency & will not pass at all here.

Teusday 11.

The morning very cold—As cold I think, and the Frost seems to be as intense & powerful as I have ever known it either at Cohansie or at Princeton. This morning I put Ben to construe some Greek, he has yet no Testament, I gave him therefore Esops Fables in Greek, and Latin. I also took out of the Library, and gave him to read Gordon, upon Geography. Ben seem'd scared with his Greek Lesson, he swore, & wished for Homer that he might kick Him, as he had been told Homer invented Greek.

Wednesday 12.

I gave *Sam* Mr Carters Barber, for shaving & dressing me, & for mending my Shoes, two pisterenes, which pass here for half a Crown —The morning is serene, pleasant, but cold yet. Miss *Hariot* this morning being over curious tasted some Mercury Mixture in Mr *Randolph's* Room, it made her very sick; I was frighted, the family was frighted! she puked, & threw it off her Stomach, & was soon relieved—

I gave *Martha* who makes my Bed, for a Christmas Box, a *Bit*, which is a pisterene cut into two equal parts—I gave to John also, who waits at Table & calls me to Supper a *Bit*. So that My whole Expence to-Day has been 3/9. Mrs Carter invited me to Day to go to the Ball, I excused myself, & declined it.

Thursday 13.

Mr Cunningham came before Noon to skait—At twelve we all went down to Mr Carters Millpond—none had skaits but Mr Cun-

ningham—we diverted ourselves on the Ice til two, when we went up
to dinner—Immediately after Dinner Mr *Carter* Miss *Prissy* & *Nancy*
rode out to Mr *Lanes.*—Mr *Cunningham* staid the Night, Prissy
play'd for us—She has since I came made great advances—

Fryday 14.

The morning very foggy, & warmer—I gave to Tom the Coach-man
who cured my Horse two *pisterenes* & half a *Bit*, which is two &
ninepence 2/9. Mr Cunningham breakfasted with us—When I went
into School there came a complaint from Miss *Sally Stanhope*[88] of
Bob that he was rude, swore, & quarrell'd at Breakfast, poor untoward, unfortunate Boy he gives me great Trouble—

Saturday 15.

I rose at seven—The morning fair the ground muddy—*Ben* asked
me to ride with him to Mr Blains Store I chose rather to stay at Home
—Ben is preparing for the approaching Ball—Bob urged me to let
him go to Mr Lees, but he is so unruly & mischeivous when abroad
that I was obliged to refuse him the liberty of going. I spent some
hours to Day with the Girls when they were practising Music on the
Guitar, & Forte-piano, Priscilla plays her tunes true and exceeding
finely—In the Evening Ben returned from Mr Blains—He told me the
Store was thronged with company—Sup'd on chocolate, & hoe-Cake,
so called because baked on a Hoe before the fire— The Colonel and
his Daughter busy at Music.

Sunday 16.

The morning frosty & cold—*Ben, Bob, Harry*, & Mr *Randolph* went
to Church—I stay at Home; Read Pictete—I feel very desirous of
seeing Home: of hearing good Mr Hunter Preach; of seeing my dear
Brothers & Sister; Indeed the very soil itself would be precious to me!
—I am shut up in my chamber; I read a while, then walk to the North
window, & look over Potowmack through Maryland towards Home;
then throw myself down into my Chair again & console myself that
I have every necessary, & convenient Accommodation here, which I
should have; nay much more than I should allow myself were I at
Home. I am contented—This whole world is only a Point almost un-
noticeable, when compared with the numerous *Systems* which com-

pose the *universe*, & yet they all are under the particular Direction & Government of *Almighty God;* How insignificant therefore is it for me and how foolish to be uneasy, & solicitous whether I live in *Cohansie*, in *Princeton*, or in *Virginiu;* Or in *America*, or in *Europe*, so long as I am still supported, & upheld by the Divine Agency!—I am fully satisfied—Guide me, propitious Heaven! Help me to Glorify my God; To honour the holy Religion which I profess; & If I shall be fitted, & introduced to the Ministry, may I still go on and be of advantage to my fellow Mortals!—

Evening, The Boys are returned; *Bob* brings me the *parsons* Compliments; Mr *Cunninghams;* & that Miss Corbin enquired If I was well!—Bob [also] informed me that the *Parson*, Mr *Blain, Cunningham, Balantine*, & others are to come to Captain *Turburvilles* Mill-Pond to Skate before they go to the Ball—

Monday 17.

At Breakfast the Colonel gave orders to the Boys concerning their conduct this Day, & through the course of the Ball—He allows them to go; to stay all this Night; to bring him an Account of all the company at the Ball; & to return tomorrow Evening—All the morning is spent in Dressing.—Mr Carter & Mrs Carter pressed me to go; But, mindful of my Promise when I left Home, I stay and enjoy myself in quiet.—I give the Children a Holiday to Day—I gave Dennis the Waiter half a Bit a Present—Mrs *Carter*, Miss *Prissy*, & *Nancy* dressed splendidly set away from Home at two.

Teusday 18.

Mrs *Carter*, & the young Ladies came Home last Night from the Ball, & brought with them Mrs *Lane*, they tell us there were upwards of Seventy at the Ball; forty one Ladies; that the company was genteel; & that Colonel *Harry Lee*,[89] from *Dumfries*, & his Son *Harrey* who was with me at College, were also there; Mrs Carter made this an argument, and it was a strong one indeed, that to-day I must dress & go with her to the Ball—She added also that She Desired my Company in the Evening when she should come Home as it would be late—After considering a while I consented to go, & was dressed —we set away from Mr Carters at two; Mrs *Carter* & the young Ladies in the Chariot, Mrs Lane in a Chair, & myself on Horseback— As soon as I had handed the Ladies out, I was saluted by Parson

Smith; I was introduced into a small Room where a number of Gentlemen were playing Cards, (the first game I have seen since I left Home) to lay off my Boots Riding-Coat&c—Next I was directed into the Dining-Room to see Young Mr *Lee;* He introduced me to his Father—With them I conversed til Dinner, which came in at half after four. The Ladies dined first, when some Good order was pre- served; when they rose, each nimblest Fellow dined first—The Dinner was as elegant as could be well expected when so great an Assembly were to be kept for so long a time.—For Drink, there was several sorts of Wine, good Lemon Punch, Toddy, Cyder, Porter &c.— About Seven the Ladies & Gentlemen begun to dance in the Ball- Room—first Minuets one Round; Second Giggs; third Reels; And last of All Country-Dances; tho' they struck several Marches occa- sionally—The Music was a French-Horn and two Violins—The Ladies were Dressed Gay, and splendid, & when dancing, their Silks & Brocades rustled and trailed behind them!—But all did not join in the Dance for there were parties in Rooms made up, some at Cards; some drinking for Pleasure; some toasting the Sons of america; some singing "Liberty Songs" as they call'd them, in which six, eight, ten or more would put their Heads near together and roar, & for the most part as unharmonious as an affronted—Among the first of these Vociferators was a young Scotch-Man, Mr *Jack Cunningham;* he was nimis bibendo appotus; noisy, droll, waggish, yet civil in his way & wholly inoffensive—I was solicited to dance by several, Captain Chelton, Colonel Lee, Harry Lee, and others; But George Lee,[90] with great Rudeness as tho' half drunk, asked me why I would come to the Ball & neither dance nor play Cards? I answered him shortly, (for his Impudence moved my resentment) that my Invitation to the Ball would Justify my Presence; & that he was ill qualified to direct my Behaviour who made so indifferent a Figure himself—Parson Smiths, & Parson Gibberns Wives danced, but I saw neither of the Clergy- men either dance or game[91]—At Eleven Mrs Carter call'd upon me to go, I listned with gladness to the summons & with Mrs Lane in the Chariot we rode Home, the Evening sharp and cold!—I handed the Ladies out, waited on them to a warm Fire, then ran over to my own Room, which was warm and had a good Fire; oh how welcome! Bet- ter this than to be at the Ball in some corner nodding, and awaked now & then with a midnight Yell!—In my Room by half after twelve; & exceeding happy that I could break away with Reputation.—

Wednesday 19.

Rose at Nine while the Bell was ringing—Breakfasted at ten, Mr *Carter* and I alone, the Ladies yet in Bed—I gave the Children the third Holiday; *Bob Ben* & *Harry* are yet at the Dance—Mrs Carter declines going to Day, I took a Walk out before Dinner, & with my Pen-knife carved *Laura's* much admired Name, upon a smooth beautiful Beech-Tree—Towards Evening Mrs Lane left us & rode home— *Bob* came Home about six, but so sleepy that he is actually stupified!—

Thursday 20.

Ben came Home late in the Night—This morning he looks fatigued out. We began to study to Day but all seem sleepy and dull. Dined with us to-day Mr *Lee* a Gentleman from Augusta County, who has lately been to the Settlements on Ohio.

Evening I began some Verses on Miss Carter for a present at the approaching Valantine[92]—But I drew the Picture from Laura.

Fryday 21.

All seem tolerably recruited this morning; we hear, the company left the Ball last Evening, quite wearied out; tho' the Colonel intreated them to stay the proposed Time.

To Day about twelve came to Mr *Carters* Captain *John Lee*, a Gentleman who seems to copy the Character of *Addisons Will Wimble.* When I was on my way to this place I saw him up in the country at Stafford; he was then just sallying out on his Winters Visit, & has got now so far as here, he stays, as I am told about eight, or ten Weeks in the year at his own House, the remaining part he lives with his waiting Man on his Friends.—

Saturday 22.

Captain Lee with us to Day—The Weather cold; I set in my Room all Day working at my Verses for Miss Carter.

Sunday 23.

None went to Church on account of the Cold—Afternoon the Sun shone fair—I took my Horse & rode about a Mile & returned—Captain *Lee* left us this Day.

Monday 24.

Still very cold snows some—Dined with us Colonel *Frank* L. *Lee*,[93] & Colonel *Harrison* of Maryland—Miss *Nancy* unwel of a cold.— There are great Professions of Liberty here expressed in Songs Toasts, &c. Yesterday News came of the Arrival of Ships with Tea; into *Boston, New-york, Philadelphia.* & of the New-Yorkers burning the House of his Excellency Governor *Tryon.* for having said that, if orders concerning the Tea had been transmitted to him he would have landed it tho' under the mouths of the Cannon!—Gentlemen here in general applaud & honour our Northern Colonies for so manly, & patriotic Resistance!—

Teusday 25.

Still sharp & cold—Miss Nancy much indisposed with a sore throat— Dined with us Mr *Cunningham.* Toasts the *King, Queen, Governor* & *Colonel,* of *Virginia.* Northern Sons of Liberty. & a good price for our comodities.—This Day the Person who carried my Letters to Baltimore returned without any Letters or Intelligence.

Wednesday 26.

The weather this morning seems to have moderated—Miss *Nancy* is poorly but better—In the Evening I ran a Foot Race with Ben & Harry fo exercise, & a prize of ten Apples to the winner. We ran from the School-House round the stable, & Kitchen & Great-House which Distance is about 70 Rod—I came out first about One Rod; but almost wholly spent; I went to my Chamber and lay down, sick, fainty, & quite distressed. I puked several times; after having rested a while, however, I revived & went well to Supper, & Spend the Evening in Writing. At Supper from the conversation I learned that the slaves in this Colony never are married, their Lords thinking them improper Subjects for so valuable an Institution!—

Thursday 27.

The morning mild Serene and moderate—The Colonel is making preparations for a Journey to *Anapolis,* where he Designs next Month. In the Evening, (for here they call the time between Dinner and day-light-End Evening,) He & Mrs Carter shewed me their

House; the original Design, the present form; & what is yet to be Done—Miss *Nancy* came down stairs to Day—

Fryday 28.

Snows this morning Briskly—Ben in a great Fever lest the Weather shall stop him from a Ride he has alloted for tomorrow—At twelve the Snow ceased, Depth about five Inches—I corrected *Harry* for the first time to-day for expressing himself indecently to *Prissy*.

Saturday 29.

Ben is preparing himself to go out—while we were dining about three it began to Snow briskly—After Dinner when I went over to my Room I was very much surprised to find my Room full of Smoke &

Flame!—A kind Providence only prevented the total Loss of our School-House & all its Furniture, & our own Clothes Books &c!—A Coal of Fire had by accident (as the Hearth is very narrow) fall'n on the floor, it took fire, & when I entered it was burning rapidly— It had burnt three Boards about eight Inches from the Hearth, & most certainly in a short time would have been inextinguishable—I put it out however speedily, & had all the fire removed—

The Weather is as wintry here in every Respect as I have ever known it in New-Jersey—Mr Carter has a Cart & three pair of Oxen which every Day bring in four Loads of Wood, Sundays excepted, & yet these very severe Days we have none to spare; And indeed I do not wonder, for in the *Great House, School* House, Kitchen, &c. there are twenty Eight steady fires! & most of these are very Large! —After Supper, when all had retired but Mrs Carter, Mr Carter & Myself, the Conversation being on serious Matters, Mr Carter observed that he much dislikes the common method of making Burying Yards round Churches, & having them almost open to every Beast— He would have them at some small distance from the Church, neatly & strongly inclosed, and the Graves kept up decent, & plain, but would have no splendid, nor magnificent Monument, nor even Stone to say "Hic jacet."—He told us he proposes to make his own Coffin & use it for a Chest til its proper use shall be required—That no Stone, nor Inscription to be put over him—And that he would choose to be laid under a shady Tree where he might be undisturbed, & sleep in peace & obscurity—He told us, that with his own hands he planted, & is with great diligence raising a *Catalpa*-Tree at the Head of his Father who lies in his Garden—Mrs Carter beg'd that She might have a Stone, with this only for a Monument, "Here lies *Ann Tasker Carter.*" [94] with these things for my consideration I left them about ten and went to my cold Room, & was hurried soon to Bed; Not however without reflecting on the importance of our preparation for this great Change!

Sunday 30.

Very stormy this morning with Rain and Hail which instantly freezes; the trees hang bending with Ice, & the ways are all glassy & slippery—None think of going to Church this day—Mrs Carter & I after Breakfast had a long conversation on religious affairs—Particularly on differing Denominations of Protestants—She thinks the Religion of the established Church without Exception the best of any invented or practised in the world. & indeed she converses with great propriety on these things, & discovers her very extensive Knowledge; She allows the Difference between the Church, & Presbyterianism to be only exceeding small, & wishes they were both intirely united! Through this whole Day it storms but the Evening is terrible! almost an Inundation of Rain; The wind violent at North-East; The Snow, Hail, and Rain freezing together on the Ground! This Evening the

Negroes collected themselves into the School-Room, & began to play the *Fiddle*, & dance—I was in Mr Randolphs Room;—I went among them, *Ben*, & *Harry* were of the company—*Harry* was dancing with his Coat off—I dispersed them however immediately.

Monday 31.

Excessive sloppy—Miss *Nancy* came to School to Day—I finished my verses which are to be presented as a Valantine to Miss *Prissy Carter.*

Teusday February 1st 1774.

Fair & mild but vastly muddy—About twelve Squire *Lee* & young *Harry Lee*, who was a College-Fellow, came to see us. They staid while about five. The Toasts at Dinner were as usual—The Colonel & Mrs Carter seem Much pleased with Harry, & with his manner.

Wednesday 2.

The weather vastly fine. At twelve o-Clock the Colonel & Miss *Prissy* rode out for an airing—*Prissy* This day began Multiplication. We had also a large elegant Writing Table brought to us, so high that the Writers must stand.

Thursday 3.

Prissy, & Nancy practising music—We had last night Thunder, Lightning, & a very great shower.

Fryday 4.

I put Ben this day into virgil—We had our Room mended & came into it—at twelve I rode out to Mr Taylors about two Miles, in again by Dinner-Time—Dined with us one Mrs Hut—This Evening, in the School-Room, which is below my Chamber, several Negroes & *Ben*, & *Harry* are playing on a *Banjo* & dancing!—

Saturday 5:

I spent the morning in my Room, *Ben*, & *Bob* are gone out. About twelve came on a visit Mr *Goodlett*, & *Saml Fantleroy*;[95] I spent the remainder of the day with them.—At Dinner when call'd upon for a Toast I gave Miss *Sally Hollinshead.*

Mr Goodlett told me he has had an Invitation, to accept a School in *Leeds*,[96] a town on the River Rapahannock, about 25 Miles from this up & across the Country.

Sunday 6.

I rode to Church; Mrs Carter & Miss Prissy & Nancy were out—Mr Smith gave us a Sermon 14 Minutes long on Charite—But poor Fellow he seem'd Cold as his Subject! Mr Fantleroy; & Mr Goodlett dined with us and set off for Home as soon as we rose from Dinner —This day two Negro Fellows the Gardiner & cooper, wrangled; & at last fought; It happened hard however for the Cooper, who is likely to lose one of his Eyes by that Diabolical Custom of gouging which is in common practise among those who fight here—Evening Ben returned; he has been into Northumland to see one Mr *Jones*. Mr Goodlett, to Day, shewed me a piece of his own performance, a paraphrase on part of the Book of Job, done in Lattin-Verse.

Monday 7.

The Day pleasant, & seems to have some appearance of Spring— Mr Blain call'd this Aftternoon, & told us that by a Letter he hears Lady *Dunmore* is arrived from New-York[97]—and that many good & wealthy Families arrived in the same Ship—It is indeed amazing, & it will soon astonish the whole World, to consider the Rapidity of the growth of these Colonies—

At Supper, Mr Carter informed me it is his purpose to manifacture 30,000 Bushels of wheat in his New-Mill which is yet scarcely finished.

Teusday 8.

Before Breakfast *Nancy* & *Fanny* had a Fight about a Shoe Brush which they both wanted—Fanny pull'd off her Shoe & threw at Nancy, which missed her and broke a pane of glass of our School Room. they then enter'd upon close scratching &c. which methods seem instinctive in Women. Harry happen'd to be present & affraid lest he should be brought in, ran and informed me—I made peace, but with many threats—

Mrs Carter has ordered the Gardener to sew Lettice, & plant Peas this Day in the Garden.—

Wednesday 9.

This day very blustry & cold—I gave Prissy a Coppy of Secretary-Hand, at her particular Request—

Thursday 10.

We had the Virginia Gazette[98] to day in which the accounts concerning the destroying the Tea at Boston are confirm'd—& also an account of the Burning of the House of Governor Tryon. Dined with us Colonel *Frank Lee;* his Wife & Captain *John Lee.* Toasts after Dinner, the *King. Queen.* Absent Friends, Governor of Virginia, & his Lady just arrived, & Success to American Trade & Commerce

Fryday 11.

The Company staid all Night—at Breakfast the conversation was on a terrible Distemper which is in this County at present; & which in Maryland last year about this time carried off hundreds, and is call'd the "putrid Quinsy." Mr Carter has a Man lying now dangerously ill of it!

Illness spreading

What they do in the Disorder is, when the Inflamation is first observ'd, bleeding; then give the *Bark* & *Salt-petre,* or *Nitre,* and *Gargles* to cleanse the mouth—

Our company left us before dinner—Last night I took Bob to my Room, after having in the course of the Day corrected him thrice, & reasoned with him concerning the impropriety of his Behaviour; at the same time I acquainted him with my final resolution to send him over for correction every Day to his Papa's Study, which had so strong an Effect on him (as all the Children are in remarkable Subjection to their Parents) that he firmly pomised to attend to my advice, & thro' this Day has been punctual to his word.

I spent the evening with the Family to hear the music. For every evening Prissy & Nancy play the whole Evening for practice & besides every Week half of Teusday, Thursday, & Saturday. We were informed that the *Carter* who goes with the Team is ill of the sore Throat!—

Saturday 12.

After having dismised the School I went over to Mr Carters Study—We conversed on many things, & at length on the College of William

& Mary at *Williamsburg*. He informed me that it is in such confusion at present, & so badly directed, that he cannot send his Children with propriety there for Improvement & useful Education—That he has known the Professors to play all Night at Cards in publick Houses in the City, and has often seen them drunken in the Street!—That the Charter of the College is vastly Extensive, & the yearly income sufficient to support a University being about 4.000 £. Sterling. —That the Necessary Expence for each Scholar yearly is only 15 £ Currency.

Two of the officers of the Institution, Mr Bracker, & Mr Henly [99] Clergymen are at present engaged in a paper War published weekly in the Williamsburg Gazette's.

Miss Fanny quite unwell of a Cold with a pain in her Breast. Evening Mrs Carter complain'd of a sore throat; and *Ben* also, complains that his Throat is quite troublesome—Mr Randolph too is confin'd in his Room all day! We seem to be all sickning!—

Sunday 13.

Things look better this morning Mrs Carter, & *Ben* seem relieved, Mr Randolph, & Fanny are better. The morning very blustry with wind & Snow—None go to Church from here to day—In my Room I read *Pictete*.

Monday 14.

Mr *Randolph* this Morning happens to be Miss *Nancy's Valentine;* & Miss *Prissy* mine,—The morning sharp & very cold—

Teusday 15.

I have a call this morning from *Bob* & *Harry* for a Holiday, for Shrove Teusday; I shall dismiss them at twelve o-Clock. I gave Miss Carter my Verses for her Valentine, Dined with us Mrs *Ford*. I finished reading the first, & began the Second Volume of *Pictete*.

Wednesday 16.

I happened last monday to offend *Prissy*, She retains her anger & seems peculiarly resentful!—*Ben* agreed for half a Bit a Week to play the Flute every Night, or read, for me, twenty Minutes after I am in Bed.

Thursday 17.

Prissy seems much affronted; The Cause was as follows Monday afternoon, by Chance I tapp'd her on the Head, & wholly in Jest; She seem'd vex'd, but Teusday morning which is her day for practice on

the Forte-Piano, after Breakfast, I desir'd her to walk over to the School, she refused, & gave for an Excuse that She must begin to play—Both these things laid together were the cause of her resentment.

Fryday 18.

The Weather pleasant and moderate—*Bob, Nancy,* & *Prissy,* are setting off this morning to the Dance, which is at Mr *Washingtons*[100]—

Saturday 19.

at Dinner we were conversing on Reading, among many remarks the Colonel observed that, He would bet a Guinea that Mrs Carter reads more than the Parson of the parish! No panegyrick on the Gentleman? Mr Christian the Dancing Master, Came home with the young Ladies.

Sunday 20.

Last Evening the virginia News-papers came; but nothing from the Northward.

Rode to Nomini Church; Parson Smith read Prayers, but it was too Cold a Day to give us a Sermon; After Service *Mr & Mrs Carter*, the Parson, his wife & Sister; *Mr Camel* the Comptroler; *Ben, Bob*, Miss *Pierce* Miss *Sanford*, and My self were invited to Colonel Washingtons to Dinner. His House has the most agreeable Situation, of any I have yet seen in Maryland or Virginia; the broad Potowmack, which they account between 7 and 8 Miles over, washes his Garden on the North. the River Nomini is within a stones throw on the West, a levil open Country on the East; a Lane of a mile & three quarters accurately measur'd. lies from the House South-East it has from the House the whole distance a uniform Descent, & at the Gate at the End of this Lane the Situation is just six feet lower than at the House —There are no Marshes near, which altogether make the place exceeding Description. The Roads are now miry & disagreeable.

Monday 21.

Prissy seems again reconciled—Miss *Stanhope* the Housekeeper is ill of a Rheumatism—They are begining to work in the Garden with vigor. Dined with us Docter *Franks.*

Teusday 22.

Mr *Carter* rode to the County-Court I read to day several chapters in the Greek testament. Mr *Carter* has given orders to his Hands to rigg, & fit his Schooner a Vessel of about 40 Tons for Business. Docter Franks with us yet. Mrs *Carter* was taken ill last Evening & has not been out of her chamber to Day. Miss *Stanhope* the Housekeeper is also confin'd to her Room with Rheumatic Pains.

Wednesday. 23.

Mr *Carter* has an invitation to dine at Lee-Hall to Day, which he accepts—before Dinner came in Miss *Corbin*, & Miss *Booth;* two young Ladies pretty well gone in what we call the Bloom of Life; Mr Carter was out, Mrs Carter is ill, & Ben was not Drest; Bob & I therefore at Dinner must be Directors of the ceremonies at Table! But happily for me I have them at last all by heart—At five Bob & I had the Pleasure to walk home with them, (for they were on foot) to Assist them in Crossing the River Nomini which lies between us & Mr Turburville's. Evening Mrs Carter seems no better—Miss Sally came out of her Room—

Thursday 24.

Frogs croaked last Evening. This morning the Birds of several kinds are singing; and some presages of Spring seem visible. Mrs Carter continues no better, A messenger is sent for Docter *Jones*, with orders, that if he is from Home to pursue him.—

Mr *Gregory*,[101] the Colonels Gardiner came this morning & began with Mr *Carters* two Fellows who have been in the Garden all winter —They planted this day the common garden Peas.
The Colonel at Dinner gave Ben & I a Piece of Music to prepare on our Flutes, in which he is to perform the thorough Bass—Evening Mrs Carter Some Better.

Fryday 25.

Mrs Carter better—The Day pleasant—There is a report that the Jail-Fever, or Yellow or putrid Fever, is at one Mr Atwel's on potowmack, in this County; that it was brought in a Ship which came lately with convict Servants; that two have already died, one this morning: & that many of Mr Atwells Slaves are infected!—

Docter Jones spent the Evening with us; He complimented *Ben Bob*, & myself with an invitation to dine with him next Sunday.

Saturday 26.

Mr *Carter's* Merchant Mill begins to run to-day—She is calculated to manufacture 25.000 Bushels of Wheat a Year—I walked at twelve with the Colonel to view her; it is amazing to consider the work and Ingenuity—He told me his Bill for the materials and work was 1450 £.!—

Ben to day Rode to Mr *Fantleroys*. Evening the Colonel & I performed the *Sonata*. I had the Pleasure to hear the Colonel say that I have my part perfect.

Sunday 27.

I rode to day to Richmond Church, Parson Gibbern preached about 20 Minutes on the Text "he that walketh uprightly walketh wisely"

—this seems to be a polite part of the parish.—After Sermon Ben &
I rode to Docter *Jones's;* he was from home. Mrs Jones a young,
Handsome, polite Lady, received & entertained us exceeding civilly.
—On our return home, we called to see Mr Hamilton, who by a
accident was thrown from a Horse, & received a sad cut in his Face!
he lies at Mr Lanes.

Monday 28.

Mrs Carter confined yet to her Room, but much better—Prissy &
I on good terms once more —Breakfasted with us Mr *Taylor*.[102] Ben
determines to ask his Papa to-morrow for Liberty to go home with
me in April. Evening we performed the Sonata I the first; Ben the
second; & Mr Carter the thorough Bass on the *Forte Piano.*

Teusday March 1st 1774.

By one of Mr Carters Sailors we heard this morning that the Fever
mentioned some Days ago continues. Afternoon Mr Lane[103] a young
Gentleman, formerly my acquaintance at Princeton came to see me;
with one Mr Harison—He stays all night.

Wednesday 2.

I gave my little family a Holiday, with an intention to ride with Mr
Lane after Dinner—We walked to the Mill, & about the works, but
before twelve it began to rain, & prevented our going out—Mrs
Carter came out of her chamber & dined with us, & seems to be well
over Illness.
Mr Lane lives in Louden County 20 Miles from Dumfries; & is to return to Princeton towards the close of this month.

Thursday 3.

Late last Evening the Packets came in: In the Pennsylvania Gazette
I saw that Docter *Elmer* of my acquaintance in Jersey; & Docter
Jones at whose House I dined Last Sunday are created members of
the American Philosophical Society.—In the virginia Papers there is
an Account of an Earthquake felt on monday the 21 ult. at *Williamsburg, Richmond,* & *Fredericksburg*—After Breakfast Mr Lane left
us, He was drest in black superfine Broadcloth; Gold-Laced hat;
laced Ruffles; black Silk Stockings; & to his Broach on his Bosom he
wore a Masons Badge inscrib'd "Virtute and Silentio" cut in a

Golden Medal! Certainly he was fine!— Mrs Carter continues better. Evening we performed again in the several parts our Sonata— *Ben* mentioned to his Mama, as Mr Lane's coming hindred his asking his *Papa* for his Consent to go to Philadelphia.
She seems to be not unwilling.
Expence to Day for Paper a Bitt, or 7½ d.

Fryday 4.

I gave the *Hostler* directions for preparing my Horse for the approaching expedition. In a Ship arrived last week in Potowmack Mr Carter received half a Dozen of the latest Gent. Magazines with several other new Books,

This day I wrote two Letters to be forwarded by Mr Lane, one to a young Lady in Philadelphia the other to my Sister.

No news of beautiful *Laura;* perhaps I may say of her, to myself: Quid insanis, Philippe, tua lura *Laura,*—Alium—secuta est! Keep her, kind Heaven, & in her Friendship make me happy! After School at Evening, on account of some difference about the Key of the School-Room Ben gave Harry a smart, but just correction; I kept in my Room that I might be wholly unconcerned in the matter.

There came in about eight o-Clock a man very drunk, & grew exceeding noisy & troublesome, & as the Evening was cold & stormy Mr Carter thought it improper to send him away; he was therefore ordered into the Kitchen, to stay the Night: Him Bob soon after persuaded to the School-house; I soon heard from my Room the noise & guesed immediately the Cause. I waited however 'til half after ten, when all seemed silent; I then took a candle & went into the School-Room, And before the Fire Bob had brought a matt, & Several Blankets, & was himself in a sound sleep covered with the Blankets on the same Matt between the drunken Man, & a Negro Fellow, his Papas Postilion! I mention this as one Example among a thousand to shew the very particular Taste of this Boy!—I could mention another which would illustrate what I have said of this passion for Horses when I gave a Scetch of his character, *Ben* has a very sightly young mare which he has in keeping for our intended Journey; this morning Bob agreed to give his Brother a Pisterene, & a rich Tortoise-Shell Handled Knife bound elegantly with Silver, only for Liberty to ride this Mare every day to Water, until his Brother sets away, & would consent to be limited as to the Gait he should use in Riding—

I borrowed the late Magazines & read them in my Leisure. I am daily more charmed & astonished with Mrs Carter. I think indeed she is to be placed in the place with Ladies of the first Degree.

Saturday 5.

Very stormy this morning, no going out: I spend the day very agreeably at Home. Mr Carter appointed to *Ben*, & I another *Sonata* to practise. He wrote for Miss *Nancy* also "Infancy" to get by Heart & sing it with the *Guitar*. The day continues stormy; *Bob*, however, has ventured out; for neither Heat, nor Cold, nor Storm can stay him!—

We dined at three—The Colonel at Dinner observed that many of the most just, & nervous sentiments are contain'd in Songs & small Sketches of Poetry; but being attended with *Frippery Folly* or *Indecency* they are many times look'd over. I am remarkably pleased with the Monument erected to the memory of General *Wolfe* in the universal Magazine for September 1773. The General is there represented in an expiring Posture, supported by an English Soldier, who seems to comfort him in his last moments, by directing his closing Eyes to a Figure representing Victory, holding in one hand a palm-Branch, the emblem of peace; & a Crown or Wreath of immortality in the other, which she offers the dying commander; while he himself seems to make a final effort to express his Sattisfaction at her Appearance. On the corners of the Base are two Lions couchant, the Emblems of the british Nation, supporting the Sarcophagus or marble Urn, & intended to express the gratitude of his native country for his eminent Services. On the first pannel of the Base is an elegant alto Relievo, representing the debarkation of the Troops at the Foot of the Heights of Abraham.

The Writer says that the Height of the Monument from the Ground-Line to the top of the Tent, is nearly twenty-seven feet; that the figures are considerably larger than the Life, & beautifully executed.

On an oval Tablet on the front of the Urn are inscribed the underwritten Lines.

To the Memory

of

James Wolfe Esqr

Major-General, & Commander in Chief of the British Land Forces on
an Expedition against Quebeck. Who, surmounting by Ability &
valour All Obstacles of Art & Nature,

Was slain,
In the moment of Victory.

At the head
of his conquering Troops, on the 13th of September 1759;

The King,
and the Parliament of Great Britain
Dedicate this Monument.

Honour is here indeed done to merit, and Valour is justly
eternized!—

I was reading in the Evening to *Bob* in the Monthly Review the
remarks on the Poetry and writings of *Phillis Wheatly* [104] of Boston;
at which he seem'd in astonishment; sometimes wanting to see her,
then to know if She knew grammer, Latin, &c. at last he expressed
himself in a manner very unusual for a Boy of his turn. & suddenly
exclaimed, Good God! I wish I was in Heaven!—The Weather is so
stormy I chose to forego my Supper, rather than venture into the
dark, & Water. In bed a little after ten which is our usual time.

Sunday 6.

I rose at eight—The morning cold & stormy—*Ben* is distressed that he
cannot go to Church; I cannot say but I enjoy myself with great
Satisfaction tho' I stay most of my time in my Chamber; & often have
to withstand the solicitations of Gentlemen to visit them.

Breakfasted at half after nine. Mr Lane the other Day informed me
that the *Anabaptists* in *Louden County* are growing very numerous;
& seem to be increasing in afluence; and as he thinks quite destroying
pleasure in the Country; for they encourage ardent Pray'r; strong &
constant faith, & an intire Banishment of *Gaming, Dancing*, & Sab-
bath-Day Diversions. I have also before understood that they are
numerous in many County's in this Province & are Generally accounted troublesome—Parson *Gibbern* has preached several Sermons
in opposition to them, in which he has labour'd to convince his People that what they say are only whimsical Fancies or at most Religion

grown to Wildness & Enthusiasm!—There is also in these counties one Mr Woddel,[105] a presbiterian Clergyman, of an irreproachable Character, who preaches to the people under Trees in summer, & in private Houses in Winter, Him, however, the people in general dont more esteem than the Anabaptists Preachers; but the People of Fashion in general countenance, & commend him. I have never had an opportunity of seeing Mr *Woddel,* as he is this Winter up in the Country, but Mr & Mrs *Carter* speak well of him, Mr & Mrs *Fantleroy* also, & all who I have ever heard mention his Name. Like *Bob* I am at once fill'd with pleasure & surprise, when I see the remarks of the Reviewers confirmed as to the Writings of that ingenious *African Phillis Wheatly* of Boston; her verses seem to discover that She is tolerably well acquainted with *Poetry, Learning,* & *Religion.* In the universal Magazine for September 1773 are the following Lines on her being brought from *Africa* to *America* by herself.

> "Twas mercy brought me from my Pagan Land,
> Taught my benighted Soul to understand,
> That there's a God; that there's a Saviour too;
> Once I Redemption neither sought nor knew,
> Some view our sable Race with scornful Eye,
> "Their Colour is a diabolic Dye."
> Remember, christians, Negroes, black as Cain,
> May be refin'd, & join the Angelic Train.

—The people Went to day as usual into the Woods with the Cart & Oxen for Wood, as the cold and stormy Weather the several days past has occasioned large, & steady fires—It seems however to be a Breach of the Law of the Sabbath. *Ben* impatient of staying at home rode out about Eleven, when the weather is more moderate; *Bob, Harry* & Mr *Randolph* also are all going out; I seem happy when intirely alone, & have undisturbed liberty to spend in Devotion God's holy Sabbath of Rest.

Before Night it grew fair when on a Sudden all are out, so that we seem like a Town; but most of the Inhabitants are black—We dined at three, no company. Evening *Bob* returned & brought Mr Turburville's Compliments, with a strong invitation for me to visit him—A little before the Sun went down I took a walk down the Poplar Avenue; which must certainly be vastly pleasant in Summer—At the farthest end of this Walk I gathered & eat some Pisimmonds from a

large Tree which were exceeding sweet, & agreeable. Supped at nine, At Supper The Colonel informed me that he has invented this Day a method for finding the difference of the value of money in this *Province* and in *Maryland*. We do not spend Sundays thus in Jersey. In Bed by ten. Ben at home.

Monday 7.

The morning vastly clear & cool—The Colonel rode to Richmond court at twelve, with Mr *Randolph*, I walked to see the Negroes make a fence; they drive into the Ground Chesnut stakes about two feet apart in a strait Row, & then twist in the Boughs of *Savin*[106]

which grows in great plenty here—Ben, to Day, began Virgils Georgics—And Prissy began Division—By accident to day in the Garden I took up Mr *Gegory* the Gardiners Spade, for which he instantly called on me for my forfeit—This Gardiner through the Summer from this Time has half a Crown daily Wages—Dined at half after two.

Teusday 8.

I rose by six—the morning fine. Breakfasted at nine. At twelve I walked, to the mill together with Mr & Mrs Carter; Miss Prissy &

Nancy, to see them bake Biscuit, & pack flour; here too I had a Forfeit for kneeding biscuit. The Colonel shewed me and explain'd the Pan of his Mill; his Canals; Waste-gates; Toll Mill, Merchant Mill: &c. The tide flows quite to the Mill & is navigable with Canoes & Flats— He told me that his Wastgate as it stands alone cost him 95 £.—And that nothing less than 5000 £ Capital can continue the works & keep them supplied. The Ovens bake 100lb of Flour at a Heating; there are in the Bake-house two Ovens. Dined half after two.

The Colonel formed last Sunday, & is yet compleating Tables for finding the Difference between *Virginia*, & *Maryland* Currency, as he is entering largely into Trade he finds it necessary to be better acquainted with the Exchange. *Ben* agreed to ask his Papa at Supper for Leave to go with me to Philadelphia but poor Boy his resolution fail'd him!

Wednesday 9.

Up by seven. very Windy—Evening I rode with Ben to Mr *Lanes* to see young Lane; he was out however, & we soon returned—Mr Warden was at Mr Lanes. Evening we played in our small Concert out old Sonata; & besides Feltons Gavott,[107] supp'd at nine.

Thursday 10.

Mrs *Carter* informed me last Evening that this Family one year with another consumes 27000 Lb of Pork; & twenty Beeves. 550 Bushels of Wheat. besides corn—4 Hogsheads of Rum, & 150 Gallons of Brandy. Breakfasted with us Mr Warden, at twelve, with Mr Randolph, I went a fishing, but we had only the luck to catch one apiece. Dined with us Mr *Cunningham*, he has lately had a severe turn of the Pleurisy—I supped with Mr Randolph on Fish—

Fryday 11.

The finest morning we have yet had: the *Robbins*, & *blue Birds* singing all around us. *Prissy, Nancy*, & *Bob* go this day to the *Dance* which is at Mr Turburville's—It come here next—I wrote a Letter to Mr Rees[108] at Trenton—At twelve with Ben I rode to Mr *Lanes* to see young Mr *Lane*, he happened to be at Home, & introduced to me Mr *Middleton* an old facetious but pofane Gentleman. We dined with Mr Lane. When call'd on for my Toast I gave Miss *Sally Hollinshead*, of Philadelphia Dined at three—

I heard a mocking Bird sing this Day. supped at eight & in Bed early for I am much fatigued with riding.

Saturday 12.

I rose by six—Breakfasted with us Captain *Blackwel;* master of a Ship lying in *Ucomico*—I heard *Harry*, Miss *Fanny*, & *Besy* repeat their catechism—At ten Mr Lane called on us to go on Board Captain Blackwels Ship to Dine—We consented and set off by Eleven; We rode to a place called Horn-Point, which is about a Mile up the River Ucomico, & in sight of the wide *Potowmac*, off this point at about a Quarter of a miles Distance lay Captain Griggs, & Captain Blackwels Ships, they sent immediately a Boat to carry us on board, but on telling us that neither of the Captains were at Home, we chose rather to turn Back—The distance from Mr *Carters* to this Point, is called twelve miles; the Land seeems to be exceeding poor, as it is covered for most of the way with Large *Pines*, & shrubby *Savins*, & destitute almost intirely of Cultivation—From Horn-Point we agreed to ride to one Mr Camels, who is Controller of the customs &c here; cheifly to see a Daughter of his to whom we were equally strangers, we arrived at Mr Camels about two o-Clock, & were severally introduced to Miss Pinkstone Camel, a young woman of about sixteen, neat, handsome, genteel, & sociable; & in my opinion she possesses as much of these as any young Lady in Virginia whom I have yet seen —It has been Mr Camels misfortune, in the course of trade, to be reduced to low circumstances, on which account his Family does not now meet with so great respect, as I am told they formerly did—

From Horn Point to the Comptrolers, the distance is call'd four miles. Before Dinner we Borrowed the Comptrolers Barge, which is an over grown Canoe, & diverted ourselves in the River which lies full fronting the House; & we were the better pleased with the sport as all our motions were in the sight of Miss Camel—We dined at half after three on Fish, & wild Duck—our drink Grogg, & Water. From the Comptrolers at 5 o-Clock we set of Homewards; we call'd on our way at Captain *Meddletons*,[109] whom I take to be exceedingly Profane in his Language; we were introduced to his two Daughters; they seemed however aukward in their Behaviour, & dull, & saturnine in their Disposition—The distance from the Comptrolers to Captain seven Miles—We left there at eight in the evening, & rode to Mr Joseph Lanes Esqr which distance is called five miles, & arrive at 9 o-Clock—here we had an elegant Supper—with good *Porter* & Madeira—after Supper, when call'd on for my Toast, I gave Miss *Betsy Beaty* of Newington, Pennsylvania—At half after ten we set off and rode home; Distance three miles, Our poor Horses went the distances which I have laid down and were not fed in the course of the day; as they have no taverns in these parts—Our whole Distance 31 Miles Expence to the Sailors for their trouble is 1s 10d. Exceedingly fatigued with Riding.

Sunday 13.

Soon after Breakfast Captain Scott (master of a Schooner laden with Wheat, & bound from Alexandria for Philadelphia, which about ten days past in a gale of wind run aground and is like to lose her Cargo) come to hire Mr Carters Schooner to assist in unloading her that the vessel may be saved; the vessel run aground, & now lies nearly opposite the mouth of the River Nomini in Potowmack!—The Colonel is engaged in taking off a Description of the River *Ucomico;* the Road from hence to Horn-Point; & Mondays-Point[110] with the Houses on the several ways—This day I declin'd going to Church, chiefly on account of my Horse, who went so far yesterday—It is however the first time that I have kept myself at home in good weather—Evening Mr Carter received a Packet of Letters from *Anopolis* by the Post, but none comes to me this long Winter—Bob to-day rode to Richmond Church, & in the Evening brought from Counsellor *Taylor*[111] a strong invitation to come and see him.

Monday 14.

Bob this morning begg'd me to learn him lattin; his Reason he tells me is that yesterday Mrs *Taylor*[112] told him he must not have either of her Daughters unless he learn'd Latin he urged me so strong that I put him some Lessons for leasure hours. Rainy most of this day, & in the afternoon from the West arose a black cloud which was attended with several pretty hard Claps of Thunder—We had with us one Mr *Neal* a good Sort of self sufficient Gentleman—

Teusday 15.

This morning, as Ben & Bob were agreeing on the price of a Rudiman Grammar, which *Bob* wanted to purchase of *Ben;* after some time when Bob would not give 2/10. Bens great demand for a Book almost worn out, which when new, may, by thousands be had in Philadelphia for 2/. that Currency- -He threw his Book into the fire, & destroy'd it at once!—An Instance of two ruling Foibles which I discover in Ben viz. obstinacy, & avarice. And another I mentioned the other day, of his agreeing, for half a Bit, or 3½d a week, to play the flute for a limited time, every night after I am in Bed; of this however he has grown tired, & given up his wages on account of the Labour, or Confinement of the Task—And I should be deceived, if a very little money would not excite him to submit to almost any menial service—Bob however; for the present is frustrated in his purpose of learning Grammer, & it seems to chagrin him as much, as tho' he actually believed in what Mrs Taylor[113] told him last Sunday, that without he understands Latin, he will never be able to win a young Lady of Family & fashion for his Wife.—At the Noon play-Hours *Bob* & *Nelson* the Boy who waits on the School had a fight, I know not on what account; it was Bobs misfortune in the course of the Battle to receive a blow on his cheek near his Eye, which is visible, & brought the intelligence of the Quarrel to me, for all were wholly silent till I made inquiry, when all in a moment seem'd to turn & try to convict him—In the Evening, after School, I took them both to my Room and examined them of the reason, Place, and manner of their fighting; from themselves it seem'd plain that they fought for mere Diversion I therefore dismiss'd Nelson, & kept Bob til near Supper & then gave him a smart correction & dismiss'd him.

Wednesday 16.

The morning cloudy & windy, Breakfasted at nine—Mr Randolph hurt himself by a Fall from a fence to day badly—Dined at half after two—Towards Evening the clouds all scattered, the wind fell, & left the air pleasant: The Birds also seemed glad and merry—The whole reminded me of a beautiful, & memorable passage in *Milton*. "If Chance the Radiant Sun with farewel-Sweet, Extend his Evening Beam the fields revive, The Birds their notes renew, the bleating Herds Attest their joy that Hill & valley rings."
After school, I had the honour of taking a walk with Mrs Carter through the Garden—It is beautiful, & I think uncommon to see at this Season peas all up two & three Inches—We gathered two or three Cowslips in full-Bloom; & as many violets—The English Honey Suckle is all out in green & tender Leaves—Mr Gregory is grafting

some figs—Mrs Carter shewed me her Apricot-Grafts; Asparagus Beds &c Before Supper a Black cloud appeared in the West, at which Mrs Carter discovered much concern as She is uncommonly affraid both of wind and Thunder.

Thursday 17.

This morning Mr Carter put Miss *Fanny* to learning the Notes— While we were breakfasting Mr *Stadley* the musician came; Miss *Prissy* is with him; *Nancy* learns the *Guitar*, under the direction of her *Papa*, as Mr Stadley does not understand playing on the *Guitar*— Dined with us a young Gentleman Mr Fantleroy from *Hobbes-Hole* —He seems to be a modest sensible, genteel young Fellow—I had the pleasure of taking a walk in the Garden at five with Mr *Stadley; Bob* along—He is a man of Sense, & has great Skill in music. I spent the Evening in the Room in the midst of music.

Fryday 18.

The morning damp & disagreeable—Mr Stadley continues to Day with Miss *Prissy*. We received this morning the *Williamsburg* Gazette's—Several Addresses appear, and poetical Encomiums on the Countess of Dunmore lately arrived there.
Mr. Bracken. & Mr. Henley, are still contending in furious Combat, but poor Henley seems to be on the verge of a Defeat—I have all along intended, & shall now attempt to give a short discription of Nomini-Hall, & the several Buildings, & improvements adjoining it; as well for my own amusement, as also to be able with certainty to inform others of a Seat as magnificent in itself & with as many surrounding Conveniences, as any I have ever seen, & perhaps equal to any in this Colony—
Mr *Carter* now possesses 60000 Acres of Land; & about 600 Negroes —But his Estate is much divided, & lies in almost every county in this Colony; He has Lands in the neighbourhood of Williamsburg, & an elegant & Spacious House in that City—He owns a great part of the well known Iron-Works near Baltimore in Maryland—And he has one or more considerable Farms not far from Anopolis. He has some large tracts of Land far to the West, at a place call'd "Bull Run," & the "Great Meadows" among the mountains. He owns Lands near Dumfries on the Potowmack; & large Tracts in this & the neighbouring Counties.—Out of these Lands, which are situated so remote

from each other in various parts of these two large Provinces, Virginia, & Maryland, Mr Carter has chosen for the place of his habitation a high spot of Ground in Westmoreland County at the Head of the Navigation of the River Nomini, where he has erected a large Elegant House, at a vast expence, which commonly goes by the name of *Nomini-Hall*. This House is built with Brick, but the bricks have been covered with strong lime Mortar; so that the building is now perfectly white; It is seventy-six Feet long from East to west; & forty-four wide from North to South, two Stories high; the Pitch of the lower story seventeen Feet, & the upper Story twelve—

It has five Stacks of Chimneys, tho two of these serve only for ornament. There is a beautiful Jutt, on the South side, eighteen feet long, & eight Feet deep from the wall which is supported by three tall pillars—On the South side, or front, in the upper story are four Windows each having twenty-four Lights of Glass. In the lower story are two Windows each having forty-two Lights of Glass, & two Doors each having Sixteen Lights—At the East end the upper story has three Windows each with eighteen Lights; & below two Windows both with eighteen Lights & a Door with nine—

The North side I think is most beautiful of all; In the upper Story is a Row of seven Windows with eighteen Lights a piece; and below six windows, with the like number of lights; besides a large Portico in the middle, at the sides of which are two Windows each with eighteen Lights.—At the West end are no Windows—The Number of Lights in all is five hundred, & forty nine—There are four Rooms on a Floor, disposed of in the following manner. Below is a dining Room where we usually sit; the second is a dining-Room for the Children; the third is Mr Carters study; & the fourth is a Ball-Room thirty Feet long—Above stairs, one Room is for Mr & Mrs Carter; the second for the young Ladies; & the other two for occasional Company—As this House is large, & stands on a high piece of Land it may be seen a considerable distance; I have seen it at the Distance of six Miles—At equal Distances from each corner of this Building stand four other considerable Houses, which I shall next a little describe. First, at the North East corner, & at 100 yards Distance stands the School-House; At the North-West Corner, & at the same Distance stands the stable; At the South-West Corner, & at the same Distance, stands the Coach-House; And lastly, at the South-East corner, & at an equal distance stands the Work-House. These four

Houses are the corner of a Square of which the Great-House is the
Center—First the School-House is forty five feet long, from East to
West, & twenty-seven from North to South; It has five well-finished,
convenient Rooms, three below stairs, & two above; It is built with
Brick a Story & a half high with Dormant Windows; In each Room
is a fire; In the large Room below-Stairs we keep our School; the
other two Rooms below which are smaller are allowed to Mr Randolph the Clerk; The Room above the School-Room Ben and I live
in; & the other Room above Stairs belongs to *Harry* & *Bob*. Five of us
live in this House with great Neatness, & convenience; each one has
a Bed to himself—And we are call'd by the Bell to the Great-House
to Breakfast &c—The Wash-House is built in the same form, & is of
the same Size of the School-House—From the front yard of the
Great House, to the Wash-House is a curious *Terrace*, covered finely
with Green turf, & about five foot high with a slope of eight feet,
which appears exceeding well to persons coming to the front of the
House—This *Terrace* is produced along the Front of the House,
and ends by the Kitchen; but before the Front-Doors is a broad flight
of steps of the same Height, & slope of the *Terrace*.

The Stable & coach-House are of the same Length & Breadth as
the School- and Wash-House, only they are higher pitched to be convenient for holding Hay & Fodder.[114]

Due East of the Great House are two Rows of tall, flourishing,
beautiful, Poplars, beginning on a Line drawn from the School to the
Wash-House; these Rows are something wider than the House, &
are about 300 yards Long, at the Eastermost end of which is the great
Road leading through Westmorland to Richmond. These Rows of
Poplars form an extreemely pleasant avenue, & at the Road, through
them, the House appears most romantic, at the same time that it does
truly elegant—The Area of the Triangle made by the Wash-House,
Stable, & School-House is perfectly livel, & designed for a bowling-
Green, laid out in rectangular Walks which are paved with Brick, &
covered over with burnt Oyster-Shells—In the other Triangle, made
by the Wash-House, Stable, & Coach House is the Kitchen, a well-
built House, as large as the School-House, Bake-House; Dairy; Store-
House & several other small Houses; all which stand due West, & at a
small distance from the great House, & form a little handsome Street.
These Building stand about a quarter of a Mile from a Fork of the
River Nomini, one Branch of which runs on the East of us, on which

are two Mills; one of them belongs to Mr Turburville, the other to Mr Washington, both within a mile -another branch of the River runs on the West of us, on which and at a small distance above the House stands Mr Carters Merchant Mill,[115] which I have in other places described; to go to the mill from the House we descend I imagine above an 100 Feet; the Dam is so broad that two carriages may pass conveniently on it; & the Pond from twelve to Eighteen Foot water—at the fork Mr Carter has a Granary, where he lands his Wheat, for the mill Iron from the Works &c—

In the Evening Mr *Carter* sent for *Ben* & I to play over the *Sonata* which we have lately learn'd; we performed it, & had not only Mr Stadleys Approbation, but his praise; he did me the honour to say that "I play a good Flute." He took a Flute also and play'd; which put me in mind, at once, of the speech of the Shepherd in virgil.— Non tu in Triviis, indocte, solebas Stridenti miserum Stipula dis- perdere cament [carmen]. For when compared to him, the best that Ben or I can do, is like Crows among Nightingales—We play'd till ten, and separated, I gave to Miss Harriot, for saying a good lesson, half a Bit—

Saturday 19.

The morning still wet & disagreeable—Last night I dreamed much of the Girl, which, I most of all others, esteem, & admire; of *Laura;* But oh! I dreamed She was treacherous!—If it be true, I must suppress the Greatness of my Disappointment by reflecting that I had not well enough considered this Sentiment of the *poet,* That,—Varium et mutabile Femina—I discover weakness when I am writing in this manner; but Anxiety, and mighty-Love carry me over the bounds which I set for the regulation of my conduct—Dreams indeed are vain & false; But perhaps *Laura* may think that Lovers vows are vain & triffling as they!—I spend the day in my Room looking over the Catalogue of the *Reviewers* for August, September, October & November 1773.—Ben, & Bob, & Harry, out tho the Day is bad— Mr *Stadley* is yet busy with the young Ladies—

Sunday 20.

The weather still cloudy, damp, and disagreeable, but it is perfectly calm; people here attribute this so long dullness to the Sun crossing the Line which is to happen to-morrow—After Breakfast Mr Stadley left us, The day is so bad none of us go to Church—Before Dinner I received from Mr Lane, by his Servant a Note, informing me that he is to set out tomorrow for home—In return, by the Same bearer, I wrote him my Compliments in a letter; desiring him to remember me to my Acquaintances in Pennsylvania, & New Jersey, as he will probably soon see many of them—I spent much of this Day in Mr Carters Library among the works of mighty-Men; I turned over *Calmets*, Scripture prints, they are beautiful, & vastly entertaining— At Dinner by some means, I know not how a conversation was introduced concerning the Souls of Women; Mrs *Carter* observed that She has heard they have no Souls—Says Miss Priscilla in a moment if I thought so I would not have spent all this morning in Reading; nor would Women, (Said the well discerning Miss) be careful to avoid any Shameful, or Sinful Action—It is not unlikly but those are the private Sentiments of many among the Fair; & no doubt they would be generally and publickly practised if it should be universally admitted that the Soul of a Woman is not to exist after the present Life.

Monday 21.

This day the days and nights are equal—The Sun enters *Aries*—Aries [Libra] dies Somniq: pares ubi fecerit Horas, Et medium suis atq: Umbris jam dividet Orbem. *Virgil.* Georgic 1.

At Breakfast Mrs Carter asked me who is foremost in Arithmetic; whether Bob, or Prissy? At which Mr Carter observed, that him of his Sons whom he finds most capable of doing Business when he leaves the World, & his Estate, Shall have the management of the whole, & support the Rest. It seemed to me to be not an ill-chosen Incentive to Diligence among the Boys—

This morning still cloudy, the wind at South—about ten a black-gloomy cloud appeared in the west; it came over like Virgils—Omnia Ventorum concurrere proelia [vidi]—The wind changed with the cloud to the westward—Dined with us Mr Washington & Mr Philip Smith, Brother to the Parson of this parish, to whom I was formally introduced—Toasts as usual—Towards Evening it grows more pleasant & after School, I had the pleasure of a walk in the Garden with Mrs Carter, Miss Stanhope, & Miss Harriot—The peas have grown admirably since my last Walk; & indeed all the Herbs seem sprouting—Harry this Day finished vulgar Fractions, & began Practice. Expence to day as Pin-Money a Bit or 7½ d

Teusday 22.

Once more the weather fine—Last night by some accident, the Main
Spring of my Watch either unhook'd or broke, for when I thought
She had run down, & trying to wind her, I found the Chain made no
Resistance As there is no oppertunity here of having her refitted, I
seem in considerable difficulty—In Spite of all my strongest opposing
efforts, my thoughts dwell on that Vixen *Laura*. I strive to refuse
them admission, or harbour them in my heart, yet like hidden fire
they introduce themselves, & seize; & overcome me when perhaps I
am pursuing some amuseing or useful Study; on giving precepts &
Directions to my little fair Seminary—At ten Mr Lane & Mr John
Simpson call'd to see us—At twelve we had a pleasant walk in the
Garden—Mr Carter, & Mrs Carter along—Mr Lane informs that he
has by particular Request, in the Absence of the Parson, Read the
funeral Service twice since he has been in the county, which is only
a few Weeks—He sets off for home soon; Mr Carter says he is in
Love, & I think it is with Miss *Camel*. I was introduced to Mr *Simp-
son:* He talks much; & often mentions his having been to England—
They Dined with us; Toasts as usual. Evening I have the Tooth Ach.

Wednesday 23.

I was almost wholly deprived of Sleep last night with a pain in my
Jaw & Teeth; which conti[n]ues this morning so bad I scarce know
what, or how to do—Frail, & weak nature; how we are forever teas'd,
& vexed with Anciety in our minds, or Pains & other distresses in our
Bodies!—We dined at half after two—It is now seven in the Evening
& I am about entering into bed, as the pain has entirely left me, that
I may satisfy my Body for last nights loss of my usual rest, I leave
Ben by the Fire, poring over a History of England, nodding Some-
times, however, & impatient of the distance of nine o-Clock.—

Thursday 24.

At Breakfast Mr Carter entertained us with an account of what he
himself saw the other Day, which is a strong Representation of the
cruelty & distress which many among the Negroes suffer in Virginia!
Mr Carter dined at Squire Lees some few Weeks ago; at the same
place, that day, dined also Mr George Turburville & his Wife—As
Mr Carter rode up he observed Mr Turburvilles Coach-Man sitting

on the Chariot-Box, the Horses off—After he had made his compliments in the House, He had Occasion soon after to go to the Door, when he saw the Coachman still sitting, & on examination found that he was there fast chained! The Fellow is inclined to run away, & this is the method which This Tyrant makes use of to keep him when abroad; & so soon as he goes home he is delivered into the pityless Hands of a bloody Overseer!—In the Language of a Heathen I query whether cunning old *Charon* will not refuse to transport this imperious, haughty Virginian Lord When he shall happen to die over the Styx to the Elysian Gardens; lest his Lordship in the passage should take affront at the treatment, & attempt to chain him also to the Stygean Galley for Life!—

Or, In the language of a Christian, I query whether he may be admitted into the peaceful Kingdom of Heaven where meekness, Holiness, & Brotherly-Love, are distinguishing Characteristicks?—

Tho the Pain in my Teeth has entirely left me, I am not therefore free from distress; for to day I am attacked with a pain in my Head, & Fever; which hinders me from Walking out at twelve as is my Custom!—

Fryday 25.

I rose by seven—& through Gods mercy I feel myself much relieved of yesterdays complaints—The weather cloudy, cold, rainy at times, & unpleasant—Evening *Ben* took courage & asked his *Papa* for his consent to allow him to go with me to Philadelphia—The Colonel very kindly, & at the same time very Politely consented—For he would not agree till he knew of me whether it is agreeable to me, & at my Request that he is to go—

Saturday 26.

Ben & *Bob* are soon after Breakfast on Horseback; Breakfasted with us one Lee, a Gentleman of what they call here the back Woods— He seems indeed a little stiff in his manner; but he has had a long Ride—I spend the Day close in my Room Reading Writing &c—

Sunday 27.

An odd Jumble of affairs happened this morning—*Bob* drest himself & came into our Room & in his usual way began to be pretty free in telling us *News.* Amongst a vast quantity of other stuff he informed *Ben* & I that he heard Mr *Randolph* has the P . . . we both join'd in

severely reprimanding for attempting to propogate so unlikely a
Tale—Why, Brother Ben, said the mischeivous Wretch I heard in
this Neighbourhood, yesterday a Report concerning you not much
to your—but I will conceal it—This inraged Ben he at first however
persuaded him but soon began to threaten loudly unless he told the
whole—why then, Brother said Bob, it is reported that two Sundays
ago you took Sukey (a young likely Negro Girl maid to Mrs Carters youngest Son) into your stable, & there for a considerable time
lock'd yourselves together!—Before Bob had done, the Bell rung
for Breakfast & we parted—All went to Church to-day but Miss
Nancy, Harry, & *Myself*—I spend the day agreeably in Mr *Carters*
Library—Evening when the Colonel returned, (for he dined at
Squire Lee's) he informed me of an affair which happened yesterday
in this County, One Smith, a Man of a Middle age who lives with his
aged Father, & his Father too is old & declining fast with disease—
This youth has lately made a will for his Father which he yesterday
compell'd him to sign; & after the Good old Man had obliged him,
he beat and abused him (tho his father) in desperate manner it is
thought with a design to destroy him! Soon after this he discharged a
musket at his own Brother who was at some distance from him &
lodged in his body eighteen large Shott!—Docters were immediately
call'd—& officers directed to take the villian but he, with his Wife
have hid themselves in a Thicket & have as yet evaded the search of
the Sheriff—

Sup'd with us one Mr Mathews a Steward for Mr Carter in Louden.

[*Monday 28*]

Breakfasted with us Mr Mathews; he seems to be a man of great
Gravity, says little, & Sighs often—The day is warm & vastly mild; it
is the first Day we have in all our Rooms been without any Fire—
At twelve I rode to Mr Taylors two miles; he was out, I sat half an
hour with Miss Taylor & returned to Dinner, the Ride exceeding
pleasant, and my Horse seems (as jockeys say) in good Flesh & well
prepar'd for our approaching & much wished for Journey—Evening
Mr *Simpson* came in, sup'd & stays the Night. He has last Week,
been destilling Mr Carter's Liquor made of Pisimonds—it is soft,
mild, of a fair pure Colour, burns clear, but does not answer the
Colonels Expectations; so that he does not propose to recommend it

to his Neighbours in this or the Neighbouring Counties as a useful experiment. When call'd on for my Toast, at Supper I gave Miss *Jenny Corbin;* Mrs *Carter* gave Captain *Lee;* & Mr *Simpson* gave Miss *Jones.*

Teusday 29.

To warm to day for fire, but we have the wind very strong from the West—Mr *Carter* rode to Court—Soon after Breakfast I receiv'd a Letter from Mr *Andrew Bryan* of Baltimore, Maryland formerly at College my Class-Mate—the Letter bears Date January 21st 1774 Dated at *Baltimore.* He informs me of his good Health, & that, he shall soon forward my Letters inclosed to him; perhaps kind oppertunity shall have before this hour favoured my wish, & brought to Laura advices of my State—At twelve I rode out, with Ben, an hour & better, the Day vastly windy. About four Colonel Philip Lee's Chariot arrived, in which came four young Misses to be ready for the Dance which happens here tomorrow—I am informed this Evening that Smith the Villian mentioned last Sunday was to day apprehended, & committed to the prison in this County

Wednesday 30.

Rainy & cold—The Colonel informed me this morning that the general Opinion of the Gentlemen at Court yesterday seem'd to be that the County would be free'd of three Villians if the old abused Father, the wounded Son & Brother, & the offending guilty Son were to be all hanged—The Day so bad Mr *Christian* does not attend—Mrs *Washington* came however, with Miss Jenny her Daughter; the two Fantleroys came also, & Miss Corbin, & Miss Turburville, & one Miss Hale[116] a new *Scholar*—Mr Carters Man play'd & the Dance goes on with great Spirit & neatness. Evening there is as common a good play. Separated all for Bed by half after nine.

Thursday 31.

All our company continue. The morning fair & cool—Yesterday & to-day I am strongly solicited to dance—I decline however & must persevere.—Mr & Mrs Turburville came in before Dinner—With the two Fantleroys, Ben, Bob, & Harry, I had a pleasant walk through the Fields, to the Mill &c. I paid my forfeit to the Baker 7½d—The Plumb-Trees are beginning to blossom—Towards Evening our company all left us.

Fryday April 1st 1774.

Good Fryday—A general Holiday here—Wednesday & thursday I gave up my School on account of the Dance, and they must have this Day for Devotion!—The Colonel, *Ben Harry*, & *myself* all go to Ucomico Church—Parson *Smith* gave the usual Prayers for the Day and a long Sermon very suitable & well chosen.

After Service we were invited and went Home with Captain Walker to dine; I was here introduced to Dr Steptoe[117] & a young Gentleman Brother to the Parson Both seem agreeable, & appear to be men of Sense Dined here also the Parson, his Wife, Sister, Mr Warder the Lawyer

Towards Evening we rode home I observed as I rode along People are universally plowing up their Land for planting Corn & for Tobacco And in one field I saw several Women planting Corn I think however, it is early even here—They raise no Flax, their Land in general being so poor that it will not produce it—And their Method of farming is slovenly, without any regard to continue their Land in heart, for future Crops—They plant large Quantities of Land, without any Manure, & work it very hard to make the best of the Crop, and when the Crop comes off they take away the Fences to inclose another Piece of Land for the next years tillage, and leave this a common to be destroyed by Winter & Beasts till they stand in need of it again to plough—The Land most commonly too is of a light sandy soil, & produces in very great quantities shrubby *Savins* & *Pines,* unless in the Vallies (for it is very hilly) & near the Potowmack where it is often vastly rich—Mr Carter has been lately solicited & was to have gone this Day with a number of Gentlemen to Horn-Point on the River Ucomico, with an intention, if they think the Situation will be proper, to establish Ware-Houses, & form a small Town—It is however, in my opinion, a fruitless Scheme—

Saturday 2.

The morning stormy. I kept the children in til twelve o-Clock then dismissed them—I spent the greater part of this Day in reading Miscellaneous Pieces out of Magazines—The weather cleared before Evening—At five with *Ben,* I rode over to Mr Turburville's, chiefly to see a young Lady[118] lately from London; who has come over at Mr Turburville's Invitation in the character of Governess to Miss Turburville She seems to be young, genteel, & is not without personal excellence—I received together with Mr *Carters* Family an Invitation from Mr Turburville to dine with him to morrow; which I propose to accept.—

Sunday 3.

The Day pleasant; I rode to church—after the Service proper for the Day, Mr Smith entertained us with a Sermon from Pauls Defence before King Agrippa "How is it thought a thing impossible with you that God should raise the dead," He in this gave us a very plain & just Discourse on the doctrine of the resurection—This being Easter-Sunday, all the Parish seem'd to meet together High, Low, black, White all come out—After Sermon the Sacrament was administered, but none are admited except communicants to see how the matter is conducted—

After Sermon I rode to Mr Turburville's (for I found to day the true spelling of his name) There dined with him, Ladies Mrs *Carter,*

& Mrs *George Turburville:* Gentlemen, Colonel *Carter*, Squire-*Lee*,
Mr *Cunningham*, & Mr *Jennings*, Merchants; Mr *George Lee*, & *Ben
Carter* & Myself—We had an elegant dinner; Beef & Greens; roast-
Pig; fine boil'd Rock-Fish, Pudding, Cheese &c—Drink: good Porter-
Beer, Cyder, Rum, & Brandy Toddy. The Virginians are so kind
one can scarce know how to dispense with, or indeed accept their
kindness shown in such a variety of instances.—I had again an oppertunity of seeing Miss *Sally Panton* which is the name of Mrs Turburville's English Governess—But the common voice seems to be
against me as to her being Handsome—But her huge *Stays* low Head
dress; enormous long *Waist,* a Dress entirely contrary to the liking
of Virginia Ladies, these I apprehend make her in their Eyes less per-
sonable, than to any one wholly unprejudiced—Her *Stays* are suited
to come up to the upper part of her shoulders, almost to her chin;
and are swaithed round her as low as they can possibly be, allowing
Her the liberty to walk at all: To be sure this is a vastly modest
Dress!—She speaks French & is to teach the Language to Miss Turburville, & also Writing, & reading English—Upon the whole, if her
Principles of Religion, & her moral behaviour, be as unexceptionable
as her person, & her Manner, let Mr and Mrs Carters opinions go
again me I shall think her agreeable—Miss *Prissy* Miss *Nancy;* &
Miss *Fanny* all stay the night at Captain Turburville's—At Church,
Mr Low, a young Scotch Gentleman, tutor in Colonel *Washingtons*
Family, solicited me to carry his Recommendations from Scotland,
to Dr Witherspoon as he is desirous to be licensed in one of our
northern Presbyteries—I shall do him the Favour.[119]—The country
begins to put on her Fowery Garment, & appear in *gaity*—The *Apri-
cots* are in their fulles Bloom; Peaches also, & Plumbs, & several sorts
of Cheries are blossoming; as I look from my Window & see Groves
of Peach Trees on the Banks of Nomini; (for the orchards here are
very Large) and other Fruit Trees in Blossom; and amongst them
interspers'd the gloomy Savin; beyond all these at a great Distance the
blue Potowmack; & over this great River, just discern the Woods
of Maryland & conceive that beyond them all lies Cohansie my native
pleasant Residence; & when I think with myself that by Gods permission, in a very few days more I shall be in the midst of Society,
quite remote from formality, and from the least fear of giving offence by being familiar, or of being aw'd to silence by ostentatious
vanity: how the thought fires me! Direct my Way, merciful God,

and keep my Feet from falling, & my Heart from disobeying thy pure & perfect commandments—And make my Way prosperous that I may go and return again, still doing thy Pleasure, & honouring thy great Name!—

Monday 4.

Easter Monday; a general holiday; Negroes now are all disbanded till Wednesday morning & are at Cock Fights through the County; This morning I make a general payment First to Sam the Barber 8/2. Second to Tom the Hostler 7/6. third to Nelson who waits on me /3½. Sum 15/11½—

Mr & Mrs *Carter*, with Mr *Cunningham* & *Ben* (as Mr Cunningham came home with us last Night) all rode to Day to Richmond Court—I was in the morning strongly solicited to go, but chose to decline it—After Breakfast, came home from Mr Turburville's our young Ladies, they inform me that Miss Panton discovered a strong inclination to be better acquainted with me; which indeed is a Curiosity that I cannot say I am altogether destitute of. I shall therefore, when I find it convenient make Miss Panton a visit—

I was before Dinner very strongly urged, by Mr Taylor, Mr Randolph, & some others to attend a Cock-Fight, where 25 Cocks are to fight, & large Sums are betted, so large at one as twenty five Pounds, but I choose rather to stay at Home. I read to day, & am much charmed with a Speech of *Plato's* over Alexander the *Great* lying dead before him—"O thou, who deceived by vain-Glory didst think of grasping at every thing, others are now going to gather the fruits of thy labours & thy Fatigues. Of so many conquests, there remains of thee but the terrible account, which thou art obliged to render unto the sovereign Judge"!—

I have also to Day with considerable attention been looking over Junius's Letters. His sentiments are strong, & bold. His language is chaste, & concise. & his Genius seems free and vast—I cannot easily omit transcribing a short passage from his Letter to the Revd Mr *Horne* in which he is speaking of Lord *Chatham*. as it pleases me vastly. "As for the common, sordid veiws of avarice, or any purpose of vulgar Ambition, I question whether the applause of *Junius*, would be of service to Lord Chatham. My vote will hardly recommend him to an increase of his pension, or to a Seat in the Cabinet. But if his Ambition be upon a levil with his understanding—If he judges of what is truely honourable for himself with the same superior Genius which animates & directs him to Eloquence in Debates, to Wisdom in Decision, even the Pen of *Junius* shall contribute to reward him. Recorded Honour shall gather round his Monument, & thicken over him. It is a solid Fabric, & will support the Lawrels that adorn it—I am not conversant in the language of panegyric—These praises are extorted from me; but they will wear well, for they have been dearly earned."—

Junius, however, does not seem to have been at all ignorant of his own merit; for in the close of the same letter he says "Such Artifices cannot long delude the understanding of the People; &, without meaning an indecent Comparison I may venture to foretell, that the *Bible* & *Junius* will be read when the Commentaries of the Jesuits are forgotten. We supped at nine—Mr Carter tired and early in Bed.

After Supper I had a long conversation with Mrs Carter concerning Negroes in Virginia, & find that She esteems their value at no higher rate than I do. We both concluded, (& I am pretty certain that the conclusion is just) that if in Mr Carters, or in any Gentlemans Estate, all the Negroes should be sold, & the Money put to Interest in safe hands, & let the Lands which these Negroes now work lie wholly uncultivated, the bare Interest of the Price of the Negroes would be a much greater yearly income than what is now received from their working the Lands, making no allowance at all for the trouble & Risk of the Masters as to the Crops, & Negroes.—How much greater then must be the value of an Estate here if these poor enslaved Africans were all in their native desired Country, & in their Room industrious Tenants, who being born in freedom, by a laudable care, would not onlyly inrich their Landlords, but would raise a hardy Offspring to be the Strength & the honour of the Colony.

Teusday 5.

It is with difficulty I am able to collect the members of our School together for Business. Holidays have become habitual, & they seem unwilling to give them over. As the Negroes have this Day for a Holiday our Schollars thinks it hard that they should be compell'd to attend to Business. I summon them together however, and shall keep them to constant Study until the time of my setting away. Miss Priscilla this morning told me, of Miss Panton, a moving story: Last Sunday Evening after we left there She took a lonely Walk, & being

asked why She chose to walk without a companion, she answered
that she was thinking of Home & of her Friends, & indulging her fond
Grief on account of their absence!—Such a feeling as this I have
not been a stranger to, I therefore Sympathize with the poor young
Girl. The Day agreeably pleasant—Towards Evening Miss *Corbin*
came over to pay us a visit After School I waited on the Ladies in the
Dining-Room the conversation was on Fashions, which instantly introduced the oddity of Miss *Panton*. But Miss Corbin with a *Sneer*,
& with ill-nature enough, swore She would not think of imitating
such a thing as her!—O!—Tantam Animis cælestibus Iræ?—I spent
the Evening in cheerful chat with the Ladies. I think I have not had
a more sociable & unconstrained feeling since I left Home, & my
forgiving Friends.

Wednesday 6.

Ben is making a great Bustle about going to Philadelphia—He almost
counts the Hours—We propose to go next Wednesday. But with
composure, & Patience, yet with great Satisfaction I anticipate the
near approaching Day. *Ben* begs me to acquaint him with the manners of the People in regard to Religion, and he swears he can suit
himself to any serious, or formal Visage—
Mrs *Carter*, & Miss *Corbin*, after Breakfast rode to Colonel Frank-
Lee's—We dine alone. I informed the Colonel that I do not think it
will be convenient for me to continue with him longer than one
year—He discovered some dissatisfaction; I told him my reason & he
assented—he honours me, by putting in me so much confidence as to
commission me to find out and recommend to Him some young
Gentleman to succeed me in the instruction of his Children—He
flattered my vanity also by reading a Letter to me which I am to
bear to Dr Witherspoon, the contents of it as follows—

"Robert *Carters* compliments to Dr *Witherspoon:* He has the
pleasure to acquaint Him that Mr Fithians Method of teaching, & his
conduct are highly approved here; He is about to visit his friends
in *New-Jersey*, & will bring these from Sir,

Your humble Servt"—

He informed me that he does indeed prefer a Tutor for his Children
who has been educated upon the Continent, not on a supposition that

such are better Schollars, or that they are of better principles, or of more agreeable Tempers; but only on account of pronunciation in the English Language, (as most of his Children are to be taught chiefly in this) in which he allows young Gentlemen educated in good Schools on the Continent, to excel the Scotch young Gentlemen, & indeed most of the English.—Evening came in & staid the Night Captain Blackwell.

Thursday 7.

Breakfasted with us Miss *Corbin*. The Day pleasant—Mr Carter proposes to set away soon after Dinner—He seems, however, to prepare himself for his Journey with all the sedateness of a philosopher—Besides the Commands he gave me yesterday, he desires me to wait on Mr Willing[120] Merchant in Philadelphia & know if he will trade here for either Flour or Bread in any Quantity.—He has given Ben & me an Invitation to ride & spend this Evening with him at Colonel *Tayloe's*—We set out about three; Mr *Carter* travels in a small, neat

Chair, with two waiting Men—We rode across the Country which is now in full Bloom; in every field we saw Negroes planting Corn, or plowing, or hoeing; we arrived at the Colonels about five, Distance twelve miles. Here is an elegant Seat!—The House is about the Size of Mr. *Carters,* built with Stone, & finished curiously, & ornamented with various paintings, & rich Pictures. This Gentleman owns *Yorick,*

who won the prize of 500 £ last November, from Dr Floods Horse *Gift*—In the Dining-Room, besides many other fine Pieces, are twenty four of the most celebrated among the English Race-Horses, Drawn masterly, & set in elegant gilt Frames.—He has near the great House, two fine two story stone Houses, the one is used as a Kitchen, & the other, for a nursery, & Lodging Rooms—He has also a large well formed, beautiful Garden, as fine in every Respect as any I have seen in *Virginia*. In it stand four large beautiful Marble Statues— From this House there is a good prospect of the River *Rapahannock*, which opposite here is about two miles across; We can also from the chambers easily see the Town Hobbes-Hole & the Ships which lie there. I was introduced by Mr *Carter* to the Colonel, to Miss Polly, & to Miss Kitty his Daughters—& to a Lady (Mrs Thornton,) [121] that happened there, & to a young Gentleman, Mr Corvin [122]—The young Ladies played several tunes for us, & in good Taste on the *Harpsichord;* We supp'd at nine; & had the usual Toasts.

Fryday 8.

The Ladies before breakfast gave us several tunes on the Harpsichord —About ten Mr Carter set out for *Williamsburg*, to the general Court, which sits twice a year, each Time twenty four Days Sundays excluded—We had some agreeable Conversation this morning; Horses seem to be the Colonels favourite topic—He inquired of me however, where I was born; where educated; & if I am pleased with *Virginia*—He told me he saw Dr Witherspoon, & conversed with him an Evening last Fall, & is much pleased with his manner, & Qualities—He informed me that Dr *Morgan* [123] of Philadelphia breakfasted with him a few Days ago; he calls the Docter facetious, sensible, & prudent. The Colonel desired me to enquire for some Gentleman of undoubted ability to teach in a Family—I shall apply to Mr *Saml Leek* junr [124] & if he declines I will look no further—Ben & I took our Leave about Eleven, and returned Home—The Day is cloudy and cold, the wind hard at North, & threatens Snow—This evening Ben met with a sad repulse; Mrs *Carter* proposes going to Williamsburg soon, & says She must have his company! Poor Boy, he feels the Force of Disappointment! And I confess I am a little vexed—

Saturday 9.

Mrs Carter gave Ben liberty to go with me as far as Anopolis, provided we set out soon, & accordingly we propose to set off to-morrow or Monday morning, I begin therefore to prepare for the Ride. The Day is rainy & cold, & I am in a vastly disagreeable Humour—

Sunday 10.

Mrs *Carter* yesterday, in the Character of a truely fond Mother, altered her mind concerning *Ben* many Times and in several different manners: At first she agreed for him to go with me as far as Anopolis without a waiting Man; then She concluded he was not well and had better decline going entirely; towards Evening She gave him full liberty if he will take a Waiting-Man; & will not set away till Monday morning; This I urged not being pleased from the Begining with going on the Sabbath—I gave yesterday to the Shoemaker a Bit—& a Bit to the Wash woman; half a Bit to her little Girl; & half a Bit to *Nelson* the Boy who waits on our School; the whole is 11½. This morning is extremely pleasant the Country full of Flowers, & the branches full of lovely singing Birds.—Before Breakfast, I saw a Ring of Negroes at the Stable, fighting Cocks, and in several parts of the plantation they are digging up their small Lots of ground allow'd by their Master for Potatoes, peas &c; All such work for themselves they constantly do on Sundays, as they are otherwise employed on every other Day. Sermon to Day, is at Ucomico, too far for my Horse immediately before his Journey—Neither Mrs *Carter* nor any of the Family go—At Dinner I received a Letter from Mr *Lowe*, with his Testimonials from the College in Edinburg which I am to present to the Presbytery of Philadelphia and if it shall be accepted, I am to bring such Exercises as they may appoint—

Monday 11.

Bens Mare lame; Nat must stay, Ben & I set out at eight Rode by Westmoreland Court-House, Mattox Church; fed at Mattox-Bridge,[125] Rode by round-hill Church,[126] to Tylors Ferry[127] by three o-Clock 36 Miles—passed over the Ferry 7 Miles Ferriage 6/2—At a small House in Virginia for a gallon of Corn 1/4.—At a small Tavern at the Ferry on the Maryland side Expence 9d rode from thence three Miles to Squire Lees who has the Naval office here—Spent the Evening with young Mr *Lee*, Miss Lee, Miss Booth, & Miss Washington —Toasts—I gave Miss Nancy Galloway—Between the Ferry & Mr Lees we passed through four gates.

Teusday 12.

Up soon, expence to Boy 3d. Rode to Port Tobacco[128] 13 Miles good Road—Fine Hill near the town; betwen Mr Lees & Port Tobacco 13 Gates—This is a small Town of not more than twenty or twenty Houses mostly of one story—Expence for a gallon of Oats ....8d, for bitters 4d, the Day fine—Rode thence to Piscataway;[129] the road good 15 Gates—ma[n]y fine streams of pure water—and many beautiful hills—This is a small Town of low Houses not more than two in it two Stories High; It lies however in a fine rich valey— Expence for Dinner, Wine & Oats 5/.... from Piscataway we rode to upper Marlboroug[130] the road something hilly, we passed through 15 Gates, two elegant Seats Mr Wests, & Mr Diggs[131]—arrived at Marlborough[132] by six it is a pleasant levil spot, 16 Miles from Alexandria[133]—they have a Presbyterian Meeting House which Mr Hunt supplies—They have a latin School also here; & an elegant Ball-Room —Piscataway is seven miles from Alexandria. In bed by nine—

Wednesday 13.

Up early, the morning fine. Expence here 4/11 Rode thence through a pleasant country four miles to a small Ferry over Patuxen,[134] Ferriage /6. then 12 Miles to South River three quarters of a Mile over Ferriage 6d then we rode thro a piny sandy road four miles to Anopolis 32 Gates—This is a pleasant situated Town: the Inhabitants appear gay & cheerful—I put up at the Coffee-House—An agreeable Woman keeps it Expence to a Barber for shaving & dressing 1/6— For oats Coffee &c 3/1—To Boy /10. I roved through the Town til five then I entered into a Boat the wind South West & Sailed over the Bay for *Rock-Hall*[135] distance 25 miles—the Boats are extremely good, well built, & strongly manned, & indeed there is need, for the Bay is broad, & often boistrous; we arrived at Rock Hall by half after nine; I was very sick on the passage, & I never was sick before on the water—The ferriage here for a Man & Horse is 15/.—To the Ferry Men for a Quart of Rum 1/3. And for my footing never having crossed the ferry before I paid 1/. The whole expence of this Day is 1 £ 8s 7d.

Thursday 14.

The morning fine. I have from this place a view of the broad Chesapeek—Expence here for Tea in the Evening, Oats Cordial &c 4/10, set away half after Six—To Boy /3d. Rode from Rock Hall over a delightful part of the country to Chester-Town 13 Miles[136] -this is a beautiful small Town on a River out of the Bay navigable for Ships. The Situation is low & I apprehend it is subject to summer Fevers— It has an elegant I may say grand Court-House, in which is the town Clock—Mr *Wall*[137] the Commedian, has been for several Evenings past exhibiting Lectures in Electricity, & I understand with some considerable applause. They have a lottery here on foot & to be drawn in May next for to assist them in building a market-House Town-Wharf &c.—I breakfast here, & feed, Expence 2/3. to Boy 2d —In this Town & the neighbouring Country rages at present a malig- nant, putrid Fever, & what is generally called the spotted Fever!— From chester Town I rode to George-Town, 16 miles—The Land levil, fertile, & vastly pleasant—In this Town I visited Mr *Voorhees*, an eminent Merchant here, & he seems to be a Gentleman of peculiar smartness Industry & Oconomy—The Fever I now mentioned, is also here, & the whooping-Cough is very general & malignant—I lodged with this Gentleman—We had Evening prayers—Since I left Co- hansie I have not heard the like—This is a small Town, & lies on a fine River, which divides it from another small Town directly oppo- site call'd Frederick.[138]

Fryday 15.

I rose early—After Breakfast I rode to see Miss *Rachel Stocktin,*[139] now Mrs *Ryley;* She lives on this River, about a mile higher up, in a large very elegant brick House; in considerable grandeur—Poor Girl She herself is much indisposed either of a bad Cold, (as She thinks) or of this epidemical Fever; Mrs *Ryley* introduced me ceremoniously to Miss *Ryley* her Husbands *Sister,* She has a small handsome For- tune, & is perhaps agreeable—I returned to Town, & dined with Mr *Voorhees,* & immediately after crossed over the Ferry for *Port- Penn.*[140] Expence at *George-Town* for my Horse 2/3 to Boy 4d. I rode next to small village called *Warwick,*[141] a pitful place indeed —Expence here 1/11 Boy /2. then I rode on to Port-Penn, the Country beautiful, the Land apparently very rich, the Timber strait, & large; I entered Port-Penn just as the Sun went down, but could not prevail with the Ferry-Man to carry me over before the morn- ing—In George-Town I was told the following distressing *News:* that Dr *Ward,* & my Aunt *Fithian* of Cohansie are both Dead; that my Aunt died in a very sudden unusual manner!—That Miss Polly Bullock of Philadelphia is dying in a Consumption!—In the Evening I called in to see Mr *Steward* an ancient, gray headed, wealthy Gentleman in *Port-Penn*, who, by some Weakness in his Back, has been unable to walk at all for four years, he is hearty, religious, cheerful, seemed much pleased, & thanked me often for calling to see him, & desired by me his kindest Compliments to Mr Hunters Family—I spend the Evening alone with quiet & content.—In Bed by nine—

Saturday 16.

I rose early, & expected to pass soon over the Ferry—The wind moderate at North West but the boat is aground, & I must wait until eleven, when She is expected to float—I was much alarmed in the night, thinking I had in Maryland taken the putrid Fever; I lay sleepless, felt feverish, had pains in my Head—But I feel wholly relieved this morning. At twelve the Boat came—We run over—Expence at

Port-Penn 4/8. Ferriage 5/-. Once more through Gods Mercy in New-Jersey. The Favours of God our common Parent are innumerable, & great beyond our merit—I rod with Pleasure from Elsenborough to Greenwich; I stopt to see the forsaken Mrs Ward; She seems to be truely distress'd! I arrived by Sunset at my Uncles he also seems much afflicted, with his Loss—He informed me that many

have Died in the Neighbourhood of Greenwich this winter. Dr
Ward, Squire Millar, Mr Boy'd Merchant—Aunt Fithian, aunt
Ware, Rachel Peck, Rachel Ware, David Mills, Mrs Mills &c. a very
Mortal Winter!

Sunday 17.

The morning vastly pleasant & Cohansie looks a delightsome as ever
it used I went to meeting. How unlike *Virginia*, no rings of Beaux
chatting before & after Sermon on Gallantry; no assembling in
crowds after Service to dine & bargain; no cool, spiritless harangue
from the Pulpit; Minister & people here seem in some small measure
to reverence the Day, there neither do the one or the other—I spent
the day at Home.

Monday 18.

I took a tour over to Town before dinner to see old acquaintances
The Neighbourhood looks in nothing altered Mr *Potter* took home
my Brother Amos with an intention if it shall suit to learn him the
Shopkeeping business—Afternoon I rode to Mr Hunters—And in
the Evening with Andrew to Deerfield, spent the Evening til ten at
Mr Greens in company with the amiable Miss Beatty—Mrs Green is
much indisposed, has lately had a daughter—The School here is at
the present time larger than it has ever been; there are now seven viz.
John Leek, Reading-Beatty,[142] James & John Ramsey, Stephen Ranney, Seeley Fithian, & Thomas Greenman—We rode to Mrs *Pecks.*
Joseph since I left home, has married Mrs *Hannah.*

Teusday 19.

Rose by six. Breakfasted with Mrs *Peck.* Soon after we again visited
Mr Green—I spent the Day most agreeably. Kind Heaven has in-
dulg'd my wish;—In the Evening I went up & staid the Night at
Mrs *Pecks.*

Wednesday 20.

Soon after breakfast I rode home and visited several of my acquaintances—I had my Hair cut short—Feel myself much indisposed.
Looked over, sorted & adjusted my Books.—

Thursday 21

Spent all this day in preparing for my approaching examination before the Revd Presbytery—I am to review Greek Testament—Moral & Natural Philosophy—Logic—Geography And if I have time I must look over the Lattin Classics.

Fryday 22.

Rode to the Stage early for the Papers thence I went Mr Hunters where I met with that great master of music, Mr *Lyon*[143]—He sung at my request, & sing with his usual softness & accuracy—He is about publishing a new Book of Tunes which are to be cheifly of his own Composition—He has removed out of Halifax into the Northern part of New-England, but poor Man, since he left Cohansie he has felt the hardy arm of want!—

I returned towards Evening but promised first to visit him again to-morrow afternoon—

Saturday 23.

At home drawing off some of Mr Lyons Tunes, & revising my own Exercises—The morning pleasant but the weather dry. Afternoon according to appointment I visited Mr Lyon at Mr Hunters. He sings with great accuracy I sung with him many of his Tunes & had much Conversation on music, he is vastly fond of music & musical genius's We spent the Evening with great sattisfaction to me

Sunday 24.

I left Mr Hunters Early I wrote a line to Miss Beatty, for a excuse for not seeing her yesterday Attended Sermon at Greenwich. I rode in the Evening to the Bridge to hear Mr Green, my old, much respected Tutor preach, he came & delivered himself admirably without making Use of Notes at all I staid the Night at Mr Seeleys, visited Mrs Ramsey, & Dr Elmer & spoke with many of my acquaintances—

Monday 25.

I breakfasted with Mrs Ramsey, then rode to Mrs Boyds, & by Mr Ewing I was introduced to herself & her two Daughters Miss *Matty* & Miss *Sally*—I had heard that this family is genteel, industrious & religious. I saw now & beleived it—Lately, by a sore stroke of providence Mr Boyd the Head has been remov'd by Death!—

Left Mrs Boyds & rode to Ephraim Seeleys junr—then about Eleven rode to Deerfield; dined with Mr Green. I had the pleasure to spend the afternoon and evening with Miss Beatty.

Teusday 26.

Visited Mr Nathan Leek, he seems to be still loquacious, & historical —He gave me a long and full account of the present difference between Messrs *Hunter, Greenman,* & *Brown,*—He told me likewise the Beginning & continuation of the quarrel of the Magistrates-freeholders, & other officers about raising money by taxation for repairing Cohansie-Bridge—After Dinner, with Miss *Beatty* I rode and visited Mrs Boyd—

Wednesday 27.

John Peck agreed to succeed me at Mr Carters in Virginia I spoke to Mr Samuel Leek junr concerning Mr Taylors proposal;[144] he is doubtful about an answer

Paid John Peck for postage of my Letter to him last Winter 4/. Bought a watch-seal 1/. Rode to Greenwich after Dinner.

Thursday 28.

I waited on the Miss Boyds to day to Mr *Hollinsheads,* New England-Town. His Family are in good health; there I saw the amiable Miss *Debby Pratt.*—Mr *Hollinshead* informed me that the Presbytery have been only a little pleased with the Examination of Messrs ———— probably mine will be worse! Returned to Mrs Boyds in the Evening

Fryday 29.

I rode to Mr Green's after breakfast—Mr. Dicky Howel came in; we spent the afternoon & Evening with Mr Green & Miss Beatty; Mr Green is, to be sure, vastly sensible, very intelligible, dry, witty, satirical, yet good and exceeding agreeable.

Saturday 30.

Breakfasted with the parson—Rode home soon after breakfast— proceeded in preparing for the near approaching examination—The latter part of this Day very stormy.

Sunday May 1st 1774.

Very cool the wind violent at North West—I spent the morning in looking over the Greek-Testament—To day preached for us Mr *Aiken.* He seems to be much applauded by the People.

Monday 2.

Very early I rode over to Mr Holinshead's at Miss Pratts request to carry her to Mr Hoshels to be ready to-morrow morning for the Stage—We rode to the Bridge & dined at Mrs Boyds—After dinner we rode to Mr Hoshels—Miss *Debby Pratt* according to her general character, is in every measure what I have said somewhere before, *Genteel, modest, Religious* & *cheerful*—

Teusday 3.

I conducted Miss Pratt to the Stage this morning by five & took my leave—I immediately after returned to the Bridge, thence to Mr Holinsheads by eight o Clock—Returned home by twelve.

Wednesday 4.

Last night & this morning fell a very considerable Snow, so much that I imagine had it not melted after it fell it would have been six inches deep! Afternoon I walked to Deerfield—Miss Beatty a little – thoughtful.

Thursday 5.

At the Bridge before noon to agree with Mr Potter about taking my Brother Amos prentice—We put it off some Days— Expence for a Watch Key 9d. Last Night was very cold; I shall scarce be beleived if I say that I saw, handled, & measured Ice this morning two Inches thick!

Fryday 6.

Still very cold. To Day is the fast before Sacrament. Mr Hunter gave us two Sermons. The leaves on the Trees are grown black, the Fruit must be past recovery, probably. the Flax too.

Saturday 7.

I did several errands for myself in Greenwich—Before Noon Mr Patterson call'd to see me; He is shortly to be married to Miss Amy

Ewing—She is a Girl of Reading, Taste, & Delicacy; has a good share of personal Beauty, open, sociable, & kind in her manner, & on the whole agreeable—Mr Paterson seemed always to me formal, has a peculiar, universal Fondness for the Fair is a great mathematician, a good English Scholar & Philosopher, & is frugal & industrious. I rode with Mr Patterson to Mr Hunters, he informed me many things concerning the new School or small Acadamy lately instituted at Wilmington, in which he is second Master. Evening I wrote a sentimental Letter to Miss *Beatty*.

Sunday 8.

To day at Greenwich was administred, & I received the holy Sacrament—Grant, great God, that I may have been a worthy communicant! I dined with Mrs Ward. She speaks with great Respect, Affection, and Sincerity of her late worthy Partner.

Monday 9.

Til Eleven I am busy in looking over Exercises for the approaching Presbytery. After Dinner I made Mrs Brewster a Visit. Mr Ben Peck in my opinion is rashly entering on an important matter; he is going to begin in a few Days the Study of Phisic under the direction of Dr Bowen; whose kowledge & Practice, by those who are in fact Judges in the Art seems to be wholly exploded. There is a Report that Mrs Brewster is in prospect of being married to a Gentleman from Maryland; She talks freely of it, says She can fancy him; that he is a man of Fortune, of character & to her agreeable—But there is one She regards more who has left her, however, without hope!—

Teusday 10.

Yesterday, in a private lonely manner, at nine in the morning, were married Mr Patterson & Miss Amy Ewing. I wish them from my heart a long, unbroken, & strong friendship for each other, & mutual, unmixed happiness. After breakfast according to a previous appointment, I rode to Deerfield Dine at Mrs Pecks. I am ashamed that I may record here what does no honour to my old Aunt, I saw her with three Partners round a Table playing Cards at that vulgar game fit only for the meanest gamblers "all Fours"[145]—At three I visited Miss *Beatty* that amiable Girl, I always see with pleasure, am happy where She is & feel uneasy & disturbed always when I must leave her.

Since June in the year 1770 I have had an acquaintance with her—& since May in the year 1771 I have happily had an Intimacy. Her Goodness has at length indulged my importunate Solicitations & in her Society I hope to be happy—I spent the Evening til eleven with her, & in the most entertaining manner, Mr Howel & Mr John Peck call'd in a small Time.

Wednesday 11.

I rose a little after seven. It is not my custom to lie in bed so long, but I was with Lazy Boys, *Reading Beatty*, and *Stephen Ranney*. Mrs Green is better, but Miss *Beatty* says she has the *Hipp*—Soon after breakfast I returned Home—Mrs Pecks Family Mr Howel, & Miss Beatty at the same time set out on a visit to Mr Hoshels. There came a report to Day that Mr Stephen Reeve Silver Smith of Philadelphia is broken up, & has left the City; disagreeable News this to his Relations here—There was an Ox killed this Day at Bridge-Town which weighed upwards of a thousand weight, supposed to be the largest ever kill'd in the County.

Thursday 12.

I wrote a chronological Letter to Miss *Beatty*. Spent the Day at home. Feel pensive on leaving Cohansie.

Fryday 13.

I rode before Dinner to Mr *Hunters*. Andrew is finishing his Exer-cises for the Presbytery—Mrs Hunter advised me to shew my Pieces to Mr *Hunter* for correction I agreed—Four o Clock I rode to the Bridge, drank Tea with Mrs Boyd. They are Girls of Great prudence, & good breeding—

Saturday 14.

After breakfast I wrote a private Letter to Laura. befor Dinner rode to Mr *Hunters* gave him my Pieces; he examined them, made some small alterations, & advised me to present them to the Presbytery—Took my Leave of several Friends in Greenwich—

Sunday 15.

I wrote a Letter to Dr Beatty, & a Letter to Charles Beatty [146] of the Junior Class at Nassau Hall—To Day is the yearly Meeting with the

Baptists—Last Evening was the first thunder Gust we have had this Season, it was not however Severe.

Mr James Ward was excommunicated this Day from our Church—

Monday 16.

We set out for Philadelphia from Mr Hunters by five Expence by the way 3/6. In Town by five.

Teusday 17.

Took lodgings at Mrs Cheesmans—Expence for a Register 3/9.— Spoke for a mourning Ring. Motto I. & H. ob: Feb: 1772.—

Met in Presbytery at eleven A. M.—Business of last Session looked over, at one adjourn'd til three—at three met. Mr Evans[147] pronounced his first exercise a Sermon length an hour—After him Mr Keith produced his length 44 Minutes. Afternoon I spent several hours with the Miss Sprouts

Wednesday 18.

I passed my first examination before the Presbytery; after which I read my thesis & Sermon both which were accepted—In this examination I was questioned on my personal Religion, & on the Latin, & Greek Languages. I spent the evening at Mr Armitages.

Thursday 19.

Waited on the Synod—Preparing to set out to-morrow. Visited several Ladies—Spent the afternoon agreeably with the Miss Holinsheads—Evening I visit Miss Bedford—Waited on Dr Witherspoon on Colonel Carters & on Mr Lowes account.

Fryday 20.

Before noon I waited on the agreeable Miss Debby Pratt. I spoke with Miss Sally Boyd. Afternoon I took my Leave at Mr McCalla's, & Mrs Cheesemans where I lodge—At six with Miss *Ruth Webster*, her Sister *Alhe* [Althea], & Betsy, & Polly Armitage I walked to a lovely Garden near the Hospital call'd Lebanon, drank some Mead, & had a most agreeable Ramble—At ten the same Evening I entered on Board the *Swallow* Captain Balinger for Cohansie—

Saturday 21.

I waked & found myself only a little below the Fort—The morning pleasant—the Wind a head—I wrote a Letter on Board to Johnny Peck to acquaint him with Dr Withespoons Opinion—I wrote also to Miss *Webster*. About five in the evening we anchored off *Marcus Hook,* we went on Shore; Drank a bowl of punch with Mr Andrew Ferguson who has lately moved here—He informed me that two young Gentlemen of Fashion & Substance in Town are making their addresses to *Laura*—She is worthy the Regard of the most worthy on Earth.

Sunday 22.

I found myself this morning a few miles above Port Penn. Perfectly calm—I wrote a Letter this morning to Miss Beatty—The *Sea Nymph* Captain Blewer came in Sight, Mr Cook & Mr Howel are passengers —About twelve a Breese sprung up at South—& with the Tide we entered our Creek by four, & I was at Home by five—Spent the evening in writing—

Monday 23.

Busy in getting ready to set away. Wrote a Letter to Dr *Beatty*—& one to Miss *Pratt.* The morning warm. I took my leave of the People in town of my acquaintance & set out for Virginia a little after noon —Mr Donaldson is very ill—There are strange & rediculous reports concerning him—That he has sent since his illness to Mr Ewing to be married to Tempy Fithian—Left Home about two o Clock—at the Ferry by five. The Boat is on the other side—Half after five she set off, the wind fair over by half after six—We left the shore at Seven. The wind light at West North West before we were over the wind fell—I was obliged to take to the Oar—& pull like a Turk— The flood strong against us—I rowed thus a full hour—My poor hands, when I got ashore were sore enough—I was set ashore more than a mile above *Port Penn*—Had to ride down on high rotten Bank through the dark—Once I got mired—On the whole it has been the worst adventure I have had in my travels.—I reached the Tavern in Port Penn by half after Nine. Call'd for half a Gill of bitters to qualify my humours; & a dish of Tea to cheer me, & soon to Bed. Ferriage 5/.

Teusday 24.

The morning pleasant & cool. Expence at *Port Penn,* 3/—Rode thence by the Trap five miles thence to middleton[148] five miles. Thence to Warwick four miles. Here I breakfasted. Expence for myself & Horse 1/7.—Thence I rode to George Town. Expence for oats 6d—Thence I rode to *New-Town*[149] fifteen Miles expence for —2/—For having my Coat altered in the Sleeves and Shoulders 2/. Expence for a pair of black worsted Stockings 6/.—Mr *Stephen Reeve*[150] is in George Town Working for Money Money to Gamble —This evening I feel more fatigued & dispirited than since I first went to Virginia—

Wednesday 25.

Expence at Newtown 4/9. Rode befor Breakfast to Rock-Hall the morning rainy—The Day calm & (hard Disappointment) I must stay til to-morrow!—My Land-Lord invited me to a race about four miles off, & as the day grew better I went; the Purse was fifty Dollars. I was surprised to see that almost, I think quite one third of the of the People were in mourning—A discouraging aspect for one who has any intention to settle in this part of Maryland, but none to leave the World—Many who wore black & Scarfs I took notice swore most desperately!—Not Death the formidable King of terrors can frighten men from provoking God by Sin!—Afternoon I was troubled with a Tooth Ach—I returned about two—Laid down til six—Slept but little—A thousand things perplex me. I am unwilling to leave Home.—I have already overstaid my Time—I am vexed at having to continue here—I have left the Girl I love—I am keeping myself out of publick business—O ten thousand difficulties embarrass me!—Heavenly Father, to thee in trouble I fly, comfort, sustain, guide & uphold me—Evening Seven Gentlemen came in— They went to Cards—I to Bed—Troubled much with a Tooth Ach—

Thursday 26.

Slept but little—Breakfasted—Set off at seven—four in company expence 26s/6. Arrived at Annopolis—Bought at Annopolis a pair of buckles 2/9. Expence ....10d—Left Annapolis at five for Marlborough—Ferriage 6d—Rode to a point of Patuxen 22 Miles— Tooth-Ach still troubles me—In Bed by eleven, tired & discouraged!

Fryday 27.

Expence at this little Town 2/9—Ferriage a full mile up the River
Patuxen 1/. Rode from the River to upper Marlborough three miles
thence without stoping to Piscataway 15 miles—Here I dined—My
pain has wholly left me—Two young Ladies Daughters of the Landlady, rather gay & noisy than discreet, very forward in discourse,
both in Love with Scotch Merchants & both willing to be talked to,
gave me much Diversion—Expence here 3/4—Rode thence in the
Evening to Port Tobacco 15 miles. staid here the night—For company all the night in my Room I had Bugs in every part of my Bed
—& in the next Room several noisy Fellows playing at Billiards.

Saturday 28.

Left Port Tobacco by six, rode to Mrs Laidlers Ferry. At Port Tobacco expence 3/10. 12 Miles Breakfasted with Mrs. Laidler Breakfast & Oats 1/7 Ferriage 6/. The broad beautiful Potowmack looks
smooth & unbroken as tho' it was fettered in Ice: it is to where we
land on the other Side eight miles a little down the River the passage
over, in the best time of this loveliest month was vastly agreeable—

From Tylers[151] in Virginia where I landed about twelve o-Clock I rode to Mattox Bridge eight miles; thence to Mattox Church six miles—Here I bought some Ears of corn for my Horse—Thence to Westmorland Court House 16 miles—Here is a Tavern I got a Bowl of Punch & fed *2/6*—Thence I rode to Nomini Hall about Eeight in the Evening 10 miles—I found Mr & Mrs Carter at home sitting together—They received me with great welcome—*Ben, Bob,* Miss *Fanny* & *Betsy* came in to see me—The others in bed—sup'd on *Crabs* & an elegant dish of Strawberries & cream—How natural, how agreeable, how majestic this place seems!

Sunday 29.

I rose by half after six—Ben informed me that Bob has behaved vastly ill since I left him—He has reported several mischievous & false stories of his brother; That has been intimate in some bad families—That he has injured his own fathers Servants &c—The morning pleasant—I did not attend Church, Ben out of kindness kept me company at Home—I had however chosen to stay alone—The family is invited to dine with Mr Turburville—Mr & Mrs *Carter,* Miss Priscilla & Nancy with three Servants went from Church— *Ben, Bob,* Miss *Fanny, Betsy* & *Harriot* with two Servants cross'd the River—Miss *Sally* with *Tasker* & one Servant rode in a Chair— Dined with us Captain Dennis, of the Ship Peggy; Dr *Steptoe;* & Mr *Cunningham.* Politicks were the topic—and indeed the Gentlemen seemed warm—The Governor of this province dissolved the Assembly last week after they had made a resolve that a general & solemn fast be observed thro' this whole Colony, on Account of the melancholy aspect of American Affairs at present, to be kept the first day of June, which is next Wednesday, when the alarming Act of Parliament which has lately come over is to take place at Boston— Parson Smith accordingly gave it out at the Church to Day & it is to be observed—I only saw Miss Sally Panton, she did not dine with us—I am told She has an Estate in England of 50 £ Sterling pr Annum, but for some unknown cause came over, probably the same as drew me from home—After dinner we had a Grand & agreeable Walk in & through the Gardens—There is great plenty of Strawberries, some Cherries, Goose berries &c—Drank Coffee at four, they are now too patriotic to use tea—Soon after we set out for Home— The young Ladies chose to walk and Cross the water with us—I am much more pleas'd with the Face of the Country since my return than I have ever been before—It is indeed delightsome!—

Monday 30.

Our little beautiful Seminary collected They seem all glad to see me, & willing to enter on business—I am truely fond of the young growing beauties—Soon they will be the admiration of the world, & ornaments in their family—This morning I asked & received four Guineas of Mr Carter to satisfy Mr Taylor of whom I had a small Sum. Mr Randolph is yet here, & is recovered of the hurt I formerly mentioned—After Dinner my Toast was the amiable *Laura*—Evening called in & staid only a few minutes Captain Dennis, & Parson Gibbern—At Supper I had an agreeable conversation with Mr & Mrs Carter on the *Times manners,* &c.

Teusday 31.

Very warm—I feel well reliev'd of the Fatigues of my ride—The lower Class of People here are in a tumult on the account of Reports from Boston, many of them expect to be press'd & compell'd to go and fight the Britains!—Evening I asked the Colonel if he proposes to observe the fast, & attend Sermon tomorrow; he answered that "No one must go from hence to Church, or observe the Fast at all"—By this, (for it is hard to know his opinion from any thing he declares) I conclude he is a courtier.—Last Night, & this evening the Colonel sup'd with us, which is more than he has done before since I have been in the Family—

Wednesday June 1st 1774.

Cool & pleasant—I began my English Exegesis—or Thesis.

Thursday 2.

I took out of the Colonels Library for Assistance in making my pieces Biblia-Sacra, & Mr Hammonds Exposition of the New Testament. I toasted Miss *Beatty* to day in a Bumpper of old Medaira—Evening Mr Carter at the Harpsichord.

Fryday 3.

The dancing School happens in course to day at Mr Washingtons—Mrs *Carter* takes *Bob* & *Nancy* with her—Our School seems silent—

Writing at my English Thesis—I put *Harry* & *Bob* this week to read Popes Homer but Homers inimitable fire cannot charm or move them!—Evening *Ben* rode to the Dance—We were informed that in Queen-Anns in Maryland many die at present, of a Fever that follows a slight Ague!—I took a Ramble, in the evening, as usual, through the Garden.

[LETTER OF PHILIP V. FITHIAN TO JOHN PECK]

Nomini Hall June 3d. 1774.
Virginia.

SIR.

I have the pleasure to inform you I arriv'd safe and had a pleasant ride; I expect to hear from you by every post but have received no letter yet—If you did not receive my letter dated "Delaware-River, on board the Swallow," this is to request you to apply immediately to Dr Witherspoon who promised me in Philadelphia that he would recommend you here; the reason of my demanding dispatch is, that Mr Carter proposes to write to England for a Tutor if he cannot be speedily satisfied of having one from the Northward—If I attempt to write news I must inform you that the Assembly of this province is dissolved on passing a resolve to keep the first day of June through the whole province a solemn fast, the resolve past however, and the day was kept—The frost of the 4th. of May was much more fatal here than to the Northward, for not only Garden produce, but Wheat and Rye in the upper parts of the province are blasted and the owners mow them down for fodder; and here the Woods look like winter!—I expect to hear from you several times this summer, I beg you will not disappoint me.

My compliments to acquaintances—

From, Sir,

yours

PHILIP V. FITHIAN

[LETTER OF PHILIP V. FITHIAN TO THE REVEREND
ANDREW HUNTER]

Nomini-Hall, Virginia. June 3d. 1774.

REVD: & DEAR SIR.

It will not be wonderful if I inform you that this Colony is in great tumult and confusion. The general Voice is *Boston*. You will have heard before the reception of this, that the Governor dissolved the Assembly in this province on their making a resolve to keep the first day of June on which the Act of Parliament is to take place at Boston, (excepting the days of grace) a solemn fast. The people agree however in general to unite with the people of Boston and the other northern trading Cities, and by their example to influence all the Colonies, not to make any resistance to the Britains, but to keep themselves independant, and refuse to receive their comodities, and keep within themselves, their own more valuable comodities, because they are for the support of life—So stedfast are the people here that the Captain of a Ship belonging to an eminent house in London was yesterday refused any more Tobacco til' there is intelligence from the Northward—

The frost which happened the 4th. of May, was by far more severe and fatal here than either in Maryland, New-Jersey, or Pennsylvania—The expected produce of Gardens and Peaches, (which were some planters chief dependance) are not only almost wholly destroy'd, but in the upper parts of the province Wheat and Rye are so much cut off that the owners think it best to mow it down for fodder!—

I have the pleasure to inform you that I had a speedy and pleasant ride; found the family in good health; that it is a time of general health in the County—and that I am again agreeably settled to business—

Please to make my compliments to Mrs Hunter, Miss Nancy, Andrew, and to Uncles family—I am, sir

Your most obedient

Most humble Servt:

PHILIP V. FITHIAN

[JOURNAL]

Saturday 4.

The day cool & agreeable—I kept the children in til twelve tho'
with great difficulty; they were for asserting their liberty. & pleaded
the custom of las winter—I finished a rough incorrect plan of my
English Thesis, & laid it by for future examination—

After dinner I begun the Lecture, wrote an introduction—Towards evening I took my hat & a Sermon, & retired to a Shady Green
where I rambled about til dusk committing my Sermon to memory
—We have omitted Supper, & in its place substituted Coffee which
we commonly take about seven in the evening—Ben, this Afternoon
rode to Colonel Frank Lee's. The ground is very dry; The Frost of
the fourth of May has been much more severe and fatal here than in
the northern colonies—The peaches here, except on Farms lying
near the Potowmack are wholly destroy'd, & these were the choisest
expectation of some, who think Brandy their most valuable comod-
ity!—And I am told that in Louden, & the other upper counties,
(which indeed are the best for grain) Wheat & Rie are cut off, so
intirely that the owners mow it down for fodder!—And in these
lower Counties in many places the Woods appear like November, &
the Leaves are actually dropping!—To be sure it is unusual & melancholy!—

Sunday 5.

The weather cool & agreeable—Sermon is to Day at Ucomico, at
the lower church, I choose therefore to stay in my Room—How
pleasant is retirement! And how easy is it to enjoy it—This may
seem strange, but it is true—I have but very few acquaintances, &
they easily dispense with my Absence—I have an elegant inviting
apartment for Study—I have plenty of valuable & entertaining
Books—And I hav business of my own that requires my attention—
At Home my Relations call me proud and morose if I do not visit
them—My own private business often calls me off & unsettles my
mind—There too lives the Girl who has subdued my heart!—All
these put together, when they operate at once, are a strong incitement to divert me from Study. Yet I love Cohansie! And in spite
of my resolution, when I am convinced that my situation is more advantageous here, yet I wish to be there—How exceedingly capricious

is fancy! When I am Home I then seem willing to remove, for other places seem to be full as desirable—It is then Society which makes places seem agreeable or the Contrary—It can be nothing else —Adam when he had no troublesome painful thoughts within him; and had a flowery Paradise for his habitation & enjoyment, was not yet fully happy while he possessed it alone; much less can we his offspring, frail, & variable, enjoy much sattisfaction without inter-course with one another—I have just spoken in praise of Society & retirement; And I now observe we are of such a make that, if we be happy, these must alternately succeed each other—It is something like the opinion of *Socrates* concerning pleasure & pain, that if we possess the one, we may expect it will not be long before we shall meet with the other—Towards evening At Mrs Carters request I waited on Miss *Priscilla, Nancy,* & *Fanny* who rode on Horse-back for an airing—Wrote a Letter to the Revd Mr Andrew Hunter, Cohansie New Jersey—In the evening Ben returned full of news of *Boston*, that we must fight that the troops are arrived & impudent &c, &c.

[LETTER OF PHILIP V. FITHIAN TO ELIZABETH BEATTY]

Nominy-Hall Virginia June 5: 1774.

To LAURA.

I have the Pleasure, since you allow me the Honour of correspond-ing with you, to acquaint you that I had a speedy & delightsome Passage from Home to this Place: It was you know, in the best Time of the lovliest of Months.

The Delaware, the broad Chesapeak, & the beautiful Potowmack were mild & lovely as a handsome, Woman's Presence when her Mind is at Rest—But are fine Women, Laura, as easily thrown into Confusion & Tumult as they—?

I expect these, if you receive them at all, will find you at N—n. If they should, please to make my kind Respects to your Brother—& compliment him on his new Alliance.

I shall wish, very much, to see you at C—e in the Fall, but if it be inconvenient I do not ask you to pay any Manner of Regard, in this Case, to my Inclination. The Face of this Part of Virginia is now in-deed beautiful. I wish often that you was here for a While to see, because I am unable to describe, the charming Landskips, & long delightsome Prospects of our winding River which we have from the high Hills! But especially in the Evening when I commonly (as it is the Custom of the Family) walk for half an hour through the Garden in Company generally with three brisk mischievous Girls you would I am certain, for you delight in Gardens, & love the Company of noisy, gay, & agreeable young Girls, be highly entertain'd.—And as for myself, if you was here, I should take these Walks & Arbours to be a verdant flowery Elysium!—I must not omit to thank you for your Letter of Feb: last; because a Line from you is rare & valuable as as the Phenix of Arabia.

Write to me, best of Girls, the Moment you receive this, that I may know how, & where you be; & let me hear often from you this Summer.

You may rest assured of my Constancy in continuing a free & full Correspondence.

PHILIP V. FITHIAN.

[JOURNAL]

Monday 6.

Mr *Carter* rode to richmond court—At Dinner I had a long and useful conversation with Mrs Carter She told me openly & candidly the Several failings of her children, & indeed She knows them perfectly—In particular she knows not what to do with her perverse Son *Bob*—He abuses his Mama, Miss Sally, the children, Family, and is much given to slander. Poor unhappy youth, I fear he will come to an unhappy end! This afternoon I found it necessary to correct Bob severely for impertinence in School—Mr Carter at Court received his Invoice from London for this Spring, in which was a gold Seal for *Ben* with a Coat of Arms price five Guineas!—

Teusday 7.

The morning pleasant, cool & agreeable—I corrected Harry this morning for telling me a Lie—Stomachful & sullen as any youth—The day warm but very bearable—Breakfasted with us Mr Blain & Mr Warden, all the conversation is Politicks; But People seem moderate & yet settled in their determinations to stand out

Wednesday 8.

The morning pleasant—Mr *Carter* rode to the Ucomiko Ware-houses to examine in the Shipping some of his Tobacco—We have no Company. The day is very warm—A flaming sultry Sun, a dusty scorched Ground, Mr *Carter* returned, the day being smoky intro-duced, at Coffee, a conversation on Philosophy, on Eclipses; the man-ner of viewing them; Thence to Telescopes, & the information which they afforded us of the Solar System; Whether the planets be ac-tually inhabited &c.

[LETTER OF PHILIP V. FITHIAN TO SAMUEL FITHIAN]

Nomini Hall Virginia June 8th. 1774.

SIR.

After I acquaint you that, by the kindness of providence I arrived safe and am in good health, I shall not neglect to inform you that the virginians are warm and active in supporting the liberties of America; the first day of June throughout this Colony, by a resolve of the House of Burgesses, or Assembly of Representatives for the province was kept a solemn Fast, and kept religiously too, to invoke almighty God to assist our falling country, and save us from oppression and Tyranny—The ware-Houses are already hindring the Shipping To-bacco, and it is expected there will shortly be a general embargo laid on all exportable commodities—The people here wish for the union of all the Colonies, and for firm perseverance in what shall seem most conducive to the good of America, notwithstanding this Colony and Maryland will suffer vastly, because Tobacco is a comod-ity less saleable among ourselves than most of the produce of the Northern Colonies, and it is in these the staple—

I am seated once more to great sattisfaction in my business, the family and neighbourhood are well, but I propose and expect by the permission of providence to return home the latter end of October; in the mean time, I am,

Dear Unkle

Your most obliged Nephew

PHILIP V FITHIAN

P. S. Please to remember me to the family, &c.

[JOURNAL]

Thursday 9.

The morning haizy, no Wind, & very warm—I wrote a Letter to
Uncle *Samuel Fithian*—After Dinner Mr Carter set out for Wil-
liamsburg—by him I sent to the Post-office at *Hobbes-Hole*, My
Letters to Mr *Hunter*, Uncle *Fithian*, Miss *Beatty*. & Mr *Peck*—
After School in the evening I had an agreeable walk with Mrs *Carter*
in the Garden—

Fryday 10.

Cool but exceeding dry—Writing at my Lecture. Mrs *Carter* was to
day sadly frighted with a Lizard, that lives under the House—After
School, with Ben I wakked over to Mr Turburville's to gather
Cheries, which are there in great plenty—Mrs *Carter* in the evening
after our return, gave me a Lecture for taking *Ben* to *Annapolis* when
I went last Home without a waiting-Man—Wrote at my Lecture
til eleven. Ben sleeps at the Great-House in the absence of his *Papa*.

Saturday 11.

I was sitting in the Colonels Library I took a Catalogue of the whole of His Books—& he tells me he has left behind him at Williamsburg, with many other things 458 volumes besides Music & Pamphlets.[152]

It is with considerable Difficulty that I keep the Children in School til twelve o Clock as they used to go out all the last winter at Breakfast—*Bob* especially is vastly vociferous on the Occasion—Our Bells for School & play-Hours are at present under good Regulations. The Children come in as soon as they rise and are Drest which is usually about seven—The Bell rings at eight for Breakfast—At nine it Rings for two purposes; for the Children to enter School, & for the Gardiners, Carpenters, & other workmen to come into Breakfast—At ten it Rings them to work. At twelve it rings for the School play hours—At two it rings for us to Dine, & the workmen—And the las[t] bell is at three for School & for the workmen to go to Labour—I dismiss them by my watch at half after Five.—After Dinner I rode alone to Mr Blains Store; bought a pen-knife, nine Jacket-Buttons, & a primmer for Miss *Harriot* 3/. It is alarming to observe how hard, & dusty the Country is; towards evening some clouds arose & looked promising in the West, but they bring no rain—No rain has fell here since the 24th of May, & then but a Scanty Shower, & most of the time since windy.

Sunday 12.

Ben & Mr *Randolph* had a small wrangle about Horses: The Day is vastly hot, the wind small at West, clear & very Dry I choose therefore to stay at Home—I lent my Horse to *Ben*, & staid myself at Home to write my Lecture, Mrs *Carter* the two Misses, & Ben went to Church, Mr Randolph went on Board Captain Blackwells Ship to dine—*Bob* pleaded hard with me for Leave to go on Board the Ship, but I kept him at home with me—Evening I finished my Lecture & laid it by for future examination. Some Clouds & Lightning in the west but no rain.

Monday 13.

Ben gave *Bob*, for some imprudent Language a drubbing this morning—About nine we had a Shower but soon over & of little use; be

to God, however, that we have any—I begun, to day my Sermon
for the Presbytery—The change in the weather since yesterday is
remarkable. This afternoon is so cool that I should be glad of a
winter suit—yesterday afternoon was so hot I could not be com-
fortably cool in a thin gown, with all the windows of my chamber
up. Evening, John the waiting Man play'd, & the young Ladies spent
the evening merrily in dancing—I staid til ten, saw them & Conversed
with Mrs Carter.

Teusday 14.

I added last night to my Bed-Clothes a Quilt, Blanket, & my own
Clothes & lay under them all, none too warm—The children call'd
for a Fire in the school-Room, & were so cold I was obliged to dismiss them before the Bell—I believe there is no Frost—Befor Breakfast, Mr *Stadley* the musician came from Colonel *Taylors* at *mount
Airy*.
Miss Priscilla & Nancy attend his instructions. Mr Stadley shewed me
some Verses he is carrying from Mr Washingtons to His Daughter
they seem good and are as follow.

> A Hymn for a dying Believer.

> 1st Happy Soul thy Days are ended,
> All thy mourning Days below,
> Go by Angel-Guards attended
> To the Sight of Jesus, go.

> 2d Waiting to recieve my Spirit,
> Lo thy Saviour stands above,
> Shews the purchase of his merit
> Reaches out the Crown of Love.

> 3d For the Joy he Sets before thee
> Bear a momentary pain,
> Die to live the Life of Glory
> Suffer, with thy Lord to reign.

Spent the evening very agreeably with Mrs Carter & Mr Stadley, we
sat about a good Fire in the Dining-Room, and it seems as necessary
& agreeable as in November or December.—

Wednesday 15.

So cold that I ordered a Fire in the School-Room—Mr Stadley with us yet—I took out of the Library to read for entertainment the "Amusement of the *German Spa;* it is a well written piece—Designed entirely for Amusement Before dinner Mrs Taylor,[153] with her two Daughters Miss Polly, & Kitty came in a Chariot—*Bob* was in a moment on Fire; He is deeply Smitten with Polly's Charms—beg'd me for Leave to go out of School & dress—I allow'd him, The Day was vastly windy & the drouth is alarming!—Close Attention for two weeks past has fatigued me so much, that yesterday, & to Day I have laid aside Study, & read only for Relaxation—I took a whim in my head & would not go to Dinner. my Head was not dress'd, & I was too lazy to change my clothes—Mrs Carter, however, in the evening lash'd me severely. I told her I was engaged in reading a pleasant Novel.—That I was not perfectly well—But She would not hear none, & said I was rude, & censurable—Mr Stadley spent the evening in playing several songs & Sonata's on the Harpsichord & violin—

Thursday 16.

Mr Stadley left us before Breakfast—Reading at the Amusement of *Spa*—Drew off some Tunes—

Fryday 17.

Bob was missing last night I was at his Room at twelve o Clock he was absent—This morning I examined him, he told me he was at Mr Turburville's, but told me several palpable Lies—I gave him however severe correction—We had this morning about 5 o Clock a smart Gust of wind, Rain & Thunder, but soon over.

Saturday 18.

Ben not very well—At twelve *Bob* teaz'd me for leave to go to a Cock-Fight & Horse-Race about two Miles off, I gave him Leave with his promising to be home by Sun Set.—Spent the Afternoon in my room writing—Towards evening 'Squire *Lee* call'd in, & brought a late London News-Paper in which we are informed that another Act of Parliament has pass'd taking from the People of Boston all power of trying any Soldier, or Person whether for commiting any

Crime; & obliging all such offenders to be sent home for legal Tryal
—Heaven only knows where these tumults will End!—He informed
us likewise that last Saturday in Richmond (our neighbour County)
the people drest & burnt with great marks of Destestation the in-
famous Lord *North*—Mrs *Carter*, after the 'Squire left us quite
astonished me in the Course of the evening. with her perfect acquaintance with the American Constitution—

Sunday 19.

The day cool—Sermon is at Ucomico, so that we all stay at Home
Mrs Carter was in the morning frightned thinking that several of the
Negro-Girls in the Family are unwell with the Measles, but I be-
lieve it to be only a Frett of the Heat Ben is unwel; He has a sick
Stomach; at Times aguish; complains of Pains in his Breast & Side;
& in the morning Spits Blood. He keeps about however, but his fond
Mama discovers great anxiety.—I spend the Day in my Room writ-
ing at my Sermon, & reading the plain & useful *Pictete*.

Monday 20.

So cool that I sit with my Cloths buttoned, & am chilly. the children also complain of the cold; this must certainly be unwholesome
weather—Breakfasted with us Mr *Cox*—Ben continues no better,
he lays by Study to day & keeps in—I myself either conceit or in
reality have a Fever & head-Ach to Day—Before twelve we had a
moderate Shower no wind nor Thunder—Mrs *Carter* wrote a note
to Dr *Jones* & Desired him to call & See *Ben*, towards evening he
came; He thinks *Ben* has only Symptoms of an Agu approaching—
He prescribed some Physick—Drank Coffee with us, & went home
about six—I lightens in the North.

Teusday 21.

Harry is unwel, takes this morning Physick, and keeps his Room—
Ben is in the same way—*Priscilla* & Nancy are practising Musick, so
that to Day we have only four in School—At five in the Evening,
Ben, *Prissy* & I rode out on Horse back for exercise; before we returned Captain *Dobby*, of the Ship *Susannah* an agreeable, sensible,
polite Gentleman came, & 'Squire *Lee*—The conversation, at Coffee
was on American affairs, the 'Squire shew'd us one of Mr Dunlaps

papers,[154] in which are accounts that the Northern Colonies are zealous & stedfast in resolutions to maintain their Liberties—We sat til eleven—

Wednesday 22.

Breakfasted with us Captain *Dobby*, & Mr Taylor, their conversation promiscuous—Clear & warm, not sultry, *Harry* better & in School, but *Ben* continues indisposed. I wrote to Day some at my Sermon—After School, with Mrs Carter & the young Ladies & *Bob*, I walked through the Garden—But I seem not suited in being confin'd wholly at Home, yet my stay is quite voluntary—

Thursday 23.

Very warm all the morning—From twelve to two I was writing at my Sermon—While we were at dinner a very black cloud rose in the West: Mrs Carter, is fearful when it thunders, so that I did not leave the Room till it was over, about four, there was a strong Gale of wind, some thunder, & a refreshing Shower. At five with Mrs Carter & the young Ladies I took a walk; She shewed me from a high Hill several beautiful Prospects—I was diverted tho it was a little cruel, to see the Girls gather the Blossoms of some Prickly-Pears.

Fryday 24.

Lat night we had a Gust of Rain & Thunder; very acceptable—To Day in course Mr Christians Dance happens here—He came before Breakfast—Miss *Jenny Washington* came also, & Miss *Priscilla Hale* while we were at Breakfast—Miss Washington is about seventeen; She has not a handsome Face, but is neat in her Dress, of an agreeable Size, & well proportioned, & has an easy winning Behaviour; She is not forward to begin a conversation, yet when spoken to She is extremely affable, without assuming any Girlish affectation, or pretending to be overcharg'd with Wit; She has but lately had oppertunity of Instruction in Dancing, yet She moves with propriety when she dances a *Minuet* & without any *Flirts* or vulgar *Capers*, when She dances a *Reel* or *Country-Dance*: She plays well on the Harpsichord, & Spinet; understands the principles of Musick, & therefore performs her Tunes in perfect time, a Neglect of which always makes music intolerable, but it is a fault almost universal among

young Ladies in the practice; She sings likewise to her instrument, has a strong, full voice, & a well-judging Ear; but most of the Virginia-Girls think it labour quite sufficient to thump the Keys of a Harpsichord into the air of a tune mechanically, & think it would be Slavery to submit to the Drudgery of acquiring Vocal Music; Her Dress is rich & well-chosen, but not tawdry, nor yet too plain; She appears to Day in a Chintz cotton Gown with an elegant blue Stamp, a Sky-Blue silk Quilt, spotted apron; Her Hair is a light Brown, it was crap'd up, with two Rolls at each Side, & on the top a small cap of beautiful Gawze and rich Lace, with an artificial Flower interwoven—Her person & carriage at a small distance resembles not a little my much respected *Laura*. But on close examination her Features are something masculine, those of *Laura* are mild and delicate: Mr *Christien* very politely requested me to open the Dance by stepping a Minuet with this amiable Girl, but I excused myself by assuring Him that I never was taught to Dance.—Miss Hale is about fourteen; a slim, puny silent Virgin; She has black Eyes, & black Hair, a good sett of Eye-Brows, which are esteem'd in Virginia essential to Beauty; She looks innocent of every human Failing, does not speak five Words in a Week, & I dare say from her Carriage that her

Modesty is invincible; She is drest in a white Holland Gown, cotton Diaper quilt very fine, a Lawn apron, has her Hair crap'd up, & on it a small Tuft of Ribbon for a Cap She is but just innitiated into the School. and only hobbles yet Once I saw her standing; I rose immediately and begg'd her to accept my Chair; She answered most kindly, "Sir I thank you." that was all I could extract from this Wonder of the Sex for the two Days she stay'd, & I seemed to have an equal Share too in the Favours of her Conversation; so that I cannot be any way particular in describing the mental faculties of Miss *Hale*. it is sufficient to say that I think She is far removed from most of the foibles of Women—Some time after these came Colonel Lee's [155] Chariot with five young Misses—These five, with Miss Washington & Miss Hale & Miss Nancy Carter, & Bob are Mr Christiens Compliment of Scholars in this School except Miss Turburville who is just now up the country with an Uncle, where She is to Stay some time together with Miss Corbin. Miss Betsy Lee [156] is about thirteen; a tall slim genteel Girl; She is very far from Miss Hale's taciturnity, yet is by no means disagreeably forward; She dances extremely well, & is just begining to play the Spinet—She is drest in a neat shell Callico Gown, has very light Hair done up with a Feather, & her whole carriage is easy inoffensive, & graceful—The other Miss Lee's are small Towards evening came in George Lee, & Mr *Grubb*, an English Gentleman; the Company danced after candle-light a Minuet round, three Country Dances, several Reels, when we were Rung to Supper after Supper we sit til twelve drinking loyal Toasts—

Saturday 25.

Ben & I slept til eight—we breakfasted at nine, soon after Christien collected his School and gave them a Lesson round—About ten the two Gentlemen left us. They quit Dancing about two—After Dinner Mrs *Carter* & the young Ladies, with Mr *Christien* Ben & Myself walked in the garden, & through the Pasture, There are several beautiful prospects of the green Bottoms, & of the River Nominy from the High hills—By Miss Washington I wrote a letter to Mr Lowe, acquainting him with what was done for him in the business he sent me to Philadelphia. The Day is cool, & intirely agreeable & the Ground has been refreshed by a Shower or two lately—I am told that the people are already reaping not only Rye but Wheat in the Neighbourhood; certainly it is earlier than we reap to the North-ward.—

[LETTER OF PHILIP V. FITHIAN TO JOHN LOWE]

Nomini Hall June 25th 1774.
To Mr John Lowe. Bushfield.

SIR.

I should have waited on you immediately after my return from Philadelphia, to acquaint you with what was done in regard to the business you intrusted me with, and to return the certificate which I now send inclosed; but necessary business detain'd me for a few days at home, and when *Bob* was at the Dance at Mr *Washingtons* he informed me you proposed shortly to be here. As I expect to see you shortly I shall write nothing particular, but only inform you that your intention was considered and approved:

I am, Sir,

Your humble Servt:

PHILIP V FITHIAN

[JOURNAL]

Sunday 26.

Mr *Smith* to Day is out of the Parish so that we have no sermon—I shut up myself therefore in my chamber to reading—Eleven I am sent for to see Mr Lowe who is come—I invite him to my Room, where we sit til Dinner—He informed me of the Manner of Trials in Scotland, which Candidates undergo. It is similar & indeed almost the same as with our Presbytery Evening Mr Carter returned about seven o-Clock from Williamsburg; He has been unwell himself while there, & he informs us that many are indisposed in that City While we were at Coffee I was taken with a Sudden & unusual pain in my Breast, a sickness at my stomach, attended with a trembling and dizzy faintness; I retired to my Room immediately, laid myself down in bed but had a Fever most of the Night—

Monday 27.

I feel myself perfectly reliev'd blessed be God who upholds my Life Mr *Carter* says the people are reaping on the Road as he came. He opened & shewed me a curious Case of mathematical Instruments price ten Guineas; He shewed me *Bens Seal* five Guineas—We have to day several plentiful Showers—Evening at Coffee the Colonel shew'd me a book of vocal Musick which he has just imported, it is a collection of psalm-Tunes, Hymns, & Anthems set in four parts for the Voice; He seems much taken with it & says we must learn & perform some of them in their several parts with our voices & with instruments.—Lightning in several parts of the Heaven Mrs *Carter* is much afraid, & can never eat if a cloud is rising nor lie down to sleep.

Teusday 28.

Warm this morning. Mr *Carter* rode to Court. I wrote some at my sermon but it goes on slowly—*Ben* is not perfectly well, he studies, however, at times a little, to day he makes Doctr *Jones* a visit —The Day very hot; people I understand are reaping in this County —Evening we have in the West & North-West amazing Lightning— Mrs *Carter* retired to her Chamber, where She always chooses to sit quite alone in bad Weather—

Wednesday 29.

Writing at my Sermon—The day cool & agreeable. I was never so much confined as now, not even when I was at College, for I used to go with my sweet mates, as Virgil calls them, about the Fields, or to the Brooks to wash, & often ride to Trenton for exercise & pleasure —& sometimes to *Newington* & spend an Afternoon with that dear girl *Laura*—Here in Virginia I have no Call out, people seem sociable & kind but I want Spirit to improve & relish Society Soon, however, soon, if I keep my Health, I shall be again at Liberty.

Thursday 30.

The morning pleasant none too hot to be agreeable—My Charge seem rising slowly, & uniformly in their several Parts—Harry begun at Reduction & is now working Fellowship; he improves too in Writing. Bob began at Addition and is working Compound Division:

he is the best writer in the School—Ben begun with reading Salust he is now reading Virgil & the Greek-Testament. He writes extremely bad—Priscilla began Addition & is working Division; She improves in writing, & reads tolerably—Nancy mends fast in writing, but reads carelessly thick & inaccurately.

—I mentioned to Day Mr *Peck* to Mr *Carter* He objected at first to his Age as rather too young for the Duty of a Tutor, he assented however & requested me to write him word that he is desired to come by the Time I shall leave Virginia—

Fryday July 1. 1774.

I rose at six. The morning bearable Breakfasted with us 'Squire Lee. —About one came in Captain *Blackwell*, Mr *Grubb*, & *Lancelot Lee*. the two youngsters came suddenly into our Room, bold gay & noisy. We conversed with them till the Bell rung for Dinner, when we all repair'd to the dining-Room: Captain Blackwel is to sail in about ten Days for London. I gave the Children the afternoon for Recreation.

Saturday 2.

Mr *Grubb* called again about twelve with an intention to ride out to the Potowmack but there came on a Rain & kept us at Home—We spent the afternoon sociably in our Room. Miss *Nancy Carter* last Night or this morning, in some whimsical freak, clipt off her Eye-Brows; She has a very good Skin; exceeding black hair, & black-well arched, full Eye-brows, which, as I said the other day are much esteemed in Virginia—She denies positively that She cut them herself, & swears some mischievous person has done it when She was sleeping. But I am inclined to think it is an experiment She has been making on herself to see how she can vary the looks of her face. It made me laugh when I saw it first, to think how early & how truely She copies Female absurdities.

Towards evening we rode out merely for exercise, & straggled at last to Mr *Simpsons;* near his house we saw two trees standing near each other both of which have lately been struck by Lightning & are torn to shivers in several parts—

Mr Grubb agreed to stay the night. we supt on Artichoks, & Huckleberries & Milk—The toasts, after Supper, were the King,

Queen & Royal Family. the Governor & his family, & then young Ladies of our acquaintance—We were alone. Mr and Mrs Carter left us immediately, so that we spent the evening without restraint.

Sunday 3.

We were all to go to Church to day, but we were prevented by a storm of thunder & Rain; the Ground is now sufficiently wetted—I have not heard a Sermon on Sunday since the fifteenth of May; a longer Vacancy from publick worship than I have ever had since my first remembrance. About ten an old Negro Man came with a complaint to Mr Carter of the Overseer that he does not allow him his Peck of corn a Week—The humble posture in which the old Fellow placed himself before he began moved me. We were sitting in the passage, he sat himself down on the Floor clasp'd his Hands together, with his face directly to Mr *Carter*, & then began his Narration—He seem'd healthy, but very old, he was well dress'd but complained bitterly—I cannot like this thing of allowing them no meat, & only a Peck of Corn & a Pint of Salt a Week, & yet requiring of them hard & constant Service. We have several Rains this day so that the Ground is sufficiently wetted—I spent the greater part of the day writing at my Sermon.

Monday 4.

I begun to read the first Volume of Tristam-Shandy—He is droll in the account he gives us of his Birth & Family—We have several good showers to day, the weather is warm, funky, very damp, & I fear will not turn out long to be healthful. With us in Jersey wet Weather about this time not only is prejudicial to the Harvest, but is generally thought, & I believe almost never fails being a forerunner of Agues, Fall-Fevers, Fluxes, & our Horse-Distempers—Fearing these, any of which so far from Home, would be painful & expensive, I keep myself much at Home, contrary to the repeated & strong invitations of the youngsters—And indeed my Duty, seems to require my Presence pretty constantly; & I am forced to produce an Example for what I find it necessary to enforce on our Boys, in order to do it with some face, for they always call upon me for a Reason for every one of my precepts—It is now the Height of Harvest—There is at Mr Turburville's a young Lady, from the Isle-of Wight, Miss *Betsy*

Lee,[157] a Sister of *George* & *Lancelot Lee's*—It is proposed that Ben
& I go this Evening to the Captain's & Invite her here—Accordingly
after School we rode on our errand, We found besides Miss *Lee*—
Mr *George Turburville*, his *Wife*, Mr *Grubb*, & *Lancelot Lee*—After
the ceremony of Introduction, & our Congees were over, we took
our seats in a cool passage where the Company were sitting; all the
Company when we entered were laughing at Master *Lee*, who had
been gathering Mulberries, & either through *carelessness* or *Greedi-
ness* had stained his ruffles—At any Rate they looked like a scarlet
Clock in a Bunters stocking. both indilicate & impudent—The attention of the Company however being wholly taken up with Mr
Lee, I had the opportunity, which I wanted, of examining the person
of his Sister, without being interrupted either by the notice of others,
or by my own timidity—Miss *Betsy Lee*, I am told is but lately entered her twenty sixth year; She is a well set maid, of a proper
Height, neither high nor low—Her Aspect when she is sitting is
masculine & dauntless; she sits very erect; places her feet with great
propriety, her Hands She lays carelessly in her lap, & never moves
them but when she has occasion to adjust some article of her dress, or
to perform some exercise of the *Fan*—She has a full face, sanguine
Complection, her Nose is rather protuberant than otherwise; Her
Eyes are exactly such as *Homer* atributes to the Goddess *Minerva;*
& her Arms resemble those which the same Poet allows to *Juno.*
When She has a Bonnet on & Walks, She is truely elegant; her carriage neat & graceful, & her presence soft & beautiful—Her hair is a
dark Brown, which was crap'd up very high. & in it she had a Ribbon
interwoven with an artificial Flower—At each of her ears dangled a
brilliant Jewel; She was pinched up rather too near in a long pair of
new fashioned Stays, which, I think, are a Nusance both to us &
themselves—For the late importation of Stays which are said to be
now most fashionable in London, are produced upwards so high that
we can have scarce any view at all of the Ladies Snowy Bosoms; &
on the contrary, they are extended downwards so low that whenever Ladies who wear them, either young or old, have occasion to
walk, the motion necessary for Walking, must, I think, cause a disagreeable Friction of some part of the body against the lower Edge of
the Stays which is hard & unyielding—I imputed the Flush which
was visible in her Face to her being swathed up *Body* & *Soul* & *limbs*
together—She wore a light Chintz Gown, very fine, with a blue

stamp; elegantly made, & which set well upon her—She wore a blue silk Quilt—In one word Her Dress was rich & fashionable—Her Behaviour such as I should expect to find in a Lady whose education had been conducted with some care & skill; and her person, abstracted from the embelishments of Dress & good Breeding, not much handsomer than the generality of Women—

What made me desirous to see, & curious to reconnoitre this young Lady, was, a Sentence that was dropt yesterday by a respectable Member of our Family, intimating a Desire that I may, on seeing Miss Lee, after having known, by report, her faultless character, be so pleased with her person as to try to make her mine, & settle in this Province—That kind Body, who is for making me happy by settling me in Virginia, & connecting me with one of the best families in the Government, little knows how painful it would be if I was indeed compell'd by any accident of Fortune to spend the remainder of my Days in Virginia if is the pleasure of Providence that I am to continue for any length of time in the World—Strong, & sweet are the bands which tye us to our place of nativity; If it is but a beggarly Cottage, we seem not satisfied with the most elegant entertainment if we are totally seperated from it—But if a Princess should solicit me to accept, together with Herself, 50000 £ a Year—I declare, with as great *pleasure* as *truth,* that the esteem, & Fidelity which I possess for my dear, dear *Eliza* would make me without reflection, evade & refuse the Proposal—Ben & I returned Home before dark—We had the 'Squire to drink Coffee with us—He brought us a Newspaper containing the debate, of the House of Commons concerning the Repeal of the Tea-duty.

Teusday 5.

While we were at Breakfast came from Hobbes-Holes Mrs *Oakly* a Woman who has acted as nurse for several of Mrs Carters Children with great credit—All the family speak of her with Love & regard— This day is very warm, but no rain—I gave all the Girls this day to chat with their old acquaintance—Tho' the weather is warm & very Damp we have here no Musquetoes; I have not seen one, since I came into the Province as I can now recollect which seems to me a little strange; for at Princeton in Jersey some warm evenings in July & August they are so numerous as to be troublesome, & that is more than twenty miles from Salt Water, this not more than three times as many *Rod.*—In the evening, among several other things Mr Carter informed me that he has on this plantation a Negro Man called Prince who is now unwell of a Strain—This Man, he swears, he would not sell for 500 £ ready Cash—I was almost ready to say it is more Money than I would give for all he owns on his Estate—The evening is very pleasant I had an oppertunity on the Pavement before the Hall Door of shewing away on Astronomy to Mrs *Carter*, I lectured for half an hour on the Milky-Way, on several of the Stars, on Jupiter in particular, & on the Course of Comets—

In bed by half after ten as usual.

Wednesday 6.

Ben seems pretty well recovered—We dined to day on the Fish call'd the Sheeps-Head, with Crabs—Twice every Week we have fine Fish, & every Day good Fruit for Dinner, caudled Apples, Hurtle-Berries with milk &c—Yes, says Mrs Carter at Supper, this hot weather takes away all my life; the small Lightning that we now have makes me uneasy & melancholy—I love to see her in such Distress—*Beauty* & *Virtue* when combined together & Strugling against Misfortune; O how such objects move, & awaken the most delicate sensations of our Souls—Call in Nancy to her Guitar, says the Colonel. In She minces slow & silent from her supper—She scratches her Instrument, after a long preparation, into the Air of "Water parted from the Sea." What, pray Miss Nancy, what bewitched you with a desire of clipping your Eye-Brows—The Genius of Woman shines forth in this little Girlish trick—Pray Mr *Fithian*, was you ever taught Singing? Yes Sir, I attended two years—Had you any instructions in particular for using the Shake[158]—I am giving Nancy some Lessons, but She is vastly indolent—Nancy, play over and sing the Funeral Hymn—Excuse me, Papa, I have lost the Verses—Happy Soul, thy Days are ended,—Go on—How steady & how sharp it lightens in the North too—Good Night.

Thursday 7.

Yes Fanny may sit down to Breakfast—Where's Ben—The Weather is hot & Ben for enjoyment had stript himself naked—Of every thing but his shirt & Trowsers—Where's Ben— He is not very well, Madam, —This Day says the Colonel after having Prefac'd our Breakfast with a—"God bless us in what we are to recieve"—is our Rye yonder to be mown down; mown down thinks I, do they mow their Grain in Virginia—Yes two Negroes take naked Sythes & mow down the Grain; others are imploy'd in raking it into heaps, but much of it is left—Shall I help you, Mr Fithian, to a Dish of Coffee? —I choose a deep Plate, if you please, Ma'am, & Milk—Our Corn, Madam, in Jersey is inferior to yours in this Province—Or your Cooks, Sir, are less Skilful in managing it—Well, Nancy, I have tuned your Guitar; you are to practice to Day with Priscilla, who is to play the Harpsichord, till twelve o Clock; You can repeat the Verses of the Funeral Hymn?—I can Sir—What, Harry, do you hesitate at that plain Sum in Arithmetical Progression?—*Bob*, attend to your Business—When I am bedizen'd with these clamorous children, some- times I silently exclaim—Once I was told, now I know I feel how irksome the Pedagoging Scheme is—Fanny—I say, Fanny, dont you hear me, Fanny, and Betsy, sit down—pray, Sir, must I multiply here by 32—Yes, thick-Scull—But Mr Fithian, I dont know how to divide by 5½—Look, Sir, do you see what Mouth's *Harry Willis* is making?—I can say my Lesson—Buz, Buz—To divide by 5½ you must double both your Dividend & divi[sor]—Half after two we were rung to Dinner; poor *Tasker*, his Fever has continued high since yesterday afternoon, he lies quiet, and asks for nothing—If his Dis- order does not abate to night, I shall give him in the morning a dose of "James's Powder"—Will you lend me Jack, he meant my Horse, says Mr Randolph, to ride tomorrow to Captain Cheltons; Yes Mr Randolph, I will oblige Jenny so far.

Fryday 8.

I swear, says Bob, Harry belies me. I never told the Nurse that Harriot should stay in School all Day—It was Mama's order that so long as Mrs *Oakly* the Nurse stays, Harriot is to go into School after Breakfast, & after Dinner, & say a lesson each time—I was passing through the Hall from Breakfast—The Nurse, a short Stump of a [wom]an, who blundered by mere accident, when she was young, out of the road in which Virgins commonly travel, & felt the diffi- culties of being a Mother, several years before She enjoyed the Pleasures of being a Wife—She call'd to me, & begg'd me to close the Quarrel; You shall have, said I, dear Madam, with the greatest Freedom my consent—Harriot shall be with you—At Breakfast—

Where is Ben?—He breakfasts with the House-keeper Madam—At
School—What a likeness there is in the manners of Boys; Bob, &
Harry had skulk'd behind the writing-Table with their Slates on
their Knees, & their Faces close together, just as I have done a thousand Times, in our little School-House in *Greenwich*—But once I
was threshed confoundedly for a piece of such hidden play—*Tom
Parks* [blotted] asleep, poor Fellow he is now sleeping in the Dust;
—Then he was fast asleep on a Bench, with his mouth open—I fill'd
his mouth with Snuff!—He sprung up—Nature was in distress, &
found all her Avenues too scanty at that time to clear out at once
the tickling penetrating Powder—He snuffed—He coughed—He
—He told the Master, & then I was tickled—Indeed he made my Feet
beat time to his Lash—Says Bob to Harry, behind the Table, I wonder Mr *Fithian* has not fallen in Love yet with some of our Nominy-
Girls—Here here he sits from Month to Month—(Not many Months
longer said I to myself)—Mr *Marshal*[159] was always out; I suppose
Mr *Fithian* never thinks of Girls—Indeed says *Harry*, drawing his
chair clos[e &] lowering his voice, I never in my Life saw a Man
who thought so little of these things—Here Tom the Coachman
came in with a wood Tarripin which he brought to be a resident in
our Room to catch the Bugs & Cockroaches—
Yes, Harry, & Bob, *Fithian* is vulnerable by Cupids Arrows—I assure
you, Boys, he is, Not by the Girls of Westmorland—O my dear
Laura, I would not injure your friendly Spirit; So long as I breathe
Heavens vital air I am unconditionally & wholly Yours—At Dinner,
Mrs Carter call'd for the Chariot, Mrs Turburville will think me
rude, unless I welcome her Home. I will take Priscilla this Afternoon
& make her a visit—I saw in a moment that *Miss* was better pleased
with the notion of trotting off in the Carriage, than to be [blotted]
up with Multiplication & Division—O yes, says Mrs *Oakly*, I know
Dadda *Gumby* at *Williamsburg*. I think you look as brisk, as hearty
& as young now as you did ten years ago—*Gumby*—I & my old
Woman, here Master, are the two oldest Negres in Mr *Carters* Estate.
Here we live, Master, on our worthy Landlords Bounty—The *Nurse,
Betsy*, & *Harriot* were at Gumby's House which stands about twenty
Rod from the Garden—I was walking, with a Book in my Fist,
musing & stumbling along—I saw them, I went up, & with a lower
Bow than I should give to a Nurse, if Women were plenty, says I,
pray Mrs *Oakly* do you know Dadda Gumby? We stood chattering

with the old African, or rather he stood chattering with us, relating one story after another, leaving some of his Narrations half untold, beginning others in the middle having entered into the true Spirit of Loquacity—Dennis, in the Height of a Story about his Grandfathers Uncle's harpooning a *Porpoise* summoned me to Coffee—Mrs Oakly, will you walk?—Come Betsy—Where's Ben?—Says the Colonel has Ben r[e]tired from the World?—He rode out this Evening, Sir, about five o Clock for Exercise—Mrs Carter, Mr Carter, good Night—

Saturday 9.

I was waked by *Sam* the Barber thumping at my Door—I was dressed—In Powder too; for I propose to see & dine with Miss *Jenny Washington* to Day. D - - - n the Bugs & Chinches, says *Ben* rolling over on the Bed, & rubbing his Eyes, I have slept none for them—Mr Fithian, do you rest any o-Nights? Dont these cursed Bugs keep you awake?—No Sir; for you see I commonly sit & read til half after ten, or eleven—So that by the Time I lay my poor Skin & Bones on the Bed, I am so much fatigued with the tumultuous Business of the Day, & the Study of the Evening that my sleep the rest of the night is sound & unbroken—Priscilla hangs her head a little this morning, She looks feverish, dispirited, sits on a low bench, with her Elbow in her Lap, & Leaning her head upon her hand, swings backwards and forwards, just as I have seen beautiful Quaker Girls when they are weeping at the frightful distortions & Grimaces of some deep-inspired *Father*. But *Priscilla* & *Tasker* are unwell—Fanny teizes me for a Picture, I must draw her a slip, she says, on Paper like the one I drew for Her the other Day with my finger in the Sand—I love the little careless Girl, & will oblige her—On the writing-Table in the School-Room I found this morning an old Book of Esops Fables done into English Verse; In the Margins of this Book up & Down Bob had in his scribbling Way recorded the Names of several young Ladies of Westmorland & Richmond Counties. I shall set them down, as I turned over the Leaves & found them—I do not insinuate, by writing this Story, the smallest reproach to either of the Ladies; I mention it solely to shew *Bob's* Taste, & the Meditations of his heart when wholly alone. In the Life of Esop, page 23, at the Bottom of the Leaf his own Name is written at full length & in as elegant a hand as he is master of with a Dash below.

Robert Bladen Carter.

He has in the same manner introduced it a few leaves further on, he has done this to be a kind of Preface for what is to follow; he has also very cleverly interspersed it with the Ladies, either that the Ladies Names should be a foil to set his off to advantage, or that his Name be a Foil to adorn the Ladies—In the Life of Woglog the great at the first page

> Miss Lucy Carter of Sabine-Hall.
> > Page 3d at the Bottom of the Leaf
> Miss Lettitia Turberville of Hickory Hill.
> > Page 8.
> Miss Betsy Carter of Sabine-Hall.
> > Page 9.
> Miss Priscilla Carter of Nomini-Hall—his Sister:
> > Esops Fables Page 1st he writes the Name of the Girl he loves above all others
> Polly Tayloe the Lovely of Mount-Airy.
> > Page 39th Miss Betsy Lee.
> > Page 41.
> Miss Kitty Tayloe. Mount Airy.
> > Page 43.
> Miss Lydia Pettit has d—m'd ugly Freckles in her Face, otherways She is handsome & tolerable—
> > Page 45.
> Miss Betsy Gaskins.[160]
> > Page 47.
> Miss Sally Tayloe.
> > Page 50.
> Miss Jenny Washington of Bushfield is very Pretty.
Then he Bolts in
> > Robert Carter.
> > Page 57.
> Miss Polly Tolliver.[161]
> > Page 59.
> Miss Steerman is a beautiful young Lady.
> Miss Jane Corbin.
> — Aphia Fantleroy.
> — — Edwards.
> — Betsy Jones
> — Sally Panton.

But this afternoon Mrs *Oakly* is taken with a Fever; I suppose, She
was out last evening without any thing on her head rather too late,
when I saw her at Daddy Gumby's—

Sunday 10.

A Sunday in Virginia dont seem to wear the same Dress as our Sundays to the Northward—Generally here by five o-Clock on Saturday
every Face (especially the Negroes) looks festive & cheerful—All
the lower class of People, & the Servants, & the Slaves, consider it as
a Day of Pleasure & amusement, & spend it in such Diversions as they
severally choose—The Gentlemen go to Church to be sure, but they
make that itself a matter of convenience, & account the Church a
useful weekly resort to do Business—I am told, for I have not yet
been to Church since my Return, that all the Sermons are in the
forensic Style, & on political Subjects. But I shall go to Church to
Day—I am sorry that I may relate an accident which happened last
night—By some accident; or by the carelessness of some Negroes Mr
Turburville's Barn took fire and burnt Down—His loss is judged at
300 £ which is something considerable for a Man who is with the
greatest Anxiety turning every ear of Corn into Money—At Church
Parson *Smith* Read to the Congregation an Order Issued out lately by
the Governor to elect Burgesses in the several Counties—He preached
us a Sermon on Brotherly Love—Dined with us to Day Mr Parker,[162]
a Lawyer of this County, & his Son, a young Man about 20 who is
also licensed to plead Law—And Mr *Cunningham*—I am not very
well to Day. I have pains in several parts of my Body—Mr *Lowe*
informed me that Colonel Washington is unwell of a sort of *Cholic*—

Monday 11.

Indeed says Mrs Carter at Breakfast a Fire this morning would be
very pleasant—Yes says I, for I have had the look & feeling of
November all the morning; My Room shut up, My Coat buttoned,
& yet my Body cold Besides!—Mr Carter on this, advanced a strange
Assertion, that there is not a single Person on this whole Continent, if
this Change is as powerful through the Continent as it is here, who is
not to day, in a greater or less Degree affected with a Fever!—My
poor skinny Body, I know is in a prodigious Tumult; I impute it tho
to my ride Yesterday to Church in the schorching Sun; & to drink-

ing five or six Glasses of Wine extraordinary—*Priscilla* & *Harriot* are confined at Home of an eruptive Fever, some think it a Swine Pox at any Rate they are sick, & break out into Pustules—I am in such Ferment to Day that I cannot sit nor Walk, nor Write with any Stomach—I made out thu' with some Difficulty to finish a rough Draught of my Sermon, & laid by for future Perusal.

Teusday 12.

Indeed I enjoy this fine cool weather, says Ben as he lay on his Back in the Bed rubbing his Eyes, & ears about half after six o-Clock; *Lancelot Lee* had never I am sure, more sensible Pleasure in swallowing a well prepar'd Dinner—To be sure I have slept last Night with the sweetest composure in Spight of the Chinches, & in spight of my Disorder!—Get up, Lump of Indolence, said I to him; Get up & clap to *Virgil* instead of lying there & boasting—Breakfasted with us Captain Guthrie, of a Small Schooner of *Norfolk;* & Mr Stadley the Musician—I love this good German, He used to teach in *New York* & *Philadelphia*—He has much simplicity & goodness of heart—He performs extremely well—He is kind & sociable with me—Dined with us one—one—Mr—Mr—I forget his name—I know his trade tho': An Inspector—He is rather Dull, & seems unacquainted with company for when he would, at Table, drink our Health, he held the Glass of Porter fast with both his Hands, and then gave an insignificant nod to each one at the Table, in Hast, & with fear, & then drank like an Ox—The Good Inspector, at the second toast, after having seen a little our Manner "Gentlemen & Ladies (but there was none in Womans Cloathing at Table except Mrs Carter) The King"—I thought that during the Course of the Toasts, he was better pleased with the Liquor than with the manner in which he was at this Time obliged to use it—I made a b[e]gining of my Latin Thesis—"Cuinam Usui inservi: at Lex moralis sub Evangeliis." I made out to write thus much—Duabus hisce Propositionibus sequentibus simulatim Respondeo.—But if I wrote so much every Day for a twelve Month my Thesis will be short. The Day is pleasant, cool enough: & my disorder which has been for several days a growing painful *Dysentery*, seems to have subsided—

[LETTER OF PHILIP V. FITHIAN TO ELIZABETH BEATTY]

Nominy-Hall July 12. 1774.

To LAURA.

The Summer is advancing briskly on, & bringing me with it every Day still nearer to you—And to my last Change—With you I am looking for the purest Happiness in Friendship & Love that I can derive from any thing below; And it will add to measure of Felicity if I can make the Woman I choose to protect & esteem think me worthy her Regard.

I said that the swift Advances of Summer are bringing me swiftly on to Death—In Virginia there are numberless Admonitions to this Reflection, but I suppress any farther Declaration. I wrote you by Mr ———— early last Month; & at the same Time I wrote to several of my Acquaintances: but if they lived in the Moon I could hear from them as often as I do now when only a Couple of Hundred Miles, or a little more, separates us: Would it not be more agreeable to me if they did—? For then I should every Night almost, see, at least, the Place of their Habitation, tho' we could have no Correspondence.

You are such a Pilgrim, Laura; I mean such a Rover, that I am at some Loss to know how to direct a Letter to you; & I want my Letters, while they are on their Passage to go through as few Hands as possible, not because I write any *Secrecy*, or *Scandal*, for you will not allow either the one or the other; but only that you may speedily receive & read the Little I do write, fresh from my Heart.

I suppose that Miss ———— has before now seen Cohansie—And cloyed of it too, no Doubt. She is a lively, sportful Soul. But that dear Place, which ingrosses so many of my Thoughts, has not Variety enough to entertain her long—You yourself, who are not always soaring on Follie's Wing, through the Regions of Vanity & Nonsense, sometimes find the Country dull—But Miss ———— does not find Satisfaction in the City; it is plain then since that young Lady cannot find Contentment either in City or Country, that She cannot be happy at all.

Merciful, merciful Heaven! O grant me what I am trying hard to obtain; grant that my Inclinations be all duely bended to a perfect Satisfaction with my Lot here—! With such a Temper I shall be at Rest, be happy, if I continue here in Virginia; Or I shall be happy if I remove into new Jersey; But, must I declare it, Laura, that if I am destitute of this, I should be wretched, tho' your Friend & Companion—I am,

Laura, thine

PHILIP. V. FITHIAN.

[JOURNAL]

Wednesday 13.

I drew off this morning for Dadda *Gumby* a List of his Children, & their respective ages—He himself is 94—For this office I had as many *Thanks*, As I have had *blessings* before now from a Beggar for Six-pence—Thank you, thank you, thank you Master, was the language

of the old Greyheaded pair.—Call on us at any time, you shall have *Eggs, Apples, Potatoes*—You shall have every thing we can get for you—Master!—In this Torrent of Expressions of Gratitude I was rung to Breakfast; I bow'd to the venerable old Negroes, thank'd them in my Turn for their Offers, & left them—

Indeed, said the Colonel at Breakfast, cool as it was last Night, I kept my Window up the whole night—I am not fond of your hot a dust Air—Was yours up Mr Fithian no truly; so long as I can breath without panting I am for keeping my Window down, & my Room close on summer nights; especially here in Virginia, Madam, where the Dews are so heavy, and so dangerous—The Postilion keeps a fox at the Stable & I am often much diverted with his Cunning Tricks. The other Day, Mrs Carter was lying in the long room among the Books on the Couch; In jumps Reynard, through a broken Pane of Glass, & begins to frisk & hue about the Room like a Bedlam—How is Nurse, pray, says the Colonel at Dinner? She has her Ague & Fever again to Day, Sir—This is a fine Sheeps-Head, Mr Stadly shall I help you?—Or would you prefer a *Bass* or a *Perch?*—Or perhaps you will rather help yourself to some picked *Crab*—It is all extremely fine, Sir, I'll help myself—Well says the Colonel when we had almost finished our Dinner with a Glass of sparkling Porter on the Table before him, we have but fasted to Day; here stands a fine Ham, & a Shoulder of excellent Mutton yet untouched—At least, says the merry, good-hearted Man, we have kept *Lent*—Yesterday evening I scribled a little for *Laura*, & to Day I drank her Health from my Heart in generous Medaira—Yes, best of Women, when you are the Toast I drink wine with Pleasure—

Thursday 14.

To Day is the election of Burgesses in Richmond the neighbouring County—Come, Fithian, will you go? My old objection recurs; I am too busy—I met this morning in Wingates Arithmetic, with the following merry Problem—"To discover a Number which any one shall have in his mind, without requiring him to reveal any part of that or any Number whatsoever"—After any one has thought upon any number at Pleasure; bid him double it, & to that double bid him add any such even number as you please to assign: Then from the Sum of that Addition let him reject one half, & reserve the other half; Lastly, from this half bid him subtract the Number which he first thought upon; then you may boldly tell him what Number remains in his mind after that Subtraction is made, for it will be always half the Number which you assigned him to add—A Reason for the Rule is added. "Because, if to the double of any number (which number for Distinction sake I call the first) a second number be added, the half of the Sum must necessarily consist of the said first number, & half the Second: Therefore if from the said half sum the first Number be subtracted, the remainder must of necessity be half the second Number which was added—Mr Inspector dined with us again to day

—We had after Dinner, *Lime Punch* & *Madaira:* but he chose & had a Bowl of *Grogg*—You are a mean Puppy, a treacherous, ungenerous Scoundrel, says *Bob,* to Harry just as I entered the School after Dinner—you told Mr *Lowe,* you did more, you published in Mr Washingtons Family that Mr *Fithian* horsed me for Staying out all night—That he call'd in John the Waiter to help him—& that you was sent to cut & bring in Whips—After School with Ben I rode out the Day is warm, & the Ground grows to be very dry—I was not a little Surprized to see Corn out in Tassel—But the Tobacco looks dismal, it is all poor, much of it is dead with the drouth; I think, however, that the Season is ten days or two Weeks earlier here than in New Jersey.—

Mr Stadly, left us to Day. I love that Man, he is gone to Colonel Taylors[163]—

Fryday 15.

I got up a little before six & as it is very warm, I threw up the window to enjoy the Morning's fine salubrious Air—I saw a *Lady*—She was walking to the *Poplars*—She appeared small but walked genteel—She walked slow & looked on the ground—Her Dress look'd to be extremely good, but was only thrown carelessly on; She had a Silk shade thrown over her shoulders in which her hands were muffled—I had the Idea in a moment of a Woman in some kind of Difficulty —But how can such a woman have been to Mr Carters & done Business, who was not there last night.?—It was Mrs *Oakly*—She has the Ague and was walking for the benefit of the *Morning Air.*—We are rid of two *troubles* from this morning till Monday: for *Bob* & *Nancy* are gone to the Dancing School—They dance at Colonel Lee's—Two great troubles, indeed, for this hot weather I can hardly keep them in the Room, much less to any useful business—Please to excuse me from Dinner, says Mrs Carter, & retired to her Chamber—There appears in the North a black Cloud, where it Thunders—Send us a Shower in Mercy, bountiful Heaven, tho' our Sins deserve thy Frowns & Judgments.—The Cloud thickens. it rises—At last there comes a kind Shower—After the Rain about six Ben & I took a Ride for exercise, the Corn litterally looks glad—I have made a party, Says Mr Carter at Coffee, for a Trip by Water to morrow, Mr Fithian will you be one?—With all my heart Sir, if it is agreeable —We are to ride then to Mr *Atwels* says he, & there enter my new

Barge; with her we will go down the River Machodockin to Potowmack then up the Potowmack & enter the River Nomini, & up that
River Home—

[LETTER OF PHILIP V. FITHIAN TO JOHN PECK]

Nomini-Hall. July 15th. 1774.

SIR.

I have communicated your intention to Mr *Carter;* he begs you
will by no Means disappoint him.

I wrote you a letter by the post early in June possibly it was lost,
for either letters are lost, or you and the rest of my friends in *Jersey*
use me vastly ill, for I have not received a line since I have been in
Virginia—You had better go into the school and acquaint yourself
with the method of teaching, and procure some copper plate copies:
I am by the goodness of heaven very well; I hope you will remember me to all friends at Princeton to relations and friends at Cohansie;
desire *Charles* to carry my *Homer* to cohansie when he goes down in
the vacancy; tell him I shall be at home if no unforeseen accident
prevents by the last of october.

You had better provide yourself with recommendations from
several, especially from Doctor Witherspoon, something of the kind
will not be a hindrance, but may possibly at some J[u]ncture be of
eminent Service.

I am, Sir, Yours,

PHILIP V FITHIAN

Mr John Peck.
Nassau-Hall

[JOURNAL]

Saturday 16.

The *Colonel, Ben,* & *myself* rode on Horse-back about Six to Mr
Atwels; four lusty, hearty Men had gone on foot before who were
Oarsmen: Here we were to enter a Boat never Rowed before, &
proceed down the River Machodock to Mr *Carters* Store-Houses
which are now building near the mouth of that River—But I am

going to venture upon a Description of a Scene which I am sure I
shall not do Justice to—A Scetch of three Rivers—Their Beautiful
Banks—Several Gentlemens Seats—Their commodious harbours—In
particular that near which Mr *Carter* is erecting Store-Houses—The
whole is to be an account of our peregrination this 16th burning day
of July 1774—With several remarks.—What a Crack of Thunder
there was! I must run to the Window & view the Cloud—It is a small
white remote Cloud in the North-West. I am summoned to Coffee—
Mrs *Carter* gave us a Dish round—Amazing what a Flash of Lightning! how fast it rises!—Ben child, says the lovely Woman, take my
Seat & fill out the Coffee. Please to excuse me; & She then retired up
chamber—We finished our Coffee—The Gust came up, & to be sure
I have seldom seen one more terable! Long, bright, forked bolts
seemed to dart incessantly through the broken parts of the Cloud;
some of them would appear perpendicular others horizontal, and
some would split, & in a Moment seem to bespangle, with sparks of
Fire, the whole Front of the Cloud! And these were continually succeeded with alarming alternate Cracks of Thunder!—It brings, however to the scorched Earth a plenteous needful Supply—By nine it is
past, & opens a serene beautiful western Sky—I resume my Description.

I have said, that we rode on Horseback to Mr *Atwels* where we were
to go on board & have our Horses sent back. This House is called six
Miles from the mouth of Machodock—It stands on the Bank of the
River; The Boat that carried us is built for the purpose of carrying
the young Ladies and others of the Family to Nominy Church—It is
a light neat *Battoe* elegantly painted & is rowed with four Oars—We
went on board; The Sun beamed down upon us, but we had each an
Umberella—The River is here about Gunshot over; the Banks are
pretty low, but hard to the very Water—I was delighted to see Corn
& Tobacco growing, or Cattle & Sheep feeding along the Brink of
this River on both Sides, or else Groves of Pines, Savins & Oaks growing to the side of the Bank—We passed by an elegant small Seat of
Mr *Beal;*[164] it was small, but it was neat—We arrived at Mr *Carters*
Store-Houses in in 50 minutes, they are 5 Miles from Mr *Atwels,* &
one from Potowmack—These Houses are building for the reception
of Iron, Bread, Flour &c. there are two Houses each 46 Feet long by
20.—They stand at the Bottom of a Bay which is a safe & spacious
harbour—Here we Breakfasted at ten.—At twelve we pushed of

from thence & rowed by parson Smiths Glebe & in sight of his house in to the broad beautiful Potowmack—: I think it is here ten Miles or twelve over has a fine high hard Bank; no Marshes—but Cornfields, Trees, or Grass!—Up the lovely Water we were rowed six Miles in to the Mouth of Nominy—We went on Board a small Schooner from *Norfolk* which lay in Nominy-Bay—Mr Carter is loading her with Flour & Iron—Here we were in Sight of Stratford, Colonel Lee's, Seat.—We were in Sight too of Captain Cheltons—And of Colonel Washingtons Seat at Bushfield—From the Schooner we Rowed up Nominy-River—I have forgot to remark before that from the time of our setting out as we were going down Machodock, & along the Potowmack-Shore, & especially as we were rowing up Nominy we saw Fishermen in great numbers in Canoes, & almost constantly taking in Fish Bass & Perch—This was beautiful!—The entrance of Nomini is very shoal, & stony, the Channel is very narrow, & lies close to the Eastermost Side—On the edges of these shoals, or in Holes between the Rocks is plenty of Fish—The Banks of Nominy are steep and vastly high, twenty & thirty Feet, & in some places almost perpendicular; The Course of the River is crooked, & the prospects on each Side vastly romantic & diversified—We arrived at the Granary near Nominy-Hall about six—I went to my room to take off an Account of the expedition—When the Gust soon hindred.

Sunday 17.

The Air this morning serene & cool—I do not go to Church. At last I have finished my Presbyterial pieces roughly they are to be reviewed & corrected; In the mean Time tho', (as Workman say) I must blow a little, for to be sure I am fatigued—Mr *Fithian,* says Mr *Carter* at Dinner with a serious Air, you see we cannot with conveniency attend *Ucomico* Church. If I should propose having prayrs read in the great Room on that vacant Day would you encourage & assist me?—I answered him that I was heartily agreed—You then, Sir, says he, may read the *prayrs*—& I will read the *Lessons.* The Afternoon extremely hot I could not leave my Room til the Sun had hid his flaming Place behind the Earth—Then I walked through the Garden—The whole Family seem to be now out Black, White, Male, Female, all enjoying the cool evening—

Monday 18.

Pray Sir let all our Windows be put up, says Bob the Moment he came down from his chamber, & let the Doors be set open or we shall faint with Heat—Such a night I never spent before—The Heat says he, and these cursed Chinches made me intirely restless—I scribbled over a Letter to Mr *John Peck*, & one to Miss ...... pray Mr Fithian says Nancy draw me a picture such as you drew for Fanny last Week—At two, just before we sit Down to Dinner a Cloud appear'd in the West—Mrs Carter excused herself from Dinner; while we were dining the Cloud came over, very moderate tho' with plenty of Rain—It is now, says Mrs Carter at Coffee, cool enough, a fine fair evening, a Northerly breeze & lovely evening—Mrs Oakly came into my Room this evening—It was to take her leave; she is to leave us early tomorrow morning—Good night, said I to the little Woman, I wish you a safe passage over the Rappahannock, & a pleasant journey home—I drew off as well as I could a rough plan of Nominy-Hall for Nancy.

Teusday 19.

Nurse left us early this morning postilion Nat. carried her in a chair to the Ferry—The Day is fine cool enough—After School in the evening I rode out to a Corn-field, about a Mile & a half off, where I usually go for exercise, the Corn is beginning pretty generally to tassel, & I saw one hill in Silk, and in Blossom—To day I put *Harry* into decimal Arithmetic—

Wednesday 20.

Shut the Door, *Harriot*, says *Fanny* I I'm so cold I shake—indeed the morning is cool enough to sit with December clothes on!—I spent the little time I have for myself to Day in forming my Latin *Exegesis* —Mr *Taylor* the head Overseer Dined with us—At *Coffee* The Colonel & myself entered somehow into Dispute upon the advantage in working an Oar—He asserted & tried to prove that the advantage lies in having the Oar longer from the *Thole-pin* or where it lies on the Boat to the water, than from the *Thole-pin* to the Rowers hand in a mathematical sense; He allow'd the Water to be the Fulcrum or Prop, & the Boat to be the weight, & the Rower to be a secondary

Power—But the resistance of the Water to the Oar he call'd the chief & primary Power—

Thursday 21.

Lazy Fellows! *Ben, Bob, Harry*, & *Myself* all this Morning slept til near seven!—It was a sleepy Morning tho', for the Girls to give us countenance slept too—My Leisure time to Day is spent in forming my Latin Exegesis—Only just before the Sun went Down *Ben* & I had our Horses & rode to our accustomed Resort the Corn-field, now many of the Hills are in Silk—We returned to Coffee—The Day has been very warm; the evening is light & pleasant, &, Thank, to our common, & bountiful Preserver, I am in good Health—

Fryday 22.

My Exegesis goes on lustily; I have finished three pages—Indeed Sir, says *Harry* I cannot reduce 7s 6d into the decimal of a Pound Sterling—you must reduce 7s & 6d to pence; for a numerator; then you must reduce a Pound Sterling to Pence for a Denominator; this Numerator you divide by the denominator & the Quotient will be the Decimal sought—Well *Ben* you & Mr *Fithian* are invited by Mr Turberville, to a Fish feast to-morrow, said Mr Carter when we entered the Hall to Dinner—I am uncertain whether my Latinitas will not be a Shackle too heavy to allow me to favour his kind invitation.

Saturday 23.

Priscilla, & *Fanny*, each presented me with a fine Jessamine Nosegay this morning—At eight I dismissed the School: *Ben, Bob*, & *Harry* go to the *Fish-Feast*, I to making latin—While we were Dining a black turbulent Cloud came over from the West (I believe the Boys will commend my choice now) It rained, it Thundered hard, & continued exceeding stormy til after six in the Evening; I spent the Afternoon however in Quiet & to advantage—I am more & more pleased with my Situation. the Time draws nigh when I must enter on a new, & perhaps less agreable exercise—There were many at the River; the Boys tell me, among others Miss *Betsy Lee*—I do not, however, repent my having staid at Home—The Colonel shewed me some Powder which was made in *Frederick* in this Province—It seems good—He charged a *Pistol*, it fired quick & strong—

Sunday 24.

I lazy slept til seven—The Boys seem sick of their yesterdays Voyage
—I rode to Nomini-Church—The Parson invited me home but we
have company—Mr *Turberville, Mr Cunningham, George* & *Lancelot Lee* dined with us—After the ordinary Toasts we were call'd on
to Toast Ladies: I gave Miss *Jenny Washington*—The Lee's came
over to our School-Room I swear says George, there is no Devil!—
There is no Devil, I swear!— He went on in such an impious, & at the
same time whimsical & foolish manner, that I left the Room, and
went over to Mr & Mrs Carter, with whom nothing is heard indecent
or profane—After the Company were gone as we were walking near
the Poplar Avenue, says Mrs Carter how sweet, & pure the Air is;
how much the weather resembles September!—Indeed I think it
feels like the fever & Ague!—*Bob* in the Evening brought me Colonel
Taylors[165] compliments, who begs I will wait on him soon; He wants
to know if I have provided a Tutor for Mrs *Thornton* Mr *Leek* told
me something about coming, but not til next Spring, & I judge that
Mrs Thornton will be impatient before that time—Do you now indeed, sincerely, in your Heart, Sir says Ben to me after we had retired
to our Chamber, believe that there is a Devil?—For my part, tho' I
made *George Lee* think otherwise, I do not—I told him that it was
universally allowed by writers of the greatest reputation for Learning and Religion in the established Church of England, whose Canons
he profess'd to believe & adhere to—And that, if he would attend to
my advice, he ought not to doubt its Reality.

Monday 25.

Harry & *Bob* go shrugging up their backs with their Coats Buttoned
about the School, first one then the other complaining of the cold—
The Girls too, in their white Frocks, huddle close together for the
benefit of warming each other, & look like a Flock of Lambs in the
Spring—I wish they were half as innocent—I myself, after having
added a Waistcoat, am notwithstanding disagreeably Cold—The air
is clear, the wind strong from the West—I proceeded in my Latin
Exegesis, & shall, I hope, shortly be through it—I gave to *Nancy* at
her Request, my Scetch of *Nominy-Hall*—I propose to take off one
for myself—

Teusday 26.

The morning cool enough—Order me a Horse & Chair, says the Colonel after Breakfast, for I must go to Westmoreland-Court—I piddled at my Exegessis, but (as they say here in Virginia) I did a mighty little—Priscilla after School invited me to ride with her, but I had preengaged to go on Board the *Harriot;* She now lies in Nominy about half a mile Distant—*Bob* conducted me on board, She is a neat vessel, carries 1400 Bushels—*Bob* strip'd & swam round us half an hour—Coffee; Well, Sir, says the Colonel at las I can treat you with several Letters—My heart jumped—A fine Repast indeed, valuable because exceeding rare! But shall I hear any thing from—*Laura?*— On this he gave me Letters from,

1. Rev'd Enoch Green, Dated Feb: 1774.
2. From Laura, Dated Feb: 13th 1774.
3. From John Peck Dated Nassau Hall July 2. 1774
4. From John Peck dated Feb: 25th 1774.
5. From the Revd: Andrew Hunter, dated Cohansie June 24th. 1774.
6. From Andrew Hunter Junr: Dated June 24th. 1774. Cohansie.
7. From Mr James Ewing, Dated Bridge-town July 7th. 1774.

For these Letters I paid—12s 5d—Pennsylvania Currency, & I am very proud of my Bargain—

Mr Peck informs me that he is to succeed me in this place—Mr *Hunter* & Mr Ewing inform me of the Death of Uncle Ephraim Seeley! That he died of a *Diabetes* which has long troubled him! He has lett no Doubt a mourning Family—Mr *Hunter* writes me word that *Andrew* was licensed to preach about the middle of June. Laura says—They all express with Concern the great Commotions which at present exist through the Colonies.

Wednesday 27.

Somehow I have taken a bad Cold, & am low-spirited to Day—The Colonel was all the forenoon down at the *Harriot* in the Sun, so that when we went in to dine he seem'd fatigued & eat nothing—We have an Addition to our numerous Family, one Mr —— I forget his name, he is a Cooper, tho', & an Irishman, & seems to be pretty smart; I sat the Evening with him in Mr Randolphs Room.

Thursday 28.

Evening, after the Sun had gone, with *Priss* I walked in the Garden. we gathered some few Figs which are just growing ripe—My Leisure to Day I spent in finishing off my Latin Exercises.

Fryday 29.

I feell wholly relieved of my cold—I wrote & sent to the Post a Letter to Mr *John Peck*, to remind & hurry him in his way here—O! it is very hot—The wind itself seems to be heated! We have a fine Room, & sufficiently open; & I dress in a thin Waist-Coat, & a loose, light linen Gown; The *Boys*, *Harry* & *Bob* have nothing on, in School, but their shirts & Breeches; and I laugh'd cordially to see the contrivance of *Fanny*, the loveliest of them all, to grow cool, She sat on a low bench, & put her Hand in her pocket, & seem'd exceeding diligent in looking for something—But before She took out her hand She had off both her Stockings, & left them both in her pocket!— Mrs *Carter* in particular seems to be overcome with the extreme Heat & looks like a fainting, expiring yet lovely Creature!—At seven I rode out to the Corn-field, the Sun was almost down, & was hid behind a large white thick Cloud where it Thunders—The Corn is roll'd up with the heat & Drouth! Yet it is strange there is no Musquetoes—I have seen one & heard another, & this is the whole compliment I have either *seen*, *heard* or *felt* since I have been in *Virginia*—While we were drinking *Coffee* the Lightning, as it began to grow Dark, began to stream, it was at some Distance, but was incessant, bright, & awful—The Colonel, however sat, & with unmoved Composure observed it;

Saturday 30.

The weather is something cooler & bearable this Morning—*Frank Christien* one of Mr *Lowe's* Scholars came to visit *Harry* & *Bob*, so that I discharged them about eleven, & retired to my Chamber to writing—I sent Mr *George Lee* a note this morning begging him to excuse *Ben* & I from attending his Fish-Feast this Day—Captain *Dobby* dined with us; he is a Man of much Spirit and Humour: A great Mimick—He acquainted us that at Hobbs's-Hole this Day is a Boat-Race on the River Rappahannock Each Boat is to have 7 Oars: to row 2 Mile out & 2 Miles in round a Boat lying at Anchor—The

Bett 50 £—And that in the Evening there is a great Ball to be given
—I believe both the *Rowers* & *dancers*, as well *Ladies* as *Gentlemen*
will perspire freely—Or in plain English they will soak in Sweat!
The Captain invited us on Board his Ship next Teusday to Dine with
him & wish them a pleasant Passage as the Ship is to Sail the day following—If the Weather is not too burning hot I shall go provided
the Others go likewise. Ben towards evening rode to Colonel
Tayloe's—

[LETTER OF PHILIP V. FITHIAN TO GEORGE LEE]

To Mr. George Lee.   July 30th. 1774.

SIR.

With my compliments I am to inform you that *Ben:-Carter* is, of
necessity, to go this day into *Richmond;* and as my company alone
will not be equal to the trouble you must be at I give you this timely
notice that you may avoid it,

I am,

with my thanks for your
          Invitation, Sir,

Your most humble Servt:

P. V. FITHIAN.

[JOURNAL]

Sunday 31.

Daddy *Gumby* saw me walking—I had just got up, it was early I
had only a Gown thrown round me—He walked towards me—Well
Master you never call for no Eggs. I can now give you a *Water
Melon*—No, Thomas, with your Wife & family enjoy these things.
I am well provided for—Well, Master, I promised you Eggs, for
writing you will think I never designed to pay you—God yonder in
Heaven Master will burn *Lyars* with *Fire* & *Brimstone!*—I speak
Truth I will not deceive you Men are wicked, Master; look see the
Grass is burnt: God burns it to punish us! Is the ground dry, Dadda.
O! all dry, all burnt—Pray, Pray, Master, do you go to Church?—

No Dadda it is too hot—Too hot, Good God, too hot! I shall affront you, Master—Too hot to serve the Lord! Why I that am so old & worn out go on Foot.—I felt a little non plus'd, I confess, but walk'd to my Room & went none to Church—I expected that we should have had prayrs at home, but it was not mentioned—Fanny towards Evening brought me half a *Water-Melon*—I accepted & thank'd the little pretty Slut, she seems so artless, & delicate I esteem her exceedingly—I walked out about Sun-set, when it is a little cool, along the River Nominy—

Monday   August 1st 1774.

The Colonel rode to Richmond Court—The morning very hot—A Cloud appeared about two o Clock as we were going to Dinner in the West where it thundered—Mrs. *Carter* kept her Chamber—There is almost no Rain—I looked to day over Dr *Burney's* present State of Musick in Germany—I think it more entertaining than realy useful—Ben to Day begun the *Eneid*—Poor Mr *Randolph* seems to be sickening with the *Ague* & *Fever!*—Evening the Colonel returned & gave us Captain Dobby's repeated Invitation.

Teusday 2.

Ben & I drest ourselves pretty early with an intention to Breakfast with Colonel *Tayloe,* but the Servant who went with us was so slow in preparing that we breakfasted before we set out—We arrived at Colonel Tayloe's however by half after nine—The young Ladies we found in the Hall playing the Harpsichord—The morning cool with a fine Breeze from the North for I forgot to mention that about Midnight last Night a violent Gust of Blackness, Rain, & Thunder came on & gave us present Relief from the scorching Sun; there was no Dust & the riding was pleasant—The Colonel, his Lady, Miss Polly, Miss Kitty, Miss Sally, rode in their Great Coach to the Ferry—Distance about 4 miles—Ben & I on Horseback—From Colonel Tayloe's to this Ferry opposite to Hobbs's Hole the Land is levil & extremely good; Corn here looks very rank is set thick with Ears, & they are high & large, three commonly on a Stalk—Here I saw about an Acre & a half of Flax, which the people were just pulling, exceedingly out of Season—This is the only Flax I have seen since I have been in the Colony; I am told they raise much in the upper Counties

—Here too is a great Marsh covered with thick high Reed—The Face of this part of the Country looks fertile, but I apprehend it is far from being healthy—We came to the Bank of the Rappahannock; it is here about 2 Miles over the Shipping on the other Side near the Town lying at Anchor look fine; no large Vessels can haul along the Wharves on account of shoal Water—There were six Ships riding in the Harbour, and a number of Schooners & smaller Vessels—Indeed, says Mrs *Tayloe*, Captain Dobby has forgot us. here we have been waiting for a full half hour, shall we take the Ferry Boat Colonel & cross over, & not stand any longer in the burning heat?—I was pleased not a little with the proposal tho' at the same time, I laughed with myself at Mrs Tayloe's truely Womanish impatience!—At last they are coming—The long-Boat came, well furnished with a large Awning, and rowed with four Oars—We entered the Ship about half after twelve where we were received by Captain Dobby, with every possible token of welcome—Since I have been in Virginia, my inclination, & my fixed purpose before I left home, both of which were very much assisted by a strict Attention to the instructing my little Charge, these have kept me pretty constantly, almost wholly, indeed out of that kind of Company where dissipation & Pleasure have no restraint—This entertainment of Captain Dobby's, elegant indeed, & exceeding agreeable, I consider as one among a prodigeous throng of more powerful similar Causes, of the fevers & other Disorders which are common in this Colony, & generally attributed to the Climate which is thought to be noxious & unhealthy. The Weather here indeed is remarkably variable But taking away & changing the usual & necessary Time of Rest; Violent Exercise of the Body & Spirits; with drinking great quantities of variety of Liquors, these bring on Virginia Fevers—The Beaufort is a Stately Ship; Captain Dobby had an Awning from the Stern over the Quarter quite to the Mizen-Mast, which made great Room, kept off the Sun, & yet was open on each Side to give the Air a free passage. At three we had on Board about 45 Ladies, and about 60 Gentlemen besides the Ships Crew, & Waiters Servants &c. We were not throng'd at all, & dined all at twice—I was not able to inform myself, because it seemed improper to interrupt the General pleasure, with making circumstantial inquiries concerning Individuals, & saying pray, Sir, what young Lady is that yonder in a Lute-String Gown? She seems genteel; where does her Father live? Is she a Girl of Family & Breeding? Has She any Suitors? This

when one could not be out of the Inspection of the Company, would
have seemed impertinent so that I did not much enlarge my Acquaintance with the Ladies, which commonly seems pleasing & desirable to
me; But I took Notice of Several, & shall record my remarks—
The Boats were to Start, to use the Language of Jockeys, immediately after Dinner; A Boat was anchored down the River at a Mile
Distance—Captain *Dobby* and Captain *Benson* steer'd the Boats in
the Race—Captain *Benson* had 5 Oarsmen; Captain *Dobby* had 6—It
was *Ebb-Tide*—The Betts were small—& chiefly given to the
Negroes who rowed—Captain Benson won the first Race—Captain
Purchace offered to bett ten Dollars that with the same Boat & same
Hands, only having Liberty to put a small Weight in the Stern, he
would beat Captain *Benson*—He was taken, & came out best only
half the Boats Length—About Sunset we left the Ship, & went all to
Hobbs's Hole, where a *Ball* was agreed on—This is a small Village,
with only a few Stores, & Shops, it is on a beautiful River, & has I
am told commonly six, eight, & ten Ships loading before it the Crews
of which enliven the Town—Mr Ritche[166] Merchant; he has great
influence over the People, he has great Wealth; which in these scurvy
Times gives Sanction to Power; nay it seems to give countenance to
Tyranny—The Ball Room—25 Ladies—40 Gentlemen—The Room
very long, well-finished, airy & cool, & well-seated—two Fidlers—
Mr *Ritche* stalk'd about the Room—He was Director, & appointed
a sturdy two fisted Gentleman to open the Ball with Mrs *Tayloe*—
He danced midling tho'. There were about six or eight married
Ladies—At last Miss *Ritche* danced a Minuet with —— She is a
tall slim Girl, dances nimble & graceful—She was *Ben Carters* partner
—Poor Girl She has had the third Day Ague for twelve months past,
and has it yet She appeared in a blue Silk Gown; her Hair was done
up neat, without powder, it is very Black & Set her to good Advantage—Soon after he danced Miss *Dolly Edmundson*[167]—A Short
pretty Stump of a Girl; She danced well, sung a Song with great
applause, seemed to enter into the Spirit of the entertainment—A
young Spark seemed to be fond of her; She seemed to be fond of
him; they were both fond, & the Company saw it—He was Mr
Ritche's Clerk, a limber, well dress'd, pretty-handsome Chap he was
—The insinuating Rogue waited on her home, in close Hugg too, the
Moment he left the Ball-Room—Miss *Aphia Fantleroy* danced next,
the best Dancer of the whole absolutely—And the finest Girl—Her

head tho' was powdered white as Snow, & crap'd in the newest Taste—She is the Copy of the goddess of Modesty—Very handsome; she seemed to be loved by all her Acquaintances, and admir'd by every Stranger, Miss *McCall*—Miss *Ford*—Miss *Brokenberry* [168] —*Ball*—Two of the younger Miss *Ritche's*—Miss *Wade*—They danced till half after two. Captain Ritche invited Ben & I, Colonel Tayloe & his Family with him—We got to Bed by three after a Day spent in constant Violent exercise, & drinking an unusual Quantity of Liquor; for my part with Fatigue, Heat, Liquor, Noise, Want of sleep, And the exertion of my Animal spirits, I was almost brought to believe several times that I felt a Fever fixing upon me, attended with every Symptom of the Fall Disorders—

Wednesday 3.

We were call'd up to Breakfast at half after eight—We all look'd dull, pale, & haggard!—From our Beds to Breakfast—Here we must drink hot Coffee on our parching Stomachs!—But the Company was enlivening—Three of the Miss Tayloe's—Three Miss Ritche's—And Miss *Fantleroy*—This loveliest of all the Ring is yet far below— *Laura* If they were set together for the choice of an utter Stranger, he would not reflect, but in a moment spring to the Girl that I mean to regard—After Breakfast the young Ladies favoured us with several Tunes on the Harpsichord—They all play & most of them in good Taste—at eleven we went down to the River; the Ships Long Boat was waiting, Captain *Purchace* of the *Beaufort* helped us on Board— I gave the Boatswain a Pisterene for his trouble—Half a Bit for the Pasture of my Horse—We rode to Colonel Tayloe's—The Ladies all retired for a nap before Dinner. We sat in the Hall, & conversed with the Colonel a sensible, agreeable Sociable person—Miss *Garrot* is Governess of the Young Ladies; She too is chatty, satirical, neat, civil, had many merry remarks at Dinner. we staid til about six took our Leave, & rode Home—Found all well; gave an account of ourselves, of our entertainment, & of our Company to Mr & Mrs Carter at Coffee—& retired soon to Bed—

Thursday 4.

I made out to get up by seven—A little fatigued tho'—Many are sickening with a Fever, & great numbers have the Ague—Protect me if it be thy will, God of my Life, & give me a Heart to praise thy name for all my Favours—Dined with us the Inspector—I walked through the Garden, several times banishing by solitude, as much as possible reflection on several Days past.—

Fryday 5.

I have no Stockings; & I swear I wont go to the Dancing School This was the first I heard of *Bob*—Are Bob & Nancy gone to Mr *Turberville's* said the Colonel at Breakfast—*Nancy* is gone Sir, Bob stays at Home he has no shoes! poh! What nonsense! says the Colonel —Call *Bob*, & Call the Clerk—He sent Mr Randolph to the Store for a pair of Shoes, Bob he took to his Study and flogg'd severely for not having given seasonable Notice, & sent him instantly to the Dance—

Saturday 6.

Last night, & this morning haizy mistty the Wind South East threatens a Rain—Transcribing my pieces, yesterday and to Day— I had a strong invitation to Dr Thompsons Fish-Feast, but the Rainy

Weather hindred; I spent the Day in Quiet in my Chamber writing —Dadda Gumbey sent me a small Water-Melon.

Sunday 7.

I set out for Church—It was cloudy, it Thundered in the West: But I rode on Bob was with me—We arrived at the Church & had our Saddles put into a Chariot—When a violent Gust came on—We were all in the Church; many Ladies were present—The Thunder was violent! Many discovered great Terror—Neither the Parson, nor Clerk attended—There we sat in Silence til the Storm was over, when each sallied out & splashed homewards—Mr & Mrs Carter were to have gone by Water—They had set off But saw the Cloud befor they had rowed far, & wisely returned—Towards Evening Miss Betsy *Carter*, Miss Polly *Carter* of Richmond, & Miss *Turberville* came over to see our Girls. Miss Betsy plays the Harpsichord extremely well, better I think than any young Lady I have seen in Virginia.

Monday 8.

All once more in School—Dined with us *George Lee* & Mr *Grubb*— They spent the afternoon at the great House—After Coffee Lee rode Home—Mr *Grubb* staid with us all night—Dennis came into our Room to bring us a Bowl of Punch; Grubb shut the Door, and accused him of having been caught with Bett, the Dairy Girl, in the Stable last Saturday Night—Dennis seem'd in great distress, he denied the Fact tho' with great steadiness—Nelson our Boy came in with a candle—Dennis here, says *Grubb* to *Nelson*, has been accusing you, Sir, of several crimes; he says you gave him half a *Bitt* last Saturday Night, to stand at the Stable-Door while he with Bett— Nelson star'd—Grubb opened a huge *Molls Atlas* that lay in the Room; & read off their Case & indictment—The Boys seem'd crazy —We dismiss'd them when all the novelty was over, but they darted like Indians so soon as they were at liberty—We sat up til eleven— Ben drank for his Toast, Miss *Julia Stockton* of New Jersey; Grubb Miss Betsy Carter—I with pleasure the Rival of them all—

Teusday 9.

I propose to visit Dr Jones to Day say's Mrs *Carter* at Breakfast— See & have the Carriage ready for me by ten o-Clock *Benny*—She took with her *Priss*, and *Nancy*—We have a thin School—Mr *Grubb* dined with us—Staid til evening, when with Ben he rode home—I finished & glad enough I feel my Latin Thesis—The Weather is now very tolerable, we had to Day a fine Shower about twelve—

Wednesday 10.

All in School—Miss *Fanny* very much troubled with the festered Bites of *Seed Ticks*—Mr *Stadley*, whom I always see with Pleasure came towards evening—After School he gave the Girls a lesson each —About Six we have a fine Shower, with Thunder and Lightning, especiall in the evening the Lightning Sharp—

Thursday 11.

Dined with us two Gentlemen Names unknown—They informed us that a Flux is in a neighbouring County, of which many die!— The Ague too is growing frequent *Fanny* has a fit this afternoon— I begin to be a little alarmed at the early approach of these Disorders, which I fear vill be distressful here!—Through the kindness of heaven I am ‸ ɘt in perfect health—Mr *Carter* & Mr *Stadley* performed both on the *harmonica* I am charm'd with the Sounds! The melody is swelling, grave & grand! The weather vastly hot—

Fryday 12.

Very hot—*Sam* our Barber is Seized with the Ague & Fever—Fanny is confined to her chamber with a Fever occasioned, I am apt to believe, by the inflamed bites of the Seed-Ticks, which cover her like a distinct Small Pox.—Dined with us by particular invitation, Mr *Turberville's* Family, and Miss *Betsy Lee*—The conversation at Table was on the Disorders which seem growing to be epidemical, *Fevers, Agues, Fluxes*—A gloomy train!—Fearing these, I keep myself at home; make my diet sparing & uniform; Use constant moderate Exercise; Drink as little Wine as possible, & when I must drink Toasts I never fail to dilute them with well with Water; I omit almost every kind of fruit; & make my time for *Sleeping* from Night to Night the same, Viz to Bed by ten, & rise by six invariably—I never lived so much by Rule as I do this Summer; & I am taught the Art, & have a Steady Example in Mr & Mrs *Carter*—Mr *Stadley* played on the Harpsichord & harmonica several Church Tunes & Anthems, with great propriety—

[LETTER OF PHILIP V. FITHIAN TO JOHN PECK]

Nomini Hall August 12th 1774.

"Si bene moneo[Maneo], attende."—

SIR.

I never reflect, but with secret, and peculiar pleasure, on the time when I studied in *Deerfield* with you, & several other pleasant Companions, under our common, & much respected instructor, Mr *Green*. And I acknowledge now, with a thankful heart, the many favours, which I received from your family while I was a member of it. This sense of obligation to your Family. And personal friendship for you, have excited me, when it was in my power, to introduce you to the business which I now occupy; into a family, where, if you be prudent and industrious, I am confident you will speedily acquire to yourself both Honour & Profit—But inasmuch as you are wholly a stranger to this Province; & have had little or no Experience in the business which you ar[e] shortly to enter upon; & lest, from common Fame, which is often erroneous, you shall have entertained other notions of the manners of the People here, & of your business as a Tutor, than you will find, when you come, to be actually true; I hope you will not think it *vain* or *untimely*, if I venture to lay before you some Rules for your direction which I have collected from a year's observation. I shall class what I have to say in the following order. First. I shall attempt to give you some direction for the plan of your Conduct among your neighbours, & the People in General here, so long as you sustain the character of a Tutor. Then I shall advise you concerning the rules which I think will be most profitable & convenient in the management of your little lovely charge, the School. Last of all. I shall mention several Rules for your personal conduct. I choose to proceed in the order I have laid down, as well that you may more fully & speedily recieve my mind, as that you may also the more readily select out and apply what you shall find to be most necessary.

First. When you have thought of removinging, for a Time, out of the Colony in which you was born, & in which you have hitherto constantly resided, I make no doubt but you have at the same time expected to find a very considerable alteration of manners, among your new acquaintances, & some peculiarities toto Caelo different, from any you have before been accustomed to. Such a thought is natural; And you will if you come into Virginia, in much shorter time than a year, be convinced that it is just. In New-Jersey Government throughout, but especially in the Counties where you have any personal acquaintance, Gentlemen in the first rank of Dignity & Quality, of the Council, general Assembly, inferior Magistrates, Clergy-men, or independent Gentlemen, without the smallest fear of bringing any manner of reproach either on their office, or their high-born, long recorded Families associate freely & commonly with Farmers & Mechanicks tho' they be poor & industrious. Ingenuity & industry are the Strongest, & most approved recommendations to a Man in that Colony. The manners of the People seem to me, (probably I am overborn by the force of prejudice in favour of my native Soil), to bear some considerable resemblance of the manners in the ancient Spartan Common-Wealth—The Valour of its Inhabitants—was the best, & only security of that State against the enemy; & the wise laws of its renowned Legislator were the powerful Cement which kept them firm & invincible—In our Government, the laborious part of Men, who are commonly ranked in the midling or lower Class, are accounted the strenth & Honour of the Colony; & the encouragement they receive from Gentlemen in the highest stations is the spring of Industry, next to their private advantage. The Levil which is admired in New-Jersey Government, among People of every rank, arises, no doubt, from the very great division of the lands in that Province, & consequently from the near approach to an equality of Wealth amongst the Inhabitants, since it is not famous for trade. You know very well that the Lands in a small township are divided, & then again subdivided into two & three Hundred Separate, proper, creditable estates; for example *Deerfield* & *Fairfield* two Townships, or Precincts, in which you & I are tolerably well acquainted, in the former of which, are the Seats of two Judges of the Sessions; & in the latter resides one of the representatives in General Assembly for the County; But if 16000 £ would purchase the whole landed estates of these three Gentlemen, who are supposed to be the most wealthy in the County, if we rate their Land at the Low Consideration of 4 £ per acre, with all conveniences, each would have 4000 Acres. Now you may suppose how small a quantity many must have when two or three hundred Landholders reside in each of these small Precincts; Hence we see Gentlemen, when they are not actually engaged in the publick Service, on their farms, setting a laborious example to their Domesticks, & on the

other hand we see labourers at the Tables & in the Parlours of their
Betters enjoying the advantage, & honour of their society and Conversation—I do not call it an objection to this, that some few, who
have no substance but work like Slaves as nec[e]ssity drives them
for a few Months in the year; with the price of this Labour they
visit Philadelphia; & having there acquired a fashionable Coat, & a
Stock of Impudence, return home to spend the remainder of the
year, in idleness & disgrace!—But you will find the tables turned
the moment you enter this Colony. The very Slaves, in some families
here, could not be bought under 30000 £. Such amazing property,
no matter how deep it is involved, blows up the owners to an imagination, which is visible in all, but in various degrees according to
their respective virtue, that they are exalted as much above other
Men in worth & precedency, as blind stupid fortune has made a difference in their property; excepting always the value they put upon
posts of honour, & mental acquirements—For example, if you should
travel through this Colony, with a well-confirmed testimonial of
your having finished with Credit a Course of studies at Nassau-
Hall; you would be rated, without any more questions asked, either
about your family, your Estate, your business, or your intention, at
10,000 £; and you might come, & go, & converse, & keep company,
according to this value; & you would be dispised & slighted if yo[u]
rated yourself a farthing cheaper. But when I am giving directions
to you, from an expectation that you will be shortly a resident here,
altho you have gone through a College Course, & for any thing I
know, have never written a Libel, nor stolen a Turkey, yet I think
myself in duty bound to advise you, lest some powdered Coxcomb
should reproach your education, to cheapen your price about 5000 £;
because any young Gentleman travelling through the Colony, as I
said before, is presum'd to be acquainted with Dancing, Boxing, playing the Fiddle, & Small-Sword, & Cards. Several of which you was
only entering upon, when I left New-Jersey; towards the Close of
last year; and if you stay here any time your Barrenness in these must
be detected. I will however allow, that in the Family where you act
as tutor you place yourself, according to your most accute Calcula-
tion, at a perfect equidistance between the father & the eldest Son.
Or let the same distance be observed in every article of behaviour
between you & the eldest Son, as there ought to be, by the latest &
most approved precepts of Moral-Philosophy, between the eldest
Son, & his next youngest Brother. But whenever you go from Home,

where you are to act on your own footing, either to a Ball; or to a *Horse-Race*, or to a *Cock-Fight*, or to a *Fish-Feast*, I advise that you rate yourself very low, & if you bett at all, remember that 10,000 £ in Reputation & learning does not amount to a handfull of Shillings in ready Cash!—One considerable advantage which you promise yourself by coming to this Colony is to extend the Limits of your acquaintance; this is laudable, & if you have enough of prudence & firmness, it will be of singular advantage—Yet attempt slowly & with the most Jealous Circumspection—If you fix your familiarity wrong in a single instance, you are in danger of total, if not immediate ruin—You come here, it is true, with an intention to teach, but you ought likewise to have an inclination to learn. At any rate I solemnly injoin it upon you, that you never suffer the spirit of a Pedagogue to attend you without the walls of your little Seminary. In all promiscuous Company be as silent & attentive as Decency will allow you, for you have nothing to communicate, which such company, will hear with pleasure, but you may learn many things which, in after life, will do you singular service.—In regard to Company in general, if you think it worth the while to attend to my example, I can easily instruct you in the manner of my Conduct in this respect. I commonly attend Church; and often, at the request of Gentlemen, after Service according to the custom, dine abroad on Sunday—I seldom fail, when invited by Mr or Mrs *Carter*, of going out with them; but I make it a point, however strongly solicited to the contrary, to return home with them too—Except in one of these cases, I seldom go out, but with a valuable variety of books I live according to Horace's direction, & love "Secretum Iter et fallentis Semita Vitae." Close retirement and a life by Stealth. The last direction I shall venture to mention on this head, is, that you abstain totally from Women. What I would have you understand from this, is, that by a train of faultless conduct in the whole course of your tutorship, you make every Lady within the Sphere of your acquaintance, who is between twelve & forty years of age, so much pleased with your person, & so fully satisfied as to your abilities in the capacity of—a Teacher; & in short, fully convinced, that, from a principle of Duty, you have, both by night & by day endeavoured to acquit yourself honourably, in the Character of a Tutor; & that, on this account, you have their free & hearty consent, without making any manner of demand upon you, either to stay longer in the County with them, which they would choose, or whenever your business calls you away, that they may not have it in their Power either by charms or Justice to detain you, & when you must leave them, have their sincere wishes & constant prayrs for Length of days & much prosperity, I therefore beg that you will attend litterally to this advice, & abstain totally from Women. But this last precaution, which I have been at some pains to dress in the plainest language, I am much inclined to think, will be wholly useless in regard to you, notwithstanding it is founded in that *Honour* and *Equity* which is on all hands allow'd to be due from one Sex to the other, & to many of your *age*, & *Standing* no doubt would be entirely salutary. Because the necessary connections which you have had with the Fair, from your Puberty upwards have been so unfavourable & ill-fated, that instead of apprehending any danger on the score of over fondness, I am fearful your rancour has grown so inveterate at length, as, not only to preserve you, in thought & practice, pure of every Fleshly foible, but has carried you so far towards the other extream, as that you will need many persuasions, when your circumstances shall seem to require it, to bring you back to a rational & manly habit of thinking & acting with respect to the Sex; which yet, after all (& eternally will continue to be, tho it is so much courted & whined after) if considered in the fullest manner, & set forth to the best advantage, never rises above its divine definition viz "The weaker Vessel." But without detaining you any longer with a matter merely depending on accident or Circumstance I pass on to the second General Head; in which "Ludis atque Jocis amotis [amatis]" I shall offer to your consideration & recommend for your practice several Rules concerning the managment of the School.

2. You will act wisely, if, from the begining, you convince all your Scholars which you may easily do, of your abilities in the several branches, which you shall profess to teach; you are not to tell them, totidem Verbis, "that you understand, perhaps as well as any man on the Continent both the Latin & Greek Classicks;" "& have gone through the usual Course in the noted College of New-Jersey, under Dr Witherspoon, so universally known & admired, where you have studied Criticism, Oratory, History, not to mention Mathematical & philosophical Studies, & dipt a good way into the French-Language, & that you have learn'd a smattering of Dancing, Cards &c. &c. &c." For Dun-p or Hack---n or the most profound dunce in your College or School would have too much sense to pass such impudence by, & not despise and reproach it; but you may speedily &

certainly make them think you a "Clever Fellow" (which is a phrase
in use here for a good Scholar) if you never mention any thing before them, only what you seem to be wholly master of—This will
teach them never to dispute your determination, & always to rely
upon your Judgment; two things which are most essential for your
peace, & their advantage. That you may avoid yourself of this with
certainty I shall recommend for your practice the following method,
as useful at least, if not intirely necessary. Read over carefully, the
lessons in Latin & Greek, in your leisure hours, that the story & Language be fresh in your memory, when you are hearing the respective
lessons; for your memory is treacherous, & I am pretty certain it
would confound you if you should be accosted by a pert School-
Boy, in the midst of a blunder, with "Physician heal thyself"!—You
ought likewise to do this with those who are working Figures; probably you may think that because the highest Cypherer is only in decimal arithmetic, it is not there fore worth your critical attention to be
looking previously into the several Sums. But you are to consider
that a sum in the Square-Root, or even in the Single Rule of three
direct, is to your Pupils of as great importance, as the most abstruse
problem in the Mathematicks to an able artist; & you may lay this
down for a Maxim, that they will reckon upon your abilities, according as they find you acquainted & expert in what they themselves are
studying. If therefore you have resolution (as I do not question your
ability) to carry this plan which I have laid down into execution;
you will thereby convince them of the propriety of their Subordi-
nation to you, & obedience to your instructions, so that you may
lead them, without any resistance, and fix them to the Study of whatever Science you think proper, in which they will rise according to
their respective Capacities. I have said that you ought to strive "from
the beginning" in fixing this very material article in the minds of
your Scholars, Viz a Sense of your authority; for one error of Judgment, or false determination will diminish your Ability with them
more than doing forty things with truth would increase your authority—They act in this case as you would do in the company of a
number of Strangers—A whole evenings conversation, if it was tolerable good Sense, would perhaps make little or no impression on you;
But if through hast[e] in speaking, or inattention, any one should let
fall a sentence either remarkably foolish, or grossly wicked, it would
be difficult if not impossible to persuade you presently that the author

was not either a *thick-Scull,* or a *Villain!*—The education of children requires constant unremitting attention. The meanest qualification you can mention in a useful teacher is *diligence* And without diligence no possible abilities or qualifications can bring children on either with speed or profit. There must be a Combination of qualifications which must all operate strongly & uniformly. In short, give this said Pedagogizing the softest name you will, it is still a "difficult Task." You will meet with numberless difficulties, in your new imployment, which you never dreamt had yet existence. All these you must endeavour to resist & Subdue. This I have seen compared to a Man swimming against a current of Water. But I am mistaken if you will agree, after having six months practice, that the comparison be strong as the truth: You will add to the figure, I am certain, & throw into the Current sharp fragments of *Ice,* & *Blocks,* which would make swimming not only difficult but dangerous! I am not urging these things to discourage you; they are hints for your direction, which, if you will attend to, tho' at first the practice seem rough & unpleasant, shall yet make the remainder of your task pleasing, & the whole of it useful, I will mention several of these Obstacles that you may the more easily guard against them. You will, in the first place, be often solicited, probably oftner than you would wish, to ride abroad; this, however, if you do it moderately, & in seasonable time, & go to proper company, I recommend as conducive to health to one in your sedentary manner of living. But if you go much into company, you will find it extremely difficulty to break away with any manner of credit till very late at night or in most cases for several days, & if you are wanting to your School, you do manifest injury to your Imployer. In this case, I advise you to copy Mr *Carter.* Whenever he invites you, ride. You may *stay,* and talk, & drink, & ride to as great excess as he; & may with safety associate yourself with those whom you find to be his intimates. In all other Cases, except when you ride to Church, at least till you are very intimate in the Colony, you had better ride to a certain Stump, or to some noted plantation, or pretty landscape; you will have in this every advantage of exercise, the additional advantage of undisturbed Meditation, & you will be under no Jealous apprehension in point of behaviour, nor any restraint as to the time of your return.

Another current difficulty will be petitions for holidays. You must have good deal of steadiness if you are able to evade cleverly this practice which has grown so habitual to your little charge from a false method in their early education that they absolutely claim it as a necessary right.

You must also as much as you can, avoid visible partiality. At least you must never suffer your fondness for one Scholar to grow so manifest, as that all your School shall see you look over a fault in him or her which same fault, if commited by another, you severely chastise. This will certainly produce in the others hatred & contempt. A fourth difficulty, and the last I shall mention, consists in knowing when, & in what measure to give the Boys Liberty to go from Home. The two younger Boys are wholly under your inspection; so that not only the progress they make in learning, but their moral Conduct (for both of these are critically observed & examined) either justifies or condemns your management to the World. If you keep them much at home, & close to business, they themselves will call you unfeeling and cruel; & refuse to be industrious; if you suffer them to go much abroad they are certainly out of the way of improvement by Study, probably, by discovering their gross Ignorance, they will expose to ridicule both themselves & all their former instructors, & possibly they may commit actual Crimes so as very much to injure themselves; & scandalize their family; but in each of these you will have a large share of blame, perhaps more than the parents, or even the Boys themselves—It will be said that the parents gave them no licence relying wholly on your judgment & prudence, this will in good measure justify them to the world. And as to the Boys they are full of youthful impetuosity & vigour, & these compel them, when they are free of restraint, to commit actions which with proper management they had surely avoided. I say, when you lay these things together, & view them on every side you will find so many perplexities arising in your mind, from a sense of ignorance of your duty, that you will proceed with caution & moderation, & will be carefull to examine with some precision into the circumstances of *time, company*, & *Business* when you license them to go out entirely at the risk of your Reputation—But the practice of three or four Weeks will give you a more full notion of these & many other incidents than I am able now either to recollect or express; I shall have gained my End if these hints prevent you from setting off wrong, & doing inadvertantly at first what your Scholars will assert to be precedents for your after conduct. I go on, therefore, in the third place as I proposed,

3.   To mention several Rules for your personal conduct. The happy Education which you have had in point of religion, you ought to consider as an important and distinguishing Blessing of Heaven. That train of useful *Instruction, Advice & Example* to which you have been accustomed from your infancy is a more perfect, & will be a safer guide in your future walk, than any directions I am able to give you. You have taken notice of a method for Assistance in Composition, which Longinus recommends. Place, says he, in imagination, several eminent ancient Authors before your Eyes, & suppose that they inspect your Work, a Sense of inferiority would make you diligent, & your composition accurate. Perhaps the same advice when transferr'd to Morality, would be equally salutary. Unless it be objected that a Belief of Gods presence at all times in every place is the strongest possible restraint against committing Sin. This I constantly admit; but when I consider how easily our minds are put in motion, & how strongly they are sometimes agitated merely by the senses, & that the senses are affected most by things which fall under their immediate notice, I am fully convinced that if some such plan as I have just mentioned should be fallen upon, & practised, it would make a visible and useful change in our behaviour—In this place I think it needful to caution you against hasty & ill founded prejudices. When you enter among a people, & find that their manner of living, their *Eating, Drinking, Diversions, Exercise* &c, are in many respects different from any thing you have been accustomed to, you will be apt to fix your opinion in an instant, & (as some divines deal with poor Sinners) you will condemn all before you without any meaning or distinction what seems in your Judgment disagreable at first view, when you are smitten with the novelty. You will be making ten thousand Comparisons. The face of the Country, The *Soil*, the *Buildings*, the *Slaves*, the *Tobacco*, the method of spending *Sunday* among Christians; *Ditto* among the Negroes; the three grand divisions of time at the Church on Sundays, Viz. before Service giving & receiving letters of business, reading Advertisements, consulting about the price of Tobacco, Grain &c. & settling either the lineage, Age, or qualities of favourite Horses 2. In the Church at Service, prayrs read over in haste, a Sermon seldom under & never over twenty minutes, but always made up of sound morality, or deep studied Metaphysicks. 3. After Service is over three quarters of an hour spent in strolling round the Church among the Crowd, in which time you will be invited by several different Gentlemen home with them to dinner.

The Balls, the Fish-Feasts, the Dancing-Schools, the Christnings, the Cock fights, the Horse-Races, the Chariots, the Ladies Masked, for it is a custom among the Westmorland Ladies whenever they go from home, to muffle up their heads, & Necks, leaving only a narrow passage for the Eyes, in Cotton or silk handkerchiefs; I was in distress for them when I first came into the Colony, for every Woman that I saw abroad, I looked upon as ill either with the *Mumps* or Tooth-Ach!—I say, you will be often observing & comparing these things which I have enumerated, & many more that now escape me, with the manner of spending Money time & credit at Cohansie: You are young, &, (you will allow me the Expression) in the morning of Life. But I hope you have plann'd off, and entered upon the work which is necessary to be performed in the course of your Day; if not, I think it my duty to acquaint you, that a combination of the amusements which I have just now mentioned, being always before your Eyes, & inviting your Compliance will have a strong tendency to keep you doubtful & unsetled, in your notions of Morality & Religion, or else will fix you in a false & dangerous habit of *thinking* & *acting*, which must terminate at length in Sorrow & despair. You are therefore, if you count any thing upon the value of my advice, to fix the plan in which you would spend your life; let this be done with deliberation, Candour, & precission, looking to him for direction, by fervent Prayr, who is the "Wonderful Counsellor;" & when you have done this, let no importunity of whatever kind prevail over you, & cause you to transgress your own Limitations. I have already exceeded the usual bounds of an Epistle. But you will easily pardon a little prolixity, when I assure you it flows from a heart deeply impressed with a sense of the many difficulties which you must encounter, & the dangers which will surround you when you come first out from the peaceful recess of Contemplation, & enter, young and unexperienced, into the tumultuous undiscerning World. I submit these hints to your consideration, & have nothing more than sincere & ardent wishes for your present & perpetual Felicity.

I am, Sir,

yours.

PHILIP. V FITHIAN.

To MR JOHN PECK.
On going to Virginia in
Character of a Tutor.

[JOURNAL]

Saturday 13.

Prissy took the Ague last Night. She had an easy Fit—This Morning is quite cold, & will, I fear hasten on or at least provoke the present disorders—The good Mr *Stadley* left us this Morning Breakfasted with us a Gentleman from *Maryland.* At Dinner he was join'd by another from the same Province they are both unknown—I rode out with Miss *Prissy* to the Cornfield for Exercise—We gathered & brought home some good Roasting-Ears of Corn—Evening came in Colonel *Henry Lee*[169] He is chosen to be one of the seven who represent this Colony in the general Congress to be held next Month in Philadelphia—He sets out next Sunday Sennight—

Sunday 14.

Colonel Lee stays Breakfast (to Speak in the phrase of Ladies)—The morning fine—Sermon is to Day at Ucomico so that I am to stay in my Room; *Ben*, however, & *Bob*, & *Harry*, & Mr *Randolph* all go —*Fanny* is yet confin'd to her Chamber—

Monday 15.

Began a Letter to Jack Peck, giving him advice in Respect to his coming into this Colony—The People are better, only Miss *Fanny* with her Sores continues in her Chamber; I bought & sent her however this evening a present a large *Musk Melon*—Dined with us Squire *Lee*, he talks of going to Philadelphia to the Congress; He informs us that in Maryland is a Tea-Ship, from the India Company—

Teusday 16.

The Colonel is summoned to a Meeting of Vestry-Men, at the Glebe —Nothing very extraordinary occurs, unless I mention that *Bob* in the former part of this Day kept pretty quiet in his Seat, and worked out three Sums in Reduction compound, without much direction!—About five from the South East came on suddenly a Gust of Rain & Wind, Evening the Colonel returned but a good deal vexed—One of the Members were absent so that the Remainder could do no Business—

Wednesday 17.

This Day is the annual Examination at Nassau-Hall—I wish the Candidates Success & Honour. Last year I had the Pleasure to be present & hear the Examination—I saw *Laura* too; & the Vixen abused me! She shall repent of that insult; Indeed She must feel, tho' I wound myself in the experiment, the Consequence of Slighting good-humour & Civility—There likewise I saw *Belinda* my late agreeable Correspondent. She had left town this unlovely Month, for the bene-fit of Princeton's pure salubrious Air—She laboured in a Consump-tion There too I took my last fare-well!—For soon after her return to Town the disorder fixed, & in a few Months destroy'd a *wise,*

useful, religious Girl—Her death surely was untimely, since she took with her all her virtues, which, with great pleasure & Sincerity She used to diffuse among her giddy Equals!—I am at a Loss to express my feeling for the Death of a young Lady, with whom I had only a short, yet a benificial Intimacy—The Circumstance of my first Acquaintance with her was wholly Accidental, yet I soon believed & accounted it advantageous—I thought her capable of improving me with Sentiment, & I speedily found that my expectation was true —We commenced a Litterary Correspondence, of which I only say that She always express'd herself with so much Truth, Ease & Humour as to make me read her Letters with eagerness and satisfac-tion—If I would record a Motto for her, it Should be—"Virtue without Melancholy." Breakfasted & dined with us two Gentlemen from Maryland—They come over for the benefit of Mr *Carter's*

Mill; as Mills are scarce near the Potowmack in Maryland; but the reason I am a stranger to—Read some in Dr Swift—Writing on to Mr Peck—The weather is close & this evening I heard two Musquetoes, only one of which ventured to light upon me—I dare say they are thicker at Cohansie!—Each Wednesday & Saturday we dine on Fish all the Summer, always plenty of *Rock, Perch,* & *Crabs,* & often Sheeps-Head and Trout!—

Thursday 18.

Very ill most of last night with a violent Dysentery; I fear a frequency of this disease will at-length fix & ruin me—It continues to Day, & with no less rage, I cannot eat nor drink, am low Spirited Think constantly of Home;—Sometimes repent my having come into this Colony, & blame myself for having been persuaded to turn out of my road to public Business—But when I reflect closely I justify the Conduct, & resign myself *Body* & *Soul* & *Employment* to God who has the Hearts of all in his hand, & who I am persuaded, if he has any thing for me to do in Life, will preserve, & in a measure fit me for it, if not, I am in his Hand, let him do as seemes good in his Eyes—At Dinner the Colonel invited me to ride with him to a Mill of his which is repairing, about eight miles Distance; I accepted his Invitation, gave the children a few Hours for Play, & went with the Colonel *Ben* was along The Face of the earth seems covered with mocking-Birds, but not one of them sing, they seem vastly busy but it is in collecting Food—Not a bird, except now & then *Robbin-Redbreast* is heard to sing in this Feverish Month— Nature seems cheerless and gloomy! The Evening is hot, but the Ride was agreeable, it was useful too; for I grow much better; The Jolting of the Horse seemed salutary, my Pain subsided, I returned almost wholly relieved in the evening, drank my Coffee, went soon to my Room, gave thanks to my divine *restorer* & laid me down to rest—

Fryday 19.

I slept through the night in *quiet* and ease, & rose perfectly relieved Mr *Carter* at Breakfast advised me to take with him Some *Salt-Petre,* as a useful Dieuretick but I declin'd—Mr *Grubb* came in about twelve o-Clock from *Sabine-Hall.* Colonel *Carter* gave an Entertainment Yesterday to celebrate his Birth-Day; & had a numerous & gay Company.—This young Gentleman (Mr *Grubb*) appears to be a person of Capacity & Improvement; he was Educated in England, & has been assistant to a Merchant on *James's River* in this Colony for some time past. This Summer he has been totally Idle—He proposes week after week to set out for Williamsburg, & Sail thence home, but he stays. He has much good nature, is an agreeable companion—I pity him.—He seems fond of Miss *Betsy Lee*—But he is too fluctuating in his mind to settle there, or with any Girl whatever Yet—

Saturday 20.

Ben Mr *Taylor*, Mr *Grubb*, & *Harry* went to the Potowmack to a Fish Feast—Come, Fithian, what do you mean by keeping hived up sweating in your Room—Come out & air yourself—But I choose to stick by the Stuff. The Colonel too, very kindly, offered me a Seat in his Chariot to Nomini Court-House, but I declin'd Mr Lane & Mr Warden came in towards evening—Both in high Spirits. But Mr *Lane* was (as they say) "Half Seas over"—they sat & chated noisily til nine—Evening clear a full Moon, & very light—Our neighbourhood seems alive with little Negro Boys playing in every part—

Sunday 21.

Nomini Church—Parson Smith gave us after Prayrs, which he was obliged to read himself, a useful Sermon; poor man he seemed to labour hard—Dined with us Captain *Walker*, Mr *Lane*, Mrs *Lane*, Mr *Wadman*, Mr *Warden*.

Soon after Dinner I left the company & retired to my chamber where I seem commonly most happy—

[LETTER OF PHILIP V. FITHIAN TO PALATIAH WEBSTER]

Nomini-Hall Virginia, augt 21st 1774.

SIR.

I have an oppertunity by some gentlemen, who go from this Colony to the Congress, of writing you a line according to promise, since I saw you, I have been in good health; The reigning spirit in

Virginia is liberty—And the universal topic politicks—I suppose it to be the same with you God Almighty knows where these civil tumults will end; probably not without War & Blood!—I have but little to say but to present you my best regards, remember me to your sister—To Miss Cunningham—The Miss Armitages—Miss Cooks—I hope to see you the last of october, when I expect to be in Town—Probably you can make it convenient for you to take a ramble into the country at that time. I hope to be at leisure, and shall be proud to attend you—Mr Blain, who favours me by carrying these is a Gentleman of my ac-quaintance in this Colony, a Merchant of Note, I shall thank you if you will take some notice of him,—And by him, as he is to return immedi-ately I beg you write Tell me how matters go in Town—Tell me what you know of the Country—Tell me much about the *Sex* you love —Remember to ask Mr Blain the hour he returns, and dont fail to send me a line

   I am, Sir,

     with great regard,

      Yours.

PALATIAH WEBSTER.

        PHILIP V. FITHIAN.

[LETTER OF PHILIP V. FITHIAN TO NATHANIEL DONNALD, JR.]

      Nomini Hall. Augt: 21st. 1774.

SIR.

I wrote you a line in great haste, just before I left home, and two days before that I had the pleasure of your company with ladies in an evening excursion—We have here no artificial gardens; Nor can we select out a company of sociable equals whenever we are in a humour for a walk—Here we either strain on Horseback from home to Church, or from house to House if we go out at all—Or we walk alone into a dark Meadow, or tall wood—But I love solitude, and these lonely recesses suit exactly the feeling of my mind—I recieved lately a letter from Cohansie, in which I am informed of the Death of Uncle *Seeley*—The family and neighbourhood will have suffered a great loss!—I suppose you join in the general language, and assert your liberties and oppose oppression. I hope at least you are on the right side of the question.

The City, I dare say, is in great tumult if not in consternation. I wish it was convenient for me to be in town when the gentlemen from the respective Colonies shall meet in general Congress—This is out of my power, but I can wish for their union, and usefulness. Mr *Blain*, the gentleman who forwards my letter, is a Merchant of Note, in this Colony, you will oblige me if you take notice of him while he is in Town.—You will not fail to write me a line, and give to Mr Blain the moment you recieve mine, least he leave town and I be disappointed.

My compliments to all friends,

from Sir,

Yours

P. V. FITHIAN.

Mr Nathl: Donnald Junr:

[LETTER OF PHILIP V. FITHIAN TO MISS RUTH WEBSTER]

Nomini-Hall August 21st 1774.

MADAM.

I send you these inclosed in a line to your Brother.

I do this that you may recieve the letter, for there seems to be little security in a letter directed to you, the youngsters are so curious to examine what is written for you—I understand that you never recieved my last dated "May 1774. Delaware River on board the swallow." I wish I could detect the impudent interceptor—You have then at last condescended to visit Cohansie! I hear by Mr *Ewing* that you was in the Country several weeks—Does it delight you, to hear the noise of Birds, of Lowing Cows, of Sheep, and of chatt'ring poultry, instead of the City-Cries? But I forget myself—Did you see that your Merchant, who, as I mentioned to you, is so moved with youn[g] person and manner? I suppose he was your constant and unwearied gallant—I expect that according to promise, you spent some part of your time with my sister—She a little Vixen, has never scribbled me a line, but I am level with her, for I have been as silent as she—Miss Beatty, that girl you seem so passionately fond of, is I expect, before this returned—She is indeed a lovely girl, if I say more you will call me partial—At any rate, as you correspond, I beg you will present her with my compliments, which are indeed but empty, thread-bare things—But Madam, I assure you they are the most valuable articles I can now transmit—I expect to be in town by the latter end of October, or beginning of November—If you are not too busy when you recieve this, I beg you will sit yourself instantly down and write me a friendly answer—This I think my due since I have written to you only, and to no other Lady either in town or country

I am, Madam,

P. V. Fithian

To Miss Ruth Webster.

[JOURNAL]

Monday 22.

Mr *Grubb* & Ben returned last evening—They spent their Day in *Richmond*[170]—I wrote to day several letters. to Philadephia One to Miss *Webster*. To her *Brother*. To *John McCalla* junr—To Mr *Donald*—These I send by 'Squire *Lee* who is to be of the Party—After School *Ben, Grubb,* & Myself rode to the *'Squires*—He took us into his Garden, shewed and gave us great Plenty of fine Peaches, *Nectarines* &c

He has a large Garden, & great abundance of fruit—His People were shaking the trees to prepare the Peaches for Brandy

[LETTER OF PHILIP V. FITHIAN TO JOHN McCALLA, JR.]

Nomini Hall Virginia Augt: 22d: 1774.

Sir.

Since I left you I have heard not a syllable about you, whether the ague has left you, whether you have left the City removed to Alexandria, as you proposed in the spring, in short both yourself and fame have been, as to you, wholly silent—
I have now an oppertunity which I gladly improve of sending you a line, and I beg that by the same conveyance you will send me an

Answer—There are many from this Colony to attend the general Congress, seven by appointment, the others out of curiosity, by Mr *Blain*, a gentleman of my acquaintance in this Colony, a Merchant of Note I forward this; you will oblige me if you use him with civility.—

I cannot write home at present; if you should write soon to Cohansie, please to mention to whoever you write to that I am in good health; that the neighbourhood is in good health; and that I propose to return about the latter end of october—I can transmit nothing now concerning public affairs, you will know by the gentlemen from this province that the reigning spirit is liberty—I hope Mr and Mrs Hollinshead keep clear of the fevers this fall; but I fear they will suffer in that common calamity. I think they ought to remove to the City for a few weeks in september when the disorder rages where they reside—My best compliments attend your family, and to Miss *Pratt*, Miss *Boyd* and others of my acquaintance in town as shall be convenient.

> I am, Sir, with great truth
>   and Regard your most obedient
>   Most humble Servt:

P. V. FITHIAN

Mr John McCalla Junr:

I shall thank you if you will send me the latest Journal, Gazette, and the Packet.

[JOURNAL]

Teusday 23.

Blessed be God who yet preserves me in perfect health—*Priss* has another fitt of the Ague these Disorders are giving Alarms. in a few Weeks I suppose they will grow numerous & troublesome—A violent Gust of Wind, Rain, & some Thunder we had about twelve o Clock, the Country seems to be afloat—A [I] received this Morning a Note from a School Master in the Village, who signs himself "Brother Quill" He sends me with his compliments a Question. To multiply 12 £ 12s 12½d by itself in Cross multiplication—And tells me the Answer is 160 £ 1s 6d his way, viz by Decimals—I did not alter his answer, but suffered him to continue satisfied with his own performance.—

Wednesday 24.

Stormy—A poor Man arrived from Maryland with Grain to grind. It was wet—He saw Mr Carter and Mr *Randolph*—Mr Randolph wore a red Coat—the Marylander asked *Bob* which was the master of the House—*Bob* with his usual impudence answered, the Man you see drest in a scarlet Coat—Who then says he is the other in a frowsled Wig?—He is says *Bob* my fathers Clerk—The Colonel heard this Anecdote of *Bob*, which entertained him, While we were dining. I hear nothing of the Ague abroad, it seems to go by turns, sometimes brief then exceeding scarce—all this day the wind North East rainy.

Thursday 25.

Still stormy. The Gentlemen who are sailing up the Bay to the Congress have a disagreeable time—This is a true August Northeaster, as we call it in Cohansie—*Ben* is in a wonderful *Fluster* lest he shall have no company to-morrow at the Dance—But blow high, blow low, he need not be afraid; *Virginians* are of genuine Blood—They will dance or die!—I wrote some at my Letter for Mr *Peck*—The people here pronounce Shower "Sho-er"—And what in New-Jersey we call a Vendue here they a "Sale"—All Taverns they call "Ordinary's"—When a Horse is frolicsome & brisk, they, say at once he is "gayly"—she [if he] is mischievous, they call him, "vicious."—At five, with *Ben*. I rode out for exercise—After a while we arrived at *George-Lee's*—He gave us some excellent Peaches—He returned with us to Mr Turberville's—We met here with Miss *Betsy Lee*, Mr *Grubb*, *Lancelot Lee* & here we spent the evening—*Fish-Feasts*, & *Fillies*, Loud disputes concerning the Excellence of each others Colts—Concerning their Fathers, Mothers (for so they call the Dams) Brothers, Sisters, Uncles, Aunts, Nephews, Nieces, & Cousins to the fourth Degree!—All the Evening Toddy constantly circulating —Supper came in, & at Supper I had a full, broad, sattisfying View of Miss *Sally Panton*—I wanted to hear her converse, but poor Girl any thing She attempted to say was drowned in the more polite & useful Jargon about Dogs & Horses!—For my Part, as I was unwilling to be singular, if I attempted to push in a word, I was seldom heard, & never regarded, & yet they were constantly refering their Cases to me, as to a supposed honest fellow, I suppose because I wear a black Coat, & am generally silent; at Home I am thought to be noisy enough; here I am thought to be silent & circumspect as a *Spy* —How different the Manners of the People! I try to be as cheerful as I can. & yet I am blamed for being stupid as a Nun—

Fryday 26.

Mr Christian came while we were at Breakfast—Soon after came Miss *Washington*, Miss *Hale* & the Miss *Lee's*—I kept myself in my Room pretty Close—Towards evening Mrs *Carter*, Miss *Washington*, Miss *Hale*, Mrs *Christien* & *Myself* had a thorough ramble, first thro' the Garden—We gathered some Figs, the Ladies seem fond of them, I cannot endure them—Then we stroll'd down the Pasture quite to the River, admiring the Pleasantness of the evening, & the delightsome Prospect of the River, Hills, Huts on the Summits, low Bottoms, Trees of various Kinds, and Sizes, Cattle & Sheep feeding some near us, & others at a great distance on the green sides of the Hills, People, some fishing, others working, & others in the Pasture among the Horses;—The Country emphatically in her goodly Variety! I love to walk on these high Hills where I can see the Tops of tall Trees lower than my Feet, at not half a miles Distance— Where I can have a long View of many Miles & see on the Summits of the Hills Clusters of Savin Trees, through these often a little Farm-House, or Quarter for Negroes; these airy Situations seem to me to be the Habitations of Health, and Vigor—We return'd, & all were apparently well satisfied with the walk—Evening was spent jovially in Dancing, at Supper, I left the Company, being not very well, & retired to my Chamber, Thanks to my heavenly Father, that I can enjoy a competent Measure of Health when many are sick around—A Note from Mr Lowe. Miss *Betsy Lee*, & her Brother came in just at night—Miss *Lee* seems cheerful, dances well, sings agreeably, appears free of formality, & Haughtiness the Common foible here,—

Saturday 27.

The morning spent in setting coppies, Sums &c, for the School— After Breakfast, I spent a couple of Hours in the Dancing-Room—

Mr *Lee* in our Room raved against the Scotch—He swore that if his Sister should marry a Scotchman, he would never speak with her again; & that if he ever Shall have a Daughter, if She marries a Scotchman he shoots her dead at once!—At twelve I rode to Mr Washingtons, the Country extremely pleasant Dined with the *Parson*, his *Brother*, Mrs *Smith*, Miss Pettit, Mr Blain, Mr Buckner,[171] & several of Mr *Lowes* Boys; Mr Lowe was from home. On my return I found no company, except *Grubb* who had come in my absence. We spent the Evening after sipping our Coffee in Chat with Mr & Mrs Carter.

Sunday 28.

Mr *Grubb* rose very early, having yesterday made every previous necessary preparation, & set out for Home about One hundred miles Distance. He has so much good Nature, is always so cheerful, & at the same time void of any thing malicious, clamorous & impudent, that I cannot but esteem & very much respect him—On some whimsical unsubstantial Miff or other, however, our Girls cannot endure him—he wrote them some Copies the other Day, & tho' he writes a much finer neater hand than I they would not allow it, nor hardly—Strive to imitate—I laughed at the ridiculous, the perfect Picture of Female *Caprice*, & *Obstinacy* in Miniature—Sermon is to Day at Ucomico, so that I keep my Room—I wrote several Letters which are to be forwarded by Mr *Blain*, one to *Jack Peck*, one to *John Duffield*,[172] at Dr Shippen's[173] Junr Philadelphia, & one to *Laura*. I begun also a Sermon I understand by Mrs *Carter* & *Ben* who were at Church, that the *Parson* was unable to read Prayrs or Preach, having a Fever, but that there was a thronged Assembly; many I am told, have the Ague & Fever, but none are dangerous or have it fixed—

[LETTER OF PHILIP V. FITHIAN TO ELIZABETH BEATTY]

Nominy-Hall. August 28: 1774.

To LAURA.

There is a Letter of yours lying before me, in which you say "that if I had continued writing to you, it is more than probable you had been as negligent as ever; but that my leaving off for a Time has at last extorted a Letter from you"—Mighty pretty! I dare say the

Sentiment is genuine, & you may be assured that I allow & believe it.

You are not, therefore, to account this any thing more than the Ghost, the Shade of a Letter; for, thinking this an extraordinary Case, I have gone beyond my usual Manner of speaking, in Order to convince you of my Resolution—And *swore* that I will not interrupt you til' I have received several.

If you receive this by the Conveyance I expect (I send it by Col: *Lee* who attends the Congress) it will be a few Days before I leave Virginia; for I intend, by the Permission of Heaven, being at Home by the beginning of November at farthest.

In the mean Time, since I ardently wish your constant and perpetual Felicity, from a deep-rooted Friendship, which I have discovered in a thousand Variations, suffer me to borrow a Form of Mr Addison, & put up one important Prayr in your Behalf "Ye guardian Angels to whose Care heaven has intrusted its dear Laura, guide her still forward in the Paths of Virtue, defend her from the Insolence & wrongs of this undiscerning World; At length, when we must no more converse with such Purity on Earth, lead her gently hence, innocent & unreproveable to a better Place, where by an easy Transition from what She now is, She may shine forth an Angel of Light."

It would be bold & presumptuous, or I would with Earnestness & Sincerity extend the Wish a little farther, but transfer it to Fortune, & pray that She would make you mine. I ought, however, to be cautious here—In so nice a Case, Truth & Virtue are often thought impertinent.

I advise you, upon the whole, to consult & examine the Prospect you have of substantial Happiness, when you are about to change your State for Life. Inform yourself, so far as you are able, of the *Quality* & *Measure* of what you think your chief Happiness—Your Satisfaction & Comfort will consist in.

Place this against necessary Distress & Perplexity; You will thereby have a clearer & fuller View of both; Your Judgement will be less confused; & more likely to fix to Advantage;—You are to consider that a wrong Choice brings on a Train of Curses; but view it in the other Light, & it is almost a State of unmixed Pleasures—

I am, Madam yours

PHILIP. V. FITHIAN.

[JOURNAL]

Monday 29.

Miss *Fanny* in School to Day, but not entirely well of her Sores made by the *Ticks*—*Ben* complains of a pain in his breast; he seems to have many symptoms of Weakness in his breast—I attempted to take a rough Draught of the Great House for myself—Evening after Coffee the C[o]lonel entertained us by playing on the Harmonica.

Teusday 30.

Mr *Carter* rides to Westmoreland Court. By him I send my Letters to Mr *Blain,* who is going to the Congress—*Ben* seems to be no better; has a slight Fever, pain in his Breast, & Uneasiness, I fear he is bordering on a Consumption—His fond Mother discovers great Anxiety, & true affection. Once I too had a fond indulgent Mother; when I was sick, or otherwise distress'd, She was always impatient til my Health & Ease returned; & She used to urge me likewise by precept & example to strive for an habitual Preparation for Sickness and Death! But oh! She has gone & left me, & Friendship seems to have been buried with her!—Formality & Pretence are common enough, but Sincerity & affection are exceeding rare—Mrs *Carter* thinks it better for *Ben* to sleep at the Great-House til he grows better, for the advantage of giving him medicine—I seem now when it is late in the Evening, lonely, & a little fearful, at least I think on what I made a Subject for a merry Hour, when I was at Home last, & a young Lady was complaining of being fearful at Night, & afraid to sleep in a Room alone—There are now (asleep I suppose) in this House, below Stairs Mr *Randolph,* & Mr *Burney* the Cooper; two clever lusty youngsters, & in the Room next to mine *Bob* & *Harry* sleep—I feel yet gloomy; *Ben* is missing, & which is worse, he is sick—

Wednesday 31.

Last Fryday, Saturday, Sunday, Monday, Teusday, & this Day have been perfectly fair, but yesterday & to Day are very hot—*Ben* quits reading & is quite unwell—Dined with us Mr *Wadman:* He is, I believe, a Man of a good understanding, but desperate in his religious Principles—

Thursday Septemr: 1st: 1774.

One other *Calm, sunny, sweltering* day

The Colonel says it is the hottest Day we have had—I keep myself caged up in my Room, & cannot venture out on my usual *walk* or Ride for exercise—Through divine goodness I continue in perfect Health, but as skinny & meagre as tho' I was continually sick—*Ben* seems a little more pert today—Evening it Lightens in the North West.

Fryday 2.

Extreme hot to day—Yesterday a Negro Child about six years old sickened as to appearance with the Ague & Fever, & to Day about eleven in the morning it expired! It is remarkable that the Mother has now lost seven successively, none of which have arrived to be ten years old!—The Negroes all seem much alarm'd, & our School make it a Subject for continual Speculation; They seem all to be free of any terror at the Prescence of Death; *Harry* in special signified a Wish that his turn may be next. I should be glad if his desire were wise; & he was as fit for the business of the other world, as he seems willing to leave the business of this—In the evening this unexpected Death was the Subject of Conversation in the House—Mr *Carter* observed, that he thought it the most desirable to die of a Short Illness. If he could have his Wish he would not lie longer than two days; be taken with a Fever, which should have such an unusual effect on his Body as to convince him that it would be fatal, and gradually increase till it affected a Dissolution—He told us that his affairs are in Such a state that he should be able to dictate a Will which might be written in five Minutes, & contain the disposal of his estate agreeable to his mind—He mentioned to us the Substance—"That he would leave Mrs *Carter* 6000 £ Serling; & leave the remainder of his Estate to be disposed among his children as the Law directs."—

He told us likewise, with great firmness, that if he hives [lives] to see his children grown, he will pay no regard to age, but give his wealth to Him who bids fairest to be useful to mankind—That he allows all an equal oppertunity of improvement, but the One who is found then improved shall with the Learning inherit also the Sub-stance—*Dennis* the Lad who waits at Table, I took into the School to day at his Fathers request, He can spell words of one syllable pretty readily. He is to come as he finds oppertunity.

Saturday 3.

Indeed says Mrs Carter at Breakfast, the Lightning, Rain, & Thunder, disturbed me, & kept me padding from Room to Room all Night; I first had the Girls Beds removed as far as possible from the Chimneys —then had lights placed in the passage; and then but without *rest* or *pleasure,* I wandered through the house silent & lonely like a disturbed Ghost!—It has however effected an agreeable change in the Air; which is now cool & agreeable. I was invited this morning by Captain *Fibbs* [Gibbs] to a *Barbecue:* this differs but little from the Fish Feasts, instead of Fish the Dinner is roasted *Pig,* with the proper apendages, but the Diversion & exercise are the very same at both— I declined going and pleaded in ex[c]use unusual & unexpected Business for the School—By appointment is to be fought this Day near Mr *Lanes* two fist Battles between four young Fellows. The Cause of the battles I have not yet known; I suppose either that they are lovers, & one has in Jest or reality some way supplanted the other; or has in a merry hour call'd him a *Lubber,* or a *thick-Skull,* or a *Buckskin,* or a *Scotchman,* or perhaps one has mislaid the others hat, or knocked a peach out of his Hand, or offered him a dram without wiping the mouth of the Bottle; all these, & ten thousand more quite as triffling & ridiculous, are thought & accepted as just Causes of immediate Quarrels, in which every diabolical Stratagem for Mastery is allowed & practised, of Bruising, Kicking, Scratching, Pinching, Biting, Butting, Tripping, Throtling, Gouging, Cursing, Dismembring, Howling, &c. This spectacle, (so loathsome & horrible!) generally is attended with a crowd of People! In my opinion, (others may think for themselves) animals which seek after & relish such odious and filthy amusements are not of the human species, they are destitute of the remotest pretension to humanity; I know not how they came by their form, by the help of which they are permitted to associate with Men, unless it has been (unfortunate for the World!) by an intermixture of the meaner kind of Devils with prostitute Monkeys!—This however, I cannot determine; But I think all such should be deemed by the community infectious, & suspended at least any kind of intercourse, til, either the lineage be settled & recorded, or those shrew'd Characteristicks of a spurious, illegitimate claim to kindred with men be in a good Measure abated.

Sunday 4.

We had last night a flood of rain, the wind North East stormy—No Church to Day—Mr Carter sent down to his Mill-Dam, & channel all his people to try if they can secure them; he gives them Rum, & a Shilling a man—

I read Prayrs, by the desire of the Parents, at the Grave over the deceased Child *Priscilla, Nanccy, Fanny, Betsy, Ben, Bob, Harry,* & Myself, & about forty or fifty Negroes were present. Neither the Father nor the Mother of the Child went out; imitating the example they see in others, & stay from an affectation of overflowing Grief.

Monday 5.

There is wonderful *To do,* this morning among the Housekeeper & children, at the great house. They assert that a Man or a Spirit came into the Nursery about one o-Clock this morning—That if it was indeed a Spirit the Cause of his appearance is wholly unknown; but if it was Flesh & blood they are pretty confident that the design was either to rob the House, or commit fornication with *Sukey,* (a plump, sleek, likely Negro Girl about sixteen)—That the doors & windows were well secured, but that by some secret manner, unknown to all, the *Thing* opened the Cellar door, went through the Cellar, & up the narrow dark Stairs (which are used only on necessary occasions, as when the great Stair way is washing or on some such account)—That it left the said Cellar door standing open, & besides unbar'd, & threw open the East Window in the little Room, in order, as they wisely supposed, to have, if it should be hurried, a ready passage out—That it had previously put a small wedge in the Lock of the Nursery Door, where several of the young Ladies, & the said *Sukey* sleep, so that when they were going to Bed they could not Lock nor bolt the door, but this they all believed was done in mischief by the children, & went thereupon to bed, without suspicion of harm, with the door open—That Sukey some time in the Night discovered Something lying by her Side which she knew to be a Man by his having Breeches—That She was greatly surprised, & cry'd out suddenly to the others that a Man was among

them, & that the Man *tickled* her, & said *whish, whish*—That on this
She left the Bed & run & squeased herself in by the side of Miss Sally
the House-keeper, but that by this time the Whole Room was awake
& alarmed—That when the thing knew there was a discovery it
stamped several times on the floor, shook the Bedstead by the side
of which it lay, rattled the Door several Times & went down Stairs
walking very heavy for one barefoot—That on its leaving the Room
the Hous[e]Keeper went to Ben Carters Chamber, & that he rose &
they all went down & found the Doors & window as I have mentioned—All this with many other material accidents is circulating
through the family to Day; some conclude it was a Ghost because
it would not speak—But, more probably it was one of the warm-
blooded, well fed young Negroes, trying for the company of buxom
Sukey—The Colonel however, at Breakfast gave out that if any one
be caught in the House, after the family are at Rest, on any Pretence what ever, that Person he will cause to be hanged!—This
Afternoon *Nelson* the Lad who waits in our School, was in the woods
about half a mile off, where he met with & kill'd a *Rattle-Snake* having six Rattles—He cut off the head, & brought Home the remainder
of the Body, which we have skin'd & stuff'd—Mrs Carter complains
to Day of the Tooth-Ach, & a slight Fever.

Teusday 6.

The day fine—It is whispered to Day that B... is the Ghost that
walk'd in the Nursery the other night, but I think the report is false,
and arises from calumny. We had an expectation of company to day,
but are disappointed. We dined on Fish & Crabs, which were provided for our company, to-morrow being Fish-Day—I begun a Sermon Job XXIII. 3. 4. We have too vagrant Tinkers with us mending
several articles, one of whom is this afternoon violent sick with the
Fever & Ague—I rode to my old spot, the Corn field, by chance
met with Mr Taylor. I walked with him among the Tobacco Cotton
&c. He gave me Directions for raising the latter.—Cotton must be
planted about the middle of May in rich Land, prepared with Hills,
& made very mellow. When up it must be weeded & kept clean, it
must be top'd & suckered as Tobacco, otherwise it runs too much to
vine. Towards the Fall it will begin to open, when the opened pods
mu[s]t be gathered & laid by til dry, then the Cotton pick'd out &
clean'd—

Wednesday 7.

Mrs Carter not very well; is troubled with a small tooth-Ach Fever
& a Cold—Every leisure minute I spend in writing at my Sermon—
Dined with us Mr Sorrel, & Mr . . . . on Fish, Rock, Perch, finc *Crabs,*
& a large fresh *Mackerel.* Yesterday & to day I have been a little
pained & pretty much alarmed, at an unusual feeling in my right
arm. Almost all the Summer I have felt an obstruction when I would
lift up my arm. But now it is a trembling steady *knawing* down the
under part of my arm & Wrist, without unless when I move it suddenly—Evening I walked throug the pasture to the River, the Hills
are green, since the late rains, & look fine tip'd with the setting Sun.

Thursday 8.

Cloudy & cool. I rise now by half after six—I found it necessary to
flogg *Bob* & *Harry* on account of lying in bed, after I come into
School—At twelve Mr & Mrs *Carter,* with all the Family except
Ben, Harry & Myself; Ben staid of choice, & Harry I kept at Home
on account of a sullen Impudence when I dismiss'd them—I told
them that they both had my leave to go but at the same time it was
my advice that they should stay—Harry then answered "D—n my
Soul but i'll go!" At this I informed him that he had at once dismiss'd himself from my authority. & without singular signs of Submission I should never take him under my direction more—And
therefore that he had general & unbounded Liberty to go not only
to the Horse Race, but *where* & *when* he chose—He seem'd startled,
& began to moderate his answer: I ordered him out of the Room, &
told him to use his liberty. Mrs *Carter* took with her all the young
Ladies & all her children—*Ben* & I with great satisfaction dined alone.
Nelson, to Day, kill'd another Rattle Snake; near the place where he
kill'd the other, which had twelve Rattles—Harry grew sick and refused to go to the Race, he came soon to my room & with every
Sign of Sorrow for his conduct begg'd me to forgive him, at first I
refused, but at length I took him in, yet informed him that I shall
pass over no other instance of what may be called rudeness only.—
The Colonel on his return, in the evening informed us that the Race
was curious, & that the Horses were almost an even match—That
the Betts were Drawn & no Money paid—That the Rider of one of
the Horses weighed only forty Seven pound—Strange that so little

substance in a human Creature can have strength & skill sufficient to manage a Horse in a Match of Importance—Something alarming happened a few nights ago in the Neighbourhood at Mr *Sorrels*[174] a House in sight—It is supposed that his Negres had appointed to murder him, several were found in his bed chamber in the middle of the night—his Wife waked—She heard a whispering, one perswading the other to go—On this She waked her Husband, who run to his Gun; but they escaped in the dark—Presumption is so strong together with a small confession of the Fellows, that three are now in Prison—The ill Treatment which this unhappy part of mankind receives here, would almost justify them in any desperate attempt for gaining that *Civility*, & *Plenty* which tho' denied them, is here, commonly bestowed on Horses!—Now, Laura, I sleep in fear too, though my Doors & Windows are all secured!—

Fryday 9.

Mr *Stadley* came in before Breakfast. He inform'd us that Governor *Dunmore* has gone to the Frontiers with about 400 Men to subdue the Indians—That the Indians seem disheartened, & leave their towns, & are unwilling to fight—Mrs *Carter*, out of Compliment, this morning presented to *Ben* & *I* for staying at home yesterday, a large fine *Cake*—Dined with us a Stranger—*Ben* with great Humour either out of a *Bravado* or for Revenge gave out in the Family to day that it is the opinion of a certain *Female*, of considerable Note in the family, that all the male Children which shall be born in this unlucky year, tho' they may be fair to the Sight, will be yet unable, from a Debility of Constitution, to do their Duty, with respect to Women, either married or single—That She has two reasons for this opinion,
1. Because the Air appears to her extremely *barren, weak,* & *ungenerative*—2. Because the Peaches, & other Fruit, are observed this year to have in them very few Kernels, at the same time that the Peaches are sweet & fair—I think that *Ben*, by this stratagem, whether it be real or otherwise, is levil with the invidious Vixen which suspected him of entering the Nursery to visit black-faced Sukey—

Saturday 10.

With the Boys I Surveyed a small field lying along the Richmond Road; the Colonel has a good *Theodolite* & other Aparatus for Sur-

veying—English Magazines, & Reviews arrived to Day—One of the
Books lately published I am desirous to purchase viz.—Dr *Henry's*
History of Great Britain on a new Plan. This history is to be contained in ten Books, each of which will be divided into seven chapters. In the first Chapter of every Book, the Author relates, the civil
& military History of Great Britain—The second chapter contains
the ecclesiastical History of the same period: the third presents us
with the history of our political constitution, Government, Laws, &
Courts of justice: the fourth is employed upon what relates to Learning & Learned men: the fifth investigates the State of the useful &
ornamental Arts: the sixth enquires into that of commerce, Shipping, Money, with the prices of commodities: & the last Chapter of
every Volume is alloted to a Detail of the Manners, Virtues, Vices,
remarkable Customs, Language, Dress, Diet, & Diversions of the
Great Britains—Six o-Clock, Mrs *Turberville*, Miss *Jenny Corbin*,
and Miss *Turberville* came in; Miss *Corbin* has been, all the Summer,
at her Brothers on Rapahanock forty miles distant.[175]—I saw, in the
evening, in Mr Randalls[176] Room, a Young man about twenty years
old, totally deaf, & dumb! He is well-set, lusty, & likely; he is cheerful, good natur'd, extremely dextrous, quick of apprehension, &, in
short, very conversable, & sociable by signs—he was taken to the
much famed Dr *Graham*,[177] when he was in this Colony trumpeting
about his own unproved Abilities; he fumbled with the unfortunate
Lad, by blooding, gouging, boreing &c. putting him to torture and
expence without any possible expectation of help—He Sustains
among his neighbours the Reputation of being, *honest, industrious,*
& *useful*—He supports by Labour his mother, & himself; He is remarkably fond of Cloths; & vastly curious, & nice in examining every
article of dress, where he has the smallest intimacy—He abstains entirely from strong Liquor.—And what most of all produced admiration in me, was his taking a Pen & writing his Name "*Coley Reed*,"
in a good legible Hand, better indeed, than the Bulk of planters are
able to do! But he can write nothing more—

Sunday 11.

Ben rode out yesterday after Dinner and returned this morning; but
came on foot, I begin to suspect him of being actually engaged in
what several alledge against him—But I will keep off so long as I
possibly can, so unwelcome, so unwelcome & so Base a thought of

its Reality—After Breakfast Mr *Stadley* left us; I feel always Sorry when he leaves the Family; his entire *good-Nature, Cheerfulness, Simplicity,* & *Skill* in Music have fixed him firm in my esteem— None go to Ucomico Church to day—Towards evening, I took a book in my hand, & strolled down the Pasture quite to the Bank of the River—Miss *Stanhope, Priss, Nancy, Fanny* & *Betsy Carter* were just passing by—They walked to the *Mill;* there they entered a Boat, & for exercise & amusement were rowed down the River quite to the granary, & then went to angling—I walked to them, & to-gether we all marched Home to *Coffee.*

Monday 12.

We threatned having a Fire this morning—I wrote at my Sermon —From the Ship lying at *Leeds,* arrived this afternoon our new Coach —It is a plain carriage, upper part black, lower Sage or Pea-Green— The Harness is neat strong, & suitable for the Country. Price 120 £ Sterling—In the same Ship Mrs *Carter* imports about 30 £ value in plate in a pair of fashionable Goblets; Pair of beautiful Sauce-Cups; & a Pair of elegant Decanter-holders—*Ben* introduced into our Room a plain useful Book-Case, in which we class & place our Books in order. after School, I took a Book, and walked through the Pasture strolling among Horses, Cows, & Sheep, grazing on the Hills & by the River.

Teusday 13.

We thought of Fire this morning, but put it off—Ben's mare is not yet heard of, though he has had a Boy almost constantly searching about for her—It is curious to see the Girls imitating what they see in the great House; sometimes tying a String to a Chair & then run buzzing back to imitate the Girls spinning; then getting Rags & washing them without water—Very often they are knitting with Straws, small round stockings, Garters &c—Sometimes they get sticks & splinter one end of them f[o]r *Brushes,* or as they call them here *Clamps,* & spitting on part of the floor, they scrubb away with great vigor—& often at a small game with Peach-stones which they call *checks*—Evening after School I rode to the much Frequented Corn-field, Mr Taylor was from Home the evening cloudy, cool, but fine, The Planters now begin to cut their Tobacco.

Wednesday 14.

Mr *Carter* received word to day that he has had brought very lately for his Mill 7000 Bushels of Wheat at 4s 6d pr Bushel.—I am at a Loss to know where he will dispose of such vast Quantities! The Colonel who is often pidling in some curious experiment, is to day making some Printers Ink—He tells me the Materials are Lint-seed-Oil, Wheat-Bread, Onions, & Turpentine, a rank compound truely —then for Black, Lamp-Black, red, Vermillion—*Ben*, found his mare lost in last Saturday's Visit, poor Brute! She was confin'd in the Pasture where he left her, in which being very large She had been concealed.—Mr *Smith*, who was wounded last Spring by a Shot of his Brother is lately dead, & it is said by the Wounds which he received from his Brother!—

Thursday 15.

Ben is much better: he has return'd to his Bed in my Room, but complains often of the pain in his Breast.—I put him to begin & read some select odes in Horace—He works arithmetic but is only in Reduction—He dispises Greek, & therefore makes little or no progress in that Language—He is reading in course the Eneid Lib 3—He has an unconquerable Love for Horses; he often tells me that he should have been a skilfull, & useful Groom; that he should be more fond & careful of a favourite Horse than of a *Wife*, or than his *victuals*, or than any thing whatever! I never saw a Person, in any Diversion, Recreation or amusement, who seemed so full of Pleasure & enjoyment as he is when on Horse back, or even in the company of a Horse! He seems to possess as warm a regard for them as Dr *Swift* had for the Houyhnhnms—But I cannot discover that Ben has so cordial an enmity to Mankind as *Swift* had for the Yahoos.—*Bobs* passion for the same Animal is no less strong, but it is furious, & cruel, he rides excessive hard, & would ride always—*Harry's* Genius seems towards Cocks, & low Betts, much in company with the waiting Boys, &, against my strongest Remonstrances, & frequent severe corrections, he will curse, at times, horribly, & swear fearfully! he always, however, omits it when I am Present.—

Fryday 16.

Mrs *Carter*, this morning, with *Prissy, Nancy,* & *Bob* went in the New-Coach to the *Dance* at Stratford, the morning is mild, fair &

cool—The Colonel informed me that now his Mill-House Bake-Houses, Store Houses &c. with a clear unobstructed navigation is compleated, & that, he will rent them all to a Person properly qualified—or gladly employ a person who is capable, trusty & industrious enough to be the sole Director of so great & valuable Property—Dined with us captain *Walker*—He threw out several exceeding unpopular Sentiments with regard to the present amazing Disturbances through the Colonies—One in special I think proper to record because it fixes his Character, & declares him, in Spite of all pretence, an enemy to America—He asserted that no Officers (at Boston or elsewhere) are obliged, either by Law, or Right, to question or refuse any kind of orders which they receive from their Sovereign, or commanding Officer—But I account every man, who possesses, & publishes such sentiments in this Crisis of the Fate of a vast Empire, as great an enemy to America at least, as Milton's *Arch-Devil* was to Mankind!—After School, we took the Theodolite, the Colonel along, & run several Lines, He seems perfectly well acquainted with the Art.

Saturday 17.

At eight I dismiss'd my small charge. Immediately after Breakfast I took some Boys, & went a Surveying; *Ben*, impatient of tiresome scurvy Home, strain'd off through the County—I run in to Dinner, the Colonel & I dined alone, we drank a Glass of Madeira, as a Health to absent Friends, after which I went again to the Field & survey'd till six in the evening; The Business of this Day has been to go round the inner Pasture About half an Hour after Sunset (when Women who love their Husbands & Families always come Home) Mrs Carter & the Girls arrived from Stratford She informed us that there was a large, genteel, and agreeable Company at the Dance; that the Ague & Fever have been & continue troublesome in that Neighbourhood; & that Word is arrived from Boston that Governor Gage has fired on the Town, & that it is expected his orders are to burn & beat it to Destruc-ion! *Ben* returned about seven from Westmoreland Courthouse—He informed us that Mr *Sorrels* Negroes had their trial there to Day, concerning their accusation of entering their Masters House in the night with an intention to murder Him—It was there proved (so far as Negroes evidence will go) that a Brother of this Sorrels early last Spring bribed some Negroes to Poison his Brother; & when that diabolical Attempt could not succeed, he has since tried to perswade them to murder Him!—But all Evidence against the Negroes was so weak & dark that the judges ordered them to be whiped & dismised them—Though the Law considers all Testimony given by a Negro against a White-Man as weak & unsubstantial; yet what the Negro said to Day on Oath of the younger Mr Sorrel, seems to gain much Belief with many who are candid, & unbiased Judges; & with me beyond all Scruple, it fixes on him the cursed Character of a *Fratricide!*—

Sunday 18.

The Colonel gave me, at Breakfast the offer of a Seat in his Boat to Church. The Morning was fine, & Nomini-River alive with Boats Canoes &c some going to Church, some fishing, & some Sporting— Mr *Smith* gave us a very practical Sermon against the common vices here, in particular against the practise of abusing Slaves—The report concerning Boston is much talked off & still confirmed!—We dined all at Mr Turberville's; Miss *Corbin* looks *fresh* & *plump* as ever. Towards evening arose a pretty furious Thunder-Gust, which we hardly escaped on our way home I observed that several, but in special Mr *Carter* is not pleased with Mr Smith's Sentiments of Slavery.

Monday 19.

The morning fine & cool, & produces in our School at last a fine Fire!—Fire looks & feels most welcome; and I observe it makes our children remarkably garrulous & noisy—I took cold by Saturdays unusual exercise, & to Day have a Pain through my head, sore throat, & the other common troubles in a Cold—This Day begins the examination of The Junior class at Nassau-Hall. Every time I reflect on that Place of retirement & Study, where I spent two years which I call the most pleasant as well as the most important Period in my past life—Always when I think upon the *Studies,* the *Discipline,* the *Companions,* the *Neighbourhood,* the *exercises,* & *Diversions,* it gives me a secret & real Pleasure, even the Foibles which often prevail there are pleasant on recollection; such as giving each other *names* & *characters;* Meeting & Shoving in the dark entries; knocking at Doors & going off without entering; Strowing the entries in the night with greasy Feathers; freezing the Bell; Ringing it at late Hours of the Night;—I may add that it does not seem disagreeable to think over the Mischiefs often practised by wanton Boys—Such are writing witty pointed anonymous Papers, in *Songs, Confessions, Wills, Soliliques, Proclamations, Advertisements* &c—Picking from the neighbourhood now & then a plump fat Hen or Turkey for the private entertainment of the Club "instituted for inventing & practising several new kinds of mischief in a secret polite Manner"— Parading bad Women—Burning Curse-John—Darting Sun-Beams upon the Town-People Reconoitering Houses in the Town, & ogling Women with the Telescope—Making Squibs, & other frightful compositions with Gun-Powder, & lighting them in the Rooms of timorous Boys, & new *comers*—The various methods used in naturalizing Strangers, of incivility in the Dining-Room to make them bold; writing them sharp & threatning Letters to make them smart; leading them at first with long Lessons to make them industrious—And trying them by Jeers & Repartee in order to make them choose their Companions &c &c—Evening after School with Mrs Carter, & the Girls I took a Walk thro the Pumpkin & Potatoe Vines. the Air is clear, cold & healthful. We drank our Coffee at the great House very sociably, round a fine Fire, the House And air feels like winter again.

Teusday 20.

Among the many womanish Fribbles which our little Misses daily practise, I discovered one to Day no less merry than natural; *Fanny & Harriot* by stuffing rags & other Lumber under their Gowns just below their Apron-Strings, were prodigiously charmed at their resemblanc to Pregnant Women! They blushed, however, pretty deeply on discovering that I saw them—We have to day both in the School & great-house steady Fires—Mr *Thomas Edwards* a reputable Planter in the Neighbourhood died this day about one o-Clock—I saw him last Sunday at Church when he was in good Health; was taken the same Evening, & hurried off at once!—Frail Man, how easily subdued!—

Wednesday 21.

We have a more particular account of the Death of Mr *Edwards.* About a twelve-month ago, he was suddenly siezed with a Fit of the

Palsy, his Foot, Side, Arm, & part of his Face then failed, & became useless, after some time, however, he grew better, & has since been apparently well; til Sunday evening last after the Shower, as he was walking in his Garden, he fell down in an instant, there happened to be help at hand, he only said these emphatical Words—"*Now I must die*"—He was carried in, & expired as I mentioned yesterday! —I am told that the Flux is in the upper part of this County—My cold continues; in the Evening on going to bed, I took a dose of Honey & Rum—

Thursday 22.

A pure cold northerly wind still blows, & we all keep Fires—Peaches & Fruit are omitted at Dinners, & Soup or Broth is brought in; Milk and Hominy at Breakfast too are laid by & Coffee & Sage Tea brought in; Our Suppers are Coffee & Bred & butter—*Neatness variety* & *Plenty* are reigning Characters in our worthy oconomist Mrs Carter. I read to Day, & am charm'd with a——of Lord Chesterfield. Letters to his natural Son, which I propose to purchase—After School, with Ben, I took a walk to Mr Turberville's—He has received a line from Colonel Lee at Philadelphia that the Congress is going on—That the account concerning Boston is false—Evening Lancelot Lee came in, & staid the night— He gave Ben & myself an Invitation to dine with him tomorrow, I took out of the Library & began to read Watts's Logic—

Fryday 23.

I spent some time in reviewing Geography & Logic—Mr Lee left us about twelve, & Ben rode out with him—Evening from Mr Turberville's I saw some *Barberry's, Sloes,* & *Pomegranates,* neither of which I had seen before—

Saturday 24.

Together with my Cold I have to Day a most disagreeable gathering on my middle Finger—I keep myself at home reading Logic—Evening the Colonel invited me to walk with him; he took me to his Mill, *Coopers, House, Channel, Meadows* &c, and was vastly particular in describing to me their particular uses—I begin to look with

eager Sollicitude to the time of my revisiting my friends & Relations
—It is, happily near—

Sunday 25.

The morning clear cool & very dry—I rode to Ucomico-Church, I was
surprised when the Psalm begun, to hear a large Collection of voices
singing at the same time, from a Gallery, entirely contrary to what
I have seen befor in the Colony, for it is seldom in the fullest Congregation's, that more sing than the Clerk, & about two others!—I am
told that a singing Master of good abilities has been among this
society lately & put them on the respectable Method which they, at
present pursue—I dined at *Mr Fishers,* among others I saw there, Dr
Steptoe, & Mr *Hamilton* who have lately been to Philadelphia—
They give various Reports concerning political affairs, & as to the
Congress nothing certain, so that I say nothing on that Score—
Their Remarks on the City & Inhabitants; The Country &c are curious—They allow the City to be fine, neat, & large; they complain a
little of the small Rooms, Uniformity of the Buildings, & several other
like faults—They call the Inhabitants grave & reserved; & the
Women remarkably homely, hard favour'd & sour!—One Colonel
Harrison[178] from a lower County in this Colony, offer'd to give a
Guinea for every handsome Face that could be found in the City, if
any one would put a Copper on every Face that did not come up to
that Character!—This is an impeachment of the Ladies which I have
never heard before, I do not give my opinion either for or against it
—The face of the Country, & the method of farming that way de-
lights them: but at this I dont wonder.

Monday 26.

Yesterday the Inspector, whom I have named & described before, desired the Parson to wait on them in his family and christen his Child
—Is the child sick? No Sir—Why then today? it is the Mothers Desire Sir—Why was it not brought to Church? The Mother is unwell, Sir—The Parson excused himself, & promised to come some
Days hence, but the long winded officer, inured to Stubbornness,
hung on, &, without moderation or Apology *demanded* his presence!
—And prevail'd.—Something in our palace this Evening, very merry
happened—Mrs *Carter* made a dish of Tea. At Coffee, she sent me a

dish—& the Colonel both ignorant—He smelt, sipt—look'd—At last with great gravity he asks what's this?—Do you ask Sir—Poh!—And out he throws it splash a sacrifice to Vulcan—

Teusday 27.

This morning the Colonel with his Theodolite observed the Centre of the Sun at his rising, & found it bore East 5° South—This he is doing to fix a true East & West Line for regulating the Needle at any

time. This Bearing he corrected by finding the Suns Declination, & fixed his Points—After the morning we let our fire go down—Both yesterday, & this evening I rode out to exercise myself & horse against our approaching Journey—Mr *Hodge,* a Merchant of *Leeds* & Mr *Leech* a Merchant of Dumfries came Home with the Colonel from Westmoreland-Court—Both chatty, in special Mr Leech; both well-bred, sensible, & sociable—The loyal Toast was *Wisdom* & *unity* to the Conferences now assembled—And when Women were to be toasted, I gave Miss *Jenny Washington.*—

Wednesday 28.

The weather remarkably dry, since Sunday sennight, we have not had a drop of Rain, nor even a cloudy Sky, and till yesterday, & steady, cold, serene northerly Wind—To Day is the annual Commencement at Nassau Hall—

[LETTER OF PHILIP V. FITHIAN TO MR. LARKIN RANDALL]

[Nomini Hall. September 28 (?) 1774]

MR RANDALL.

You will please to acquaint Mr Rigmaiden[179] that I received and looked over his Note, and should have attempted to answer it but for the following reasons. I observe that the first author of the question very rudely calls Mr Rigmaiden a fool for not working it by Cross-Multiplication.

And I observe too that Mr Rigmaiden throws back the word fool, (I suppose in revenge) upon the other, and if I should intermeddle in the case it is more than probable, that I should be called the third fool, by either the one or the other, at least I think the hazard of this too great to set against any Honour I could recieve by resolving it— But since Mr *Rigmaiden* intimates in his note that he is at something of a loss to know whether himself or the other have the least claim to the character; I shall propose a question in arithmetick, which will fully decide any dispute of this nature, for I pronounce the man who can work it off at once, to be no fool in figures.

A Man has 5000 £ which he puts to interest for 30 years 6 £ per Cent. per Annum. I demand how much of this he must spend every day, to spend it all, principal and interest in the thirty years, and let the daily sums in the whole time be equal?

As to the question given, "to Multiply 12 £ 12s 12½d by itself, It must have been a punn, or from one not well skill'd in figures. If it was the former, it does not deserve to be answered at all, because that would be indulging wanton impertinence; and if it was the latter, I am not able to understand how such a person should venture to question Mr *Rigmaidens* answer—Upon the whole, I am apt to think it is all a punn which, "Brother Quill" (as he is pleased to style himself) has ventured to throw out, and on this account, until I am better satisfied that the sentiment is genuine, I decline wholly entering farther into the matter.

I am, Sir, Yours

P V FITHIAN

To MR LARKIN RANDELL
     Nomini Hall.

Thursday 29.

Warm to day, but dry & clear. Mr *Leech* & Mr *Hodge* spent last evening with us; the Conversation was on exchange—Loyal Toasts, *Agreement,* & *Firmness* through the american Colonies—Ladies. mine was Miss Corbin—The Colonel informed us that early next week he shall set out for Williamsburg—Soon after I hope to set out for Cohansie!

[LETTER OF PHILIP V. FITHIAN TO BENJAMIN CARTER]

Nomini Hall Septr: 29th. 1774.

> "Aetas Parentum, pejor avis, tulit
> Nos nequiores; mox daturos
> Progeniem vitiosiorem."

SIR.

You will comprehend, at once, the design of Horace in the Ode from which this motto was taken, And, perhaps, you may think the application of it here unmeaning, and impertinent. In order to free you wholly from every such secret suspicion, you will please to take notice, that the dignity of your very respectable family, (which is a sacred thing) depends almost entirely upon your *Capacity, improvement,* and *behaviour,* an attempt, therefore, to guide and enlarge either or all of these may not be called unmeaning; and, as you have honoured me for some time past in the character of a Tutor, by submitting to my advice and instruction, I cannot suppose you so utterly destitute of candour and gratitude as to put the name of impertinence on what is the *close* and *sum* of my duty to you: especially as there is but little probability that I shall ever see you more, and can, therefore, have no possible incitement from interest, to flatter nor oppertunity of indulging any kind of revenge. These remarks, I presume, are sufficient to remove from you any hurtfull prejudice. I thherefore go on, to make several observations with moderation and freedom, which, at least, I hope you will duely consider, and if they please you, practise. Give me leave then, first of all to tell you, That you possess a critical tho' a high station, and that in your road throug[h] life you are liable to innumerable dangerous [dev]iations. On many accounts your station is critical; I shall enumerate only a few.

—The rest is lost—

To MR BEN CARTER

[JOURNAL]

Fryday 30.

Warm, but clear & dry—Dined with us Mr *Blain;* He gave us a large account of affairs at the Congress, of the City, Country, Manners, Persons, Trade &c—But he swears the Women are coarse & hardy— Evening I informed the Colonel that it is hardly probable I shall continue in his family til his return from the general Court, & at the same time, desired him to give me a discharge so that I expect to have all things adjusted before he leaves Home—We have now entered on the Winter plan, have Coffee just at evening & Supper between eight & nine o-Clock—It is wonderful to consider the Consumption of provisions in this family—I have before spoken of Meat, & the steady Rate of flour weekly, for the great House is 100Lb of which 50 is the finest, & 50 the Seconds—But all the Negroes, & most of the Labourers eat Corn.

Saturday October 1st. 1774.

Wind South West cloudy. After Breakfast with the Boys I went a Surveying along the River round the lower pasture at twelve, *Ben, Bob, Harry* all gallop off—I spent the afternoon plotting my work— I paid Sam our Barber for *Blacking, Dressing* &c 12/.

Sunday 2.

Parson Smith is out of the Parish so that we have no service—With *Ben* I rode to Mr *Washingtons*. Mr Lowe again absent—Dined with us Mrs *Turberville*, Miss *Corbin*, Miss *Pierce*—we found the Colonel in the evening busy at his Instrument of Music—We drank our Coffee & retired early to our Room, & read til ten, then thanking our bountiful Preserver we retired to our bed.—

Monday 3.

I gave Tom the Hostler, for his care of my Horse 3s—After Breakfast the Colonel settled & paid me for my Years Service 40 £ Sterling—This is better than the scurvy annuity commonly allowed to the Presbyterian Clergy—He is very Busy in adjusting his affairs, he set out however, by twelve for Williamsburg, after taking final leave of me—*Ben* accompanies him to Richmond Court—Afternoon Miss Corbin & Miss Turberville came in to stay a while with Mrs *Carter*. Bob went yesterday to Mr Lanes there was Parson *Gibbern* ill of his last weeks Bout; he was up three nights successively drinking & playing at Cards, so that the liquor & want of sleep put quite out of his Sences—A rare tale this to relate of a Man of God!—To use the language of the vulgar, "Old Satan will sadly belabour such overgrown Sinners"!—

Teusday 4.

Dined with us Mrs Turberville and Miss *Letty* we were all Tete a Tete, vastly merry & garrulous—I gave Nelson for a Stirrup Buckle a Bit—I am preparing my Saddle. Cloth's, Bags, Horse, & myself for the intended Ride—

Wednesday 5.

Dined with us Mr Taylor, he informs us that the crops of Tobacco are like to be good—Evening I wrote a Letter to Mrs Thornton Northumberland, concerning Mr Leek's coming into her Family as a Tutor—I had a fine walk with the young Ladies through the Pasture—They make me proud by expressing much concern at my necessary Departure, throwing out many Wishes that I would continue with them—

[LETTER OF PHILIP V. FITHIAN TO MRS CHARLOTTE THORNTON]

Nomini Hall. Octr. 5th. 1774.

MADAM.

I saw Mr Leek last Spring, and, as directed by Colonel Taylor,[180] I enquired if he would undertake the education of several children in this Colony: he seem'd willing, but would make no promise, nor enter into any agreement til he is fully instructed as to the number and standing of his pupils, the conditions of the agreement, and time when he is to begin.

I expect to return shortly to Philadelphia, and write these to acquaint you that I would willingly forward a letter to him, if you are yet desirous of employing him to instruct your family.

you will please, Madam, if you think proper to write, to direct the letter thus "To Mr Samuel Leek junr: Cohansie, New Jersey—"
I shall leave this place about the 18th instant.

I am Madam, your
Most humble Servt:

P V FITHIAN

To MRS CHARLOTTE THORNTON
Northumberland

[JOURNAL]

Thursday 6.

I paid Natt who drives the Team half a Bit as a Forfeit for taking hold of his plough—And to Harry 18d for a stirrup-leather & sundry other Articles—The School presented me with a petition formally drawn up for a holiday to day on account of the race at Mr Turberville's, which I granted—*Priscilla, Nancy, Ben,* & *Bob* go Harry & I, making in my opinion the wisest choice both stay.

[PHILIP V. FITHIAN TO HARRY WILLIS AND ROBERT BLADEN CARTER]

Nomini Hall Octr: 6th. 1774.

FOR MASTERS HARRY & BOB.

I approve highly of the method you have taken in asking for liberty to attend the race this afternoon, and think myself bound to give you an answer in the same manner.

This Race happening so soon after the other, which was at the same place, and so much like it seems to promise nothing that can require your attendance, it is therefore my *desire* and *advice* that you stay contented at home. But if your inclination be stronger than either of these, and you still choose to go, you have my consent provided you return by Sun set in the Evening.

Yours

PHILIP V FITHIAN

[JOURNAL]

Fryday 7.

Nancy, & Bog go to the Dance at Schantille[181]—Mrs Carter after Breakfast took *Prissy, Fanny* & Harriot, & made Mrs Washington a Visit, *Ben, Harry*, Betsy & I are left at Home alone I spent to Day in writing off Mr Peck's Letter—Evening I am troubled with a drunken Carpenter; he saw a Light in my Chamber—up he bouzes, with a Bottle of Rum in his hand; Who keeps Home?—I asked him in—Have you any water Sir?—Not any I told him—Not a Drop, Sir?—No—My Flute was lying on the Table, he took it for a Trumpet & tooted in for two or three Minutes Then again he begs, O Sir call in a Servant & have me some Water—But I left the Room glad to be free of his foolish Impertinence. At Supper Mrs Carter informed us that Captain *Walker's* little Son has the putrid Quinsey, but we hope it is only a bad sore Throat by a Cold—I have a Complaint of a painful Jaw, for these several Days

Saturday 8.

Expence to the Smith for mending my Stirrup a Pisterene 1/3—Ben this morning Wrote a letter to his Papa—I finished off mine for Mr Peck The Pain in my face is a good deal troublesome. Dined with us Colonel Frank Lee & his Lady; Mr Turberville Mrs Turberville & Miss Letty.

Sunday 9.

Ben & *Harry* ride to Ucomico Church I at home spend the day in my Room, I walked out towards evening & saw a number of Negroes very busy at framing together a small House—Sundays they commonly spend in fishing making Potatoes &c, building & patching their Quarters or rather Cabins—

Monday 10.

The General Court at Williamsburg begins to sit this Day—We have no intelligence of the carryings on of the Congress; our Papers this Summer come vastly seldom, it is said that the Post Men are bribed & give away the News Papers. I expect that Mr Peck is about setting out from Home for this place—I wish him a speedy & successful passage, for I am now impatient of Delay til I visit again my acquaintances & Home—The day is cold, the wind at North & the ground extremely dry—

Teusday 11.

Mr *Stadley* came this morning. He brings no news of the Congress, but much of the great Race lately at Fredericksburg—Every Evening, for the Benefit of exercise I ride out, and commonly carry with me one of the small Girls, who partaking of the prevailing Spirit, are passionately fond of Riding—

Wednesday 12.

I was told often before I left Home that coming into Virginia would bring me into the midst of many dangerous Temptations: Gay Company, frequent entertainments, little practical devotion, no remote pretention to Heart religion, daily examples in Men of the highest quality, of Luxury, intemperance, & impiety: these were urged, by my kind acquaintances, as very strong dissuasions against my leaving home; the admonitions I accepted with great Thankfulness, tho' I could not allow them to turn me off from my purpose & I resolved with as much sincerity & Firmness as I could to carry them with me in every part of my behaviour. The close of the time of my Stay here is I expect now near at hand: And if I may judge myself of the carrying my resolutions into practice, I should pronounce that I have not been wanting in my duty in this respect. Some few who frequently ask me to go from home, say I am dull, unsociable, & splenetic: But the Gentlemen generally here have a good & reasonable manner of judging in this case they are well pleased with strict & rigid virtue in those who have the management of their children, if it does not grow to factious enthusiasm; so that Levity, tho perhaps they would wink at it lessens, & in a while would take away the Reputation & business of a Family Tutor—Of this I was fully convinced in a short time after my coming into the Colony, & saw too the very great advantage of the Precaution which I received from my friends, for they assisted me in setting out on a safe, and prudent Plan, which has, I hope directed me to propriety of conduct with regard to my private character, & likewise to my little lovely Charge.

Thursday 13.

Good Mr Stadley left us this morning. I took leave with great reluctance of this worthy Man, & do not expect to see him more!—After Breakfast Mrs Carter with the young Ladies, rode to Colonel Tayloe's. My jaw continues growling & keeps me uneasy, I very much fear some hurtful humours are collecting themselves there together—To day at twelve o-Clock *Bob* providentially escaped with his life—He went up into a tall Chesnut tree to cut down Boughs & gather Chesnuts & foolishly he began to cut the Limb on which he was

standing, at a little distance from his feet—Chesnut splits extremely easy, so that when the Limb was about half cut off it split down; this so weaked the part on which Bob stood that his weight instantly split it too, & down he must have tumbled upwards of thirty feet but he happily caught a bough on his way down.—

Fryday 14.

The Disorder in my face continues, slow, uniform, & Steady; it does not hinder me from rest by night or from any exercise or business by day; But It keeps me in continual doubt, & anxiety, whether it be not something gathering which will be peculiarly distressful—But my temper, I fear, in these respects is very phlegmatic; I find it unpleasing to myself, & it would be certainly unpleasant to any one who was interested in my complaints—I am of so strange a constitution that very trifles make me utterly unhappy—A mere conceit, frivolous & unsubstantial often takes away my rest—This feeling I have possest from my infancy; I remember very well that a Cuff on my Ear would make me sullen for Several days when I was too young to go out to school; Afterwards a disappointment of an hours play would mak me disrelish for a long time both play-fellows, & all Diversion! When I was at the College one Blunder at recitation, or in any performance of my duty would make one [me] dull, low-Spiritted, & peevish; In fact any disappointment, even the most inconsiderable seems to have a general Effect on my Passions & mingle fear, & anger, & rage, together with many others which are excited by different & disagreeable modifications of our Bodies, &, tho' I am conscious of this frailty in myself, I have not yet brought myself under so good subjection, as to make these humours give way intirely to Philosophy or Religion—It is, however, my constant study how I may accomplish this much wish'd for habit—While we are dining there is a large shower of rain but by no means plentiful, for the earth is uncommonly dry—Mrs *Carter* to day asked me if Mr Peck is to be here before my setting out: I answered that he is—And says she, is he grave as you?—

Saturday 15.

I rode after Breakfast to Dr Thompsons with a settled purpose of having my troublesom tooth drawn out but on examination he found

it to be too far back, & too short to be extracted—More sorry I.—
Dined with us besides the family, Mr *Munro,* young Mr Washington, and Master Christien—Here is a fine Prospect from an exceeding
high eminence, of the Potowmack; River Nominy; our House, which
is six miles distant; Lee Hall Bush-field; all remote.—Evening I rode
Home, the country pleasant   Bought several articles as presents for
the young Ladies, a neat gilt paper Snuff Box for Miss Priscilla, a
neat best clear Hair-Comb a piece for Miss Nancy & Fanny. A broad
elegant Sash a piece for Miss Betsy & Harriot   Value of all 15s. Soon
after my return, when I was in the Chamber adjusting my articles
Ben came bawling at my window Mr Peck's come, Mr Peck's come!
I step'd to the window, & saw presently that what he said was fact,
my Heart bounc'd & I with it bolted down to meet him   But he comes
empty of a letter, & barren of news, at least all he brings seems
gloomy; none at all of the great Congress; very little of the present
momentious political affairs; that it has been at Cohansie an unhealthy
season; that good & useful Mr Hunter has been ill of a disorder in his
head: that Mrs Reve is gone & left a Brood of infants! that young
Tom Jennifer of Port-Tobacco, my acquaintance at College too is
dead! that matters go in their usual course at Cohansie & Princeton;
that *Laura* is not in new Jersey! All his intelligence is similar to this,
which is to me harsh & unharmonious as a Ravens ominous Croak!—
To Day Harry boil'd up a Compound of Poke-Berries, Vinegar,
Sugar &c to make a red Ink or Liquid—I spent the evening til two in
the morning in conversation.

Sunday 16.

A fine morning—We rose by Seven but we were informed that there
is no Sermon so that out of compliment to Mr Peck's weariness we
kept close at home rathar than ride to Richmond. We spent the Day
in our chamber til towards evening when with the young Ladies we
took a turn down the River   Many we saw fishing—Mrs Carter with
Priss rode to Captain Turberville's—We all return'd and assembled
by evening at the great House—

Monday 17.

Before Breakfast I heard all the School a lesson round Mr Peck
Present—After Breakfast I heard their Tables, Grammer &c & then

in Spite of my resolution with great reluctance, I resigned up to Mr
Peck my little much-loved Charge!—The pain in my Face is quite
gone—To day I saw a Phenomenon, Mrs Carter without Stays!—
She complains of a pain in her breast, that prevents her wearing
them, she says that She is always supposing the worst, & fears it is a
Cancer breeding there—I hope it may be only fear—I am more &
more every day pleased with the manner, Temper, Oconomy, &
whole management of this good Lady—Now I am to take my final
Leave!—Towards evening we all went down on the River & had a
pleasant exercise—

Teusday 18.

Early to Day I wrote a Note to Mr Lowe and Harry Fantleroy to
dine with us to day, & soon received their promise—After Dinner
with Mr Lowe on the violin, I play'd over many tunes on the Flute,
he plays with good Taste and accuracy—At five we all walk'd over
to Mr Turberville's—I gave to our Wash-Woman some old Linen
& as a Box 2/4—We spent the evening in Music Chat & pleasantry—
But this said thing which I hear of that turn-Coat *Laura*, that She
loves & courts one Mr *Rodman* this distresses me exceedingly But
this relieves me, for I have had it always in my View that—Varium
& mutabile semper Feminae—Tho I have made a Solemn vow which
I have no inclination at all to forego, yet if it shall appear that she
has listened to another, my dearest vow is not inviolable; I will retreat
from every former Promise, I will not hearken to womanish solicitations, but I shall in return for her want of goodness treat her with
contempt; & Sincerely pity, instead of resent, her ineffectual
Caprice—

[LETTER OF PHILIP V. FITHIAN TO JOHN LOWE]

Nomini-Hall Octr: 18th: 1774.

FOR MR LOWE.

Ben: Carter's compliments with mine wait on you this morning,
and beg your company with us to day to dine, if it be convenient.

We also present our compliments and the same request to Mr
Fantleroy.

I should not have ventured to encroach upon your hours of business, but as Mr Peck, the gentleman who succeeds me in this family arrived last saturday so that I propose to set out tomorrow and should be glad to see you before I leave Virginia.

I am, Sir,

Your most humble Servt.

P V FITHIAN.

[JOURNAL]

Wednesday 19.

Mr Lowe & Fantleroy left us early But I agreed to stay till tomorrow —I gave to Nelson on going away 2/2—To Miss Sally the House-Keeper 5/.—

Thursday 20.

I rose by three, & left Home by half after four—Gave Nelson & Dennis half a Bit a piece—rode thence to Westmoreland Court House ten Miles by half after six—Fed my Horse & drank some Brandy—Expence a Bit—Rode thence to Mattox Bridge 18 miles— Fed here three quarts of Bran & Corn for a Bit—The Bloody-Flux is now extremely bad in this Neighbourhood—I am told that scarce a Family is clear of it, & of every family some die!—Rode thence to *Tylers* Ferry 8 miles the road extremely dry & dusty—At two I set off for Maryland, the wind fresh at South East arrived at Mrs Laidlers by five Ferriage 7/6 I gave the Ferrymen a Bottle of Rum—Here I dined on fryed Chicken, Ham, with good Porter—Accomodations good—I[n] Bed by half after Seven—

Fryday 21.

Directly over my Room was a sick Woman that kept a dismal groan-ing all night—My window-Shutters Clapt the Potowmack howl'd, yet I Slept—My Bill at Mrs Laidlers—A Bottle of Porter 2/. Dinner 1/3 Bed./6d—Bottle of Rum for Ferrymen 1/3—Gallon Oats./8d— Stable & Foder 1/.—A smart looking Girl at Mrs Laidlers made me smile—She was complaining to me of the unhealthy Climate, that these three months past she has had a constant Ague & Fever, & been in the Country only six months—Pray Miss said I did you come from Britain?—No Sir, I came from London—Rode thence to Port-To-

bacco—It has been extremely sickly here this Fall—Bill to Barber
1s/8—Breakfast 1/—Hay and Oats 1/3—Mrs Halkinson my Landlady, a poor aged, distress'd Widow, when she found that I was
acquainted with her little son at Princeton, seemed a little to revive;
she beg'd me to encourage her Son to be diligent & industrious, to
caution & admonish him from h[er] against bad company & wicked
practices—She told me of her great & sore loss of an only Daughter,
a young woman of 15 this Summer, since which, she told me in
tears, that She has been a stranger to health & Quiet—O relentless
Death!—How universal & severe are thy Commissions! From Mrs
Laidlers to Port Tobacco is called 13 miles—I rode thence thro' a
fog of Dust to Piscatua 14 miles. The Landlady here is very ill—
That dismal disorder the bloody-Flux has been extremely bad at
Port-Tobacco, & in the Neighbourhood of this town, but is subsided—Expence here half a Gill of Brandy./3d—Oats & Fodder./6d—
Left this Village half after four, and rode to upper-Marlborough,
almost blinded with sweat & dust!—Arrived by seven, a little tired
this Evening—Distance 16 Miles—Whole distance yesterday including the Ferry 8 miles 44 Miles—Whole Expence 8/7—That epidemical distemper above mentioned has been likewise raging in the
Neighbourhood of this Town—Bill at Marlborough To Tea 1/3—
To lodging ./8—To Oats 1/1—To stabling 1/.—

Saturday 22.

Rode thence to Patuxen Ferry 4 mile Ferriage./6d—Thence to South
River 12 miles, Ferriage./6d—To Boy ./4—Thence to Annapolis 4
miles—Bill here To Dinner & Club 4/6—To Hay & Oats 1/3—To
two Silver watch Seals 15/6 To half Gallon Rum for Ferryman 2/6
—To Hay for Horse /8—To Barber 1/——Left Annapolis at 6 no
wind returned about 8 to the Coffee-House To Ferriage across the
Bay 17/6—

Sunday 23.

Teusday evening last the people of this Town & of Baltimore obliged
one Anthony Stewart a Merchant here to set fire to a Brig of his
lately from London in which was 17 Chests of Tea—The People
seem indeed to be full of patriotic Fire—Second Bill at Annapolis—
Supper 1/6—Lodging ./9 Hay 1/3—2 Gallons Oats 1/6—Articles

for the Voyage 4/..—Landed about 5 at Kent-Island,[182] rode thence to a small Ferry for Oats & Ferriage 1/.—thence we rode to Queens Town 15 miles[183]—Bill there 5/2½

Monday 24.

Rode from Queens Town over a low levil Country 7 miles to a small Tavern—Breakfasted 1/7 rode thence by a small Town call'd Churchill—thence to the Head of Chester River 22 miles here I dined my Company gone to the Chester Races which happen to morrow—Expence 2/4 Rode thence to Warwick 12 miles My Horses feet swell this Evening

Teusday 25.

Bill at Warwick—supper 1/3—Oats ./8—Stable Hay & Lodging 2/. —Glass of Wine Bitters ./4—Rode thence to Port Penn 15 miles expence there 1/7—Ferriage 5/.—Arrived once more by Gods Kindness in New-Jersey among my friends & relations I found many of my Acquaintances have gone off the Stage Uncle *Seeley; Damon James;* Mrs *Reeve; James Boyd;* & several others—And many are Sick—Our Family through divine Goodness are in Health.—

[Letter of Philip V. Fithian to Elizabeth Beatty]

Greenwich Novem: 30: 1774.

To Laura.

—The Widow left the Room after begging that I would stay to Coffee—I was seated near the Toilet on which Miss had thrown her Piece of Drawing.—I viewed it, She saw me, & began a fine Apology —That her Situation is so lonely, being out of the Way of Entertainment by Company!—That Music & Drawing are her chief & necessary Amusements—That She was glad of the Oppertunity of an Hours Conversation even of an utter Stranger—That She came to America about the 20th: of last May, with a Brother who is since returned—That her Aunt is desirious She may stay in Mary-land & be a Companion and Intimate with her—That since July She has had the Ague and Fever, which had left her only a few Days—And, said She, I want very much to up to Philada:—I heard all this with great Attention & Patience;—When She had finished her Story, I asked her in turn several Questions which she answered with Propriety, & the greatest Apparent Frankness—Til She came to the Answer which I have before set down, then I smil'd—You came then from Britain, Miss—No Sir, I came from London!—Fearing a Proposal to wait on her down to Annapolis, & thence to Philadelphia, the moment I had drank two Dishes of Coffee, which was a few Minutes before Sunset I mounted & rode twenty Miles—

Do you know Mr ―――― who lodged at Mrs ―――― in Philada said P.―――― to me as we were sitting together in the Parlour this rainy Afternoon, she sewing at a Lawn Wrist-band, & I pouting over Watts's Logic—Yes, Madam, I have some Acquaintance with him— And he knows Miss ―――― said She, I saw him last Spring at Mr A―――― She had sometime before told him that you was remarkably & impertinently intimate with Miss Beatty—That She herself, & Miss Beatty both had disapproved of your Conduct, & had by themselves, agreed to inform you of their Sentiments & to advise you to enter upon a different Behaviour—She told him that She had at last prevailed over you so far as to declare to her that you would never make any further Addresses to Miss ―――― because She had a few Days before made a pointed and ill-natured Remark upon your going to Virginia—And pray Madam, did you believe such Trash—? But Trash or Substance it makes me feel grave—I was to Day looking over my Papers & saw Something Apropos, if I can turn to it presently you shall have it—It is an Extract from my Virginia Journal.

I have heard lately some very dull Stories, & am consequently in a very dull gloomy kind of Humour—Every Day I am expecting a more vigorous Feeling—Perhaps it will come tomorrow, but today I must tell you that my Feeling accords precisely with what I have recorded of myself last March.

—Virginia.

Teusday March 22. 1774.

—In spite of all my strongest opposing Efforts my Thoughts dwell on that Vixen Laura—I strive to refuse them Admission, or harbour them in my Heart, yet like hidden Fire they introduce themselves, & sieze & overcome me, when perhaps I am pursuing some favorite Study, amusing or useful, or giving Directions to my little lovely Charge—
I had an Invitation to go to night to hear Mr Worth, a Baptist Minister preach; Polley, Salley, Ruth, Sister, Dr King were to be along—

But it storms, & has been storming all Day so violently that I have not dared yet to venture myself so far as the Stable to see my Horse —Nature is like your Pulse Laura; There is a constant Succession of black & white, Pain & Ease, Good & Evil—Yesterday was as fair, & to Day as directly the contrary as ever I saw two—Had you ever a Swellyng on your Finger—? It throbb'd—The Pain came & went by turns—This is not my Thought, I stole it from Mr Addison—He tells us of the Conversation & Behaivour of the great Socrates the morning he was to die. "When his Fetters were knocked off, being seated in the midst of his Scholars, and laying one of his Legs over the other in a very unconcerned Posture, he began to rub it where it had been galled by the Iron: And willing to improve every Oppertunity of instructing them he observed the Pleasure of that Sensation which now arose in those very Parts of his Leg that just before had been so much pained by the Fetter. Upon this he reflected on the Nature of Pleasure & Pain in General that they constantly succeed each other" —If you are curious you may read the whole beautiful Story of their Alliance & Marriage in the Spect: No: 183.

We poor earthly Creatures are, as to fortune & Feeling, exactly like the Nails in a turning Wheel, to Day up, to morrow Down— Always either sinking or rising. I have been descending for several Days, & am this very Moment down on the cold Earth in which lowly Posture I sincerely tell you I am in good or evil Fortune—fortune kind or cross.

forever yours

PHILIP. V. FITHIAN.

[LETTER OF PHILIP V. FITHIAN TO ELIZABETH BEATTY]

Greenwich Decem: 1. 1774.

To LAURA.

—"From a Settlement made May 12: 1774 there appears a Balance due from Laura of N. n to Lucius, fifteen Letters & a Visit; the whole to be paid on or before the 20th: of Novem. next ensuing— Which Payment if not well & truely made by the said Laura, within the Time above limited, then the said Lucius is, & by these Presents shall be now & forever possest of the full Liberty of siezing, destrain- ing, or taking any or every Part of the said Delinquents Goods & Chattels, & disposing of the same, as he shall think proper til the said Balance be made up—And in Case there shall be failure of Effects, then it is & Shall be lawful for the said Lucius to take under his immediate Direction the Person of the said Laura—

This 1. Day of Decem: on which I am examining a little into my Accompts is the 11:Day since the Time of Payment allow'd to that young Lady is fully expired—"Curse not the King, said Solomon, in thy Bed-Chamber, not even in thy Heart"—Why? "The Birds of the Air will tell it."—Very fine, this! Bring Scrippture among your Pounds, Shillings, & Pence—Very fine, young black Coat—Don't be too fast, Madam, I've got a Gown on, & my Hair is cu'd—On the 4: of July 1774. about three in in the Afternoon, I was sitting alone in my Chamber, in Virginia, thinking—Among many other Conclusions I remember well, it was determined in my mind that this same Laura who is now so much in my Debt, is actually worth 50,000 £ Sterling, pr Annum—Where is the Impropriety then, of my mentioning Solomon's Advice?—Does it now hurt your Conscience, Madam?—

If you can have Patience, I will tell you, from my Virginia Journal the true Cause of that Conclusion.

—Monday. July 4th: 1774.

"Miss Nancy Carter, at Dinner, informed us that Miss Lee, a young Lady from Richmond is now at Mr Turberville's, & she begg'd that her Brother, & I would go in the Evening & invite her here—We consented, & after School took Horses & rode on our Errand; Besides Miss Lee, we found Capt: Turberville, his Lady, Daughter, & several young Gentlemen.

After the Ceremony of Introduction, & our Devoirs were over, we took Seats, in a Cool Hall where the Company were sitting;—All when we entered were smiling at young Mr——who had been gathering Mulberries, & stained his Ruffle—The Attention of the Company being wholly taken up with him, I had the Oppertunity which I wanted, of examining the Person of his Sister, without being interrupted either by the Notice of others, or by my own Timidity. Miss Lee, I am told, is now entering her 20th Year; She is handsome. Her Eyes are exactly such as *Homer*, attributes to the Goddess *Minrva*; and her Arms resemble those which the same Poet allows to *Juno*—Her Hair is a dark leaden Colour; & was craped & knotted up very high, & in it neatly-woven, a Ribband, with a Sprig of green Jessamine—She wore a light Chintz Gown, very fine, with a blue

Stamp, eligantly, & fashionably made, & which set well upon her—In one word, her Dress was neat & genteel; her Behaivour such as I should expect to find in a Lady whose Education had been conducted with Care & Skill, & her Person, abstracted from the Embellishments of Dress & Good-Breeding, not much above the Generality of Women.

What made me desirous to see, and curious to examine this young Lady, was a Sentence that was dropt yesterday by a respectable Person in our Family, intimating a Desire that I may, on seeing Miss Lee, after having known, by Report, her faultless Character, be so far pleased with her Person, as to try to make her mine, & settle in this Colony—That kind Person who is for making me happy by setling me in Virginia, & connecting me with one of the best Families in the Government little knows how painful it would be, if I was indeed compell'd by any Accident of Fortune, to spend the Remainder of my Days in Virginia, if it is the Pleasure of Providence, that I am to continue for any Length of Time in the World.

"*Strong*, & *sweet* are the Bands which tye us to our Place of Nativity; If it be but a beggarly Cottage, we seem not satisfied with the most rich & splendid Entertainment if we are separated totally from it.

"But if a Princess should ask me to accept together with herself, 50,000, £ Sterling pr Annum; I declare with as great Pleasure as Truth that the Esteem and Fidelity which I possess for my ever-dear Eliza would make me, without Reflection, evade & refuse the Offer."

This is not strained Panegyrick; it is still the faintest Image of my Heart, tho' the Sentiment may seem strong & improbable.

PHILIP. V FITHIAN.

[LETTER OF PHILIP V. FITHIAN TO PRISCILLA CARTER]

Philadelphia Octr. 12th. 1775.

MADAM.

It gave me high satisfaction when I saw your brother first in our province. I was cordially glad.—He came unexpected, and that circumstance increased my pleasure at seeing him at all. He is now in this city—Has been in several parts of East and West Jersey—Has tolerable health—And a steady cheerfulness, which I am willing to believe, arises from pretty constant entertainment.

I hear with much surprise, that none of my letters, since I left your family, have been so fortunate as to arrive safe. I impute this to the jealousy of the public, concerning the contents of letters passing through the continen[t].

Mr Peck carries you, with these, my best wishes—That you may rise rapidly in the early improvement of your mind in each useful and ornamental undertaking to which you may be directed—That you may have much real unmixed happiness in the friendships which your age and rank will soon lead you to form—And that the transporting scenes which at a distance, you discover to be painted on your future life, may, as they rise before you one after another, give you as much peaceful enjoyment as so great imperfection can bestow.

You will please to give my best duty to your dear Mama.

I shall write to Miss Nancy. Do not fail by any means whatever, to mention me to Miss *Fanny*, *Betsy*, and *Harriot*—Dear Harriot, Dear Betsy, dear Fanny—Lovely, lovely Girls! And Tasker too, if he has not forgot me, O tell him,—Tell them all howmuch I want to see them—Tell them I will surely come for such impatience as mine cannot bear disappointment.

You will also please to give my kind respects to Miss Sally Stanhope, and to all the family without one exception.

May I ask you to send me a line? My desire of se[e]ing as well as hearing from you is so strong I will venture—O write; three lines, if you send no more, will put you to some little trouble, but none can tell how welcome three lines from you would be to

Your most obliged,

And most humble Servt:

P. V. FITHIAN

To MISS PRISCILLA CARTER.

[LETTER OF PHILIP V. FITHIAN TO ANN TASKER CARTER]

Philadelphia Octobr: 13th. 1775.

MISS NANCY:

No Dances, and but little music! You will begin to ask what is the world coming to?—No Tea, nor Gause, nor Paris-net, nor lawn, nor lace, nor Silks, nor Chintzes; Good Sirs—Good Sirs!—Well

Nancy, in these hard times, I must want Stocks, and you must want Caps—But you look best, when I recollect, in your Hair; you look ten thousand thousand times over the best without any Cap at all, so that in spight of me I shall be outdone. I want to know how you and the Guitar agree yet—

Pray do you ride out often? If you do, who rides with you; or do you boldly ride alone?—Tell me who is yet mistress at Checks—I believe, if you will allow me to guess at so great a distance, it is Fanny. My dear Nancy I want much to see you. I would give this moment my hand full of half-Bits, or their value in coppers, if I thought you wish to see me.

Good-by, Good-by

PHILIP V. FITHIAN

To MISS NANCY CARTER.

[LETTER OF PHILIP V. FITHIAN TO ROBERT BLADEN CARTER]

Greenwich Octobr: 16th. 1775.

SIR.

It gives me pleasure to hear by your brother and Mr Peck, that, in continual health, you are growing rapidly to lusty Manhood—I am more pleased to hear that by growing industry you are rising faster in the progress of your education. Diligence overcomes all difficulties, Be diligent, in a proper course of business, and you will be great.

Mr Peck informs me that Henry has left the school and is in an other way of business; I wish him success in whatever course fortune shall lead him in. You will give him my kind respects. I should have written him a letter but I am drove on to the last hour of your brothers stay before I finish these.

Mr Peck or your Brother can inform you farther in any questions of my place and business,

I must now write myself dear Bob always respectfully

Yours

PHILIP V. FITHIAN

MASTER BOB CARTER
Virginia

[LETTER OF PHILIP V. FITHIAN TO COUNCILLOR ROBERT CARTER]

Greenwich Octobr. 17th. 1775.

HON: SIR.

I was much gratified at your indulgent permission of your Son to visit, for a time, these northern Provinces. I think it will on the whole, be several ways advantageous to him. When I first saw him, he was feeble, and daily feverish; now he is better—He attended the commencement at Princeton; has been some time in Philadelphia—Seems cheerful—I think entertained—And will not return home without having made some useful observations—I am however fearful, that his constitution is not sufficiently vigorous, without scrupulous attention to exercise and nourishment, to afford him lasting health.

With regard to the public concerns they are here at so high a pass, and so complex, I must refer you to *Ben* and Mr *Peck*.

I hear with great anxiety of Mrs Carters Illness; but hope, through the kindness of auspicious Heaven, that before you receive these, She will again enjoy her usual health. You will please to remind her of my constant strong esteem; it flows from the remembrance of a succession of unmerited kindness.

I have wrote frequently since I left your family, but am surprized to hear that all my letters have been intercepted or lost.

I am, Sir, with great truth & Esteem

Your most obliged
Most obedient
Servant

PHILIP V. FITHIAN

To ROBT: CARTER ESQR.
   Virginia.

APPENDIX

Appendix

[CATALOGUE OF LIBRARY OF ROBERT CARTER
COMPILED BY PHILIP FITHIAN.]

FOLIO'S

Molls large correct map of the whole world.

Chamber's Dictionary of the Arts & Sciences 2 Vols

Suplement to Ditto 2, Vol.

Millers Gardeners Dictionary.

Postlethwayts Do. of Trade & Commerce 2. Vol.

Bayley's Etymological Ditto.

Laws of Maryland.

Puffendorf's Law of Nature & Nations

Salmons universal Traveller 2. Vol.

Grotius on War & Peace.

Lockes Works 3 Vols

Wilkin's real Character.

Principle of Equity.

Homes Decisions of the Court of Sessions.

Treatise & Maxims of Equity or Chancery.

Stackhouse History of the Bible 2 Vols.

17 Volumes of Music, by various Authors.

Temples Works 2 Volumes.

Cases in Equity Abridged 2 Volumes

Ackerleys Britanick Constitution.

Spelmans Works.

Swinburne of Wills

Vavassoris omnia Opera.

Hughes's natural History of Barbadoes.

Salmons Abridgment of state Trials.

Vossii Epistolae.

Observations on Caesars Comment.

Clarendons Tracts.

Scripta Senecae Philosophi.

Books of Common Prayer.

The Surveyor in four Books.

Hortensii Enarrationes in Virgilium.

Advices from Parnassus.

Blounts Censura Authorum.

Bacons Government.

Dictionaire universel de toates les Sciences, & des Arts 3 Volumes.

Biblia Sacra.

Stephani Thesaurus 4 Volumes.

Le grand Dictionaire History 4 Volumes.
Acta Regia.
Raleighs History of the World.
Calmets historical, critical, geographical, chronological and Etymological Dictionary of the Holy Bible in 3 Volumes.
Bundys Roman History 3 Volumes.
Works of Virgil 2 Volumes.

A View of universal History.
Cooke [Coke] on Littleton.
Sidney on Government.
Cornu Copia of Terence Varra.
Calmets Prints.
Alexanders Feasts, or the Power of Music, an Ode in Honour of St. Celaelia [Cecilia] by Dryden set to Music by Handel.
Hammond on the New Testament.

QUARTO.

Bates Hebrew & English Dictionary.
Christianity as old as the Creation.
North's Examen.
Blackstones Comment. 4 Volumes.
Harris's Justinian, in Latin
Shaws Boerhave. 2 Volumes.
Simpsons Justice.
Builders Treasure of Designs.
Palladio Londenensis.
Marine Dictionary.
Newtons observations on Daniel.
Guidonis de Rebus memorabilibus.
Piscarnii Dissertationes medicae.
Carmina quadrigessimalia.
History of the London Royal Society.
Erasmus de optimo Rei Statue.
The Courtier by Castligio.
Puffendorf de la Nature, et des Gens.
Hedorici Lexicon.
Morhosii Polyhistor 2 Volumes.
Helvicus Chronology.

Hierenymi Syphilis.
Pearoes Longinus.
Boyers Dictionary.
Aurelii de Levitate Dei.
Phisica, a manuscript.
Monthly Review 24 Volumes.
Quinctiliani de Institutione Oratoris
Barcleys Argenis.
Apology of the Church of England.
Newton's Milton 3 Vols. neatly gilt.
Horatius Bentleii.
Cowleys Works.
Chubbs Tracts.
Robertsons Charles 5. 5 Vols. Gilt.
Desaguliers Experiment. Philos. 2 Vols.
Gravesande Elements of Philosophy 2 Vols.
Sheridan on Elocution.
Grotius de la Guerre & de la Paix.
Fingal; an Epic Poem.

OCTAVO'S.

Universal History 21 Vols.
Supplement to Ditto.
Smiths Moral Sentiments.
Wingates Arithmetic.

Newtons Arithmetic.
Middltons Life of Cicero.
Dissertation upon Parties.
Free-thinking with remarks.

Middletons Letter from Rome.
Watts's Logic.
Buchanans History 2 Vol's.
Atterbury's Sermons 2 Vol's.
Familiar Letters.
Chaucers Tales 2 Vol's.
Loves Surveying.
Mc.Laurin's Algebra.
Erasmus's Colloquies.
Jacob's Law-Dictionary.
Quincy's Dispensatory.
Elements of the Art of Assaying
    Metals.
Mairs Book-Keeping.
Oxford Grammar.
Preceptor 2 Volumes.
Harris's Hermes.
Sheridan on Education.
Athenean Oracle 4 Vol's.
Echard's Roman History 6 Vol's.
Patricks Terence 2 Vol's.
Watson's Horace 2 Vol's.
Johnstons Dictionary 2 Vol's.
Greys Ecclesiastical History.
Hales History of the Law.
Virginia Justice.
Elements of Criticism 2 Vol's.
Gilbert of Wills.
Terms of Law.
Trials Per Pais.
Law of Estates.
Hawkins's Crown Law.
Duty of Executors.
Law of Uses & Trusts.
Molloy's de Jure Maritimo.
Kaim's Law Tracts.
Montesque's Spirit of Laws
    2 Vol's.
Laws of ordinance 2 Vol's.
Attorney's Practice of Kings-
    Bench.
Harrison's accomplished practiser
    2 Vol's.
Burns Justice 4 Vol's.

Ladies Compleat letter Writer.
Compleat Guide to London
    Trader.
Letter to Serena.
Poetical Works of the Earl of Hali-
    fax.
A Voyage to Cacklogallinia.
Kennets Roman Antiquities.
Fresnays Art of Painting.
Heridiani History Libri 8.
Zenophon in Latin.
Stillingfleet, & Burnet Conf: of Rel:
Discovery of celestial Worlds.
Minucii Felicis Octavianus.
Wards Mathematics.
Demetrii Phalerii de Elicutione.
Submission to the civil Magistrate.
Sacerdotism display'd.
Platonis Dialogi selecti.
Lexicon Plautinium.
The compleat Gentleman.
Ovid de Tristibus.
Valerius Maximus.
Wyckerleys Works.
Salmons History of England.
Hist poeticae Scripteres antiqui.
Bowdens Poetical Essays.
Noetica & Ethica.
Van Sweetens Comment 8 Vols.
Ausonii Opera.
Ovids Metamorphosis.
Wells Geography of New Testa-
    ment 4 Vols.
Uptons observ: on Shakespear.
Spinoza reviv'd.
Hi[s]tory of the Belles Lettres.
Montaignes Essays 2 Vols.
Salmons Chronology 2 Vol's.
Lactantii Opera.
Present state of Great Britain.
Gays Fables 2 Vol's.
The Chace by Somerville.
Mitchels Poems 2 Vol's.
Cobdens Poems.

Seneca Tragediae.
Livii Historia 3 Vol's.
Rays Wisdom of God.
Terentii Delphini.
Law of Executors.
Tyndals Rights of the Church.
Youngs Poetical Works.
Gordons Geography.
Roseommons Poems.
Lynch's Guide to Health
Bladens Caesar.
Variorum Auctorum Consilia.
Poems on State Affairs.
Essays on Trade.
Nardius's Noctes Geniales.
Caesaris Comment Vossii.
Account of Denmark.
Friend on Fevers & Small Pox.
Broaches General Gazatere.
Virgils Works.
Bailies Dictionary.
Ovidii Opera 3 Vol's.
Malcolm on Music.
Woodwards nat. Hist. of the Earth.
Smith's Sermons.
Guthries Essay on English
  Tragedy.
Bishop of Bangors Reply.
Flavii Aviani Fabulae.
Exposition of Roman Antiquities.
Oxford Latin Grammer.
Present State of Great Britain.
Alexandri ab Alexandro Libri sex.
Thompsons Poems.
Needlers Works.
Denhams Poems.
Ovids Metamorphosis.
Dictionary of the Holy Bible.
Spelmans Expedition of Cyrus.
Virginia Laws.
Smollets History of England 10
  Vol's.
Series of political Maxims.

Donnes Letters.
De Juramenti Obligatione.
Voltaires select Pieces.
Rapin on Gardens. (A poem)
Life & Opinions of Tristram
  Shandy.
State of Great Britain & Ireland.
Juvenals & Perseus's Satires.
Wards Mathematicks.
Littletons History of Henry
  Seventh 3 Vol's.
Locke on human understanding.
Aprol's Nepos.
Cradocks Version of the Psalms.
Terrentiae Comediae
Discours politiques sur Tacite.
Villa Burghesia.
Every Man his own Lawyer.
Chamberlanes religious Phil:
  3 Vol's.
Observations on the Resurrection.
Manwarring on the Classicks.
Fontaines Fables.
Sheridans British Education.
Oldcastles Remarks on History of
  England.
Davidsons Ovids Epistles.
Potters Greek Antiquities 2 Vol's.
Chaucers Tales 3 Vol's.
Robertsons History of Scotland.
  2 Vol's.
Thoyras's History of England.
Dennis's Miscellanies.
Dialogues of the Dead.
Of the Rupture with Spain, France
  & Eng.
Addissons Dissertation on the
  Roman Poets.
Augustini de Deitate Dei Libra 22.
Essay on the first Book of Lucre-
  tius.
The School of Man.
Book of Italian Music.

Poetices Libri septem.
Handels Operas for Flute 2 Vol's.
Enquiry concerning Virtue.
Montaignes Essays. 3 Vol's.
Epicteti Enchiridion.
Remarks on Prince Arthur.
Seneca Grutui.
The Religious Philosopher.
Tolands Works.
Memoirs of the Duke of Sully
   3 Vol's.
Virgilii Opera.
Charon of Wisdom. 3 Vol's.
Arithmetica universalis.
Le Livre des Priores communes.
Life of Mahomet.
The moral Philosopher
Gordons Tacitus. 4 Vol's.
Wagstaffes Works.
Art of Reading.
Colliers Amendments.
Life of Sethos 2 Vol's.
Kennets Roman Antiquities
Of Conformity to religious Cere-
   monies.
Ovids Metamorphosis.
Musee Sacrae Poetarum.
History of Charles twelfth of
   Sweden 3 Vol's.
Broomes Poems.
Davidsons Virgil 2 Vol's.
Parliamentary Debates 12 Vol's.
Wells Geography of old Test
   3 Vol's.
Davidsons Horace 2 Vol's.
Bakers Medulla Poet: Rom.
   2 Vol's.
Fontaines Cupid, & Pisyche.
Davidsons Ovid.
Defence of Christian Revelation.
Philosophical Letters.
Strades Prolusions.
Whaleys Poems.

Nature & consequences of Enthu-
   siasm.
Quintiliani Declamtiones.
Barcleys Apology. French.
Mitchels Poems 2 Vol's.
History of the Council of Trent.
Kerr, de Latina Ling. loquenda.
Homer, Greek & Latin.
Potters Greek Antiquities.
Tulls Husbandry.
Religious Philosopher.
Holy Bible, Longinus.
Tertullian.
View of the Court of Exchequer.
Porneys Elements of Heraldry.
Enchiridion Metaphysian.
Lactantius.
Treatise on Ventilators.
Virgil, Turners Syphilis.
Cicero's Orations. 3 Vol's.
Book of Rates
Amyntor.
Agnyppus's Vanity of Arts.
Livii Historia 6 Vol's.
Humes Essays 2 Vol's.
Humes History of England.
   8 Vol's.
(Both these Setts neatly gilt)
Vertets Revolutions of Sweden.
Ansons Voyage.
Cicero's Epistles.
Daran on the Urethra.
Virgil 2 Vol's.
Littletons Life of Henry Second
   2 Vol's.
Dictionary of plants 2 Vol's.
Salmons chronological Historian 2
   Vol's.
Smollets History of England
   8 Vol's.
Smollets Continuation 4 Vol's.
Life of prince Eugene.
Life of Duke of Marlborough.

DUODECIMO'S.

Compleat French Master.
Buchanans English Grammar.
Steeles English Grammar.
Historical Companion.
Boyers Telemachus 2 Vol's.
Eulia a Novel
Burnets History of England
  6 Vol's.
Holme's Lattin Grammer.
Rdimans Ditto.
Tennants Law.
Harvey's Meditations 2 Vol's.
Academy of Play.
Tristram Shandy, 2 Setts 4 Vol's.
  Each
Salmons Gazateer.
Rudimans Institutons Latin.
British Grammar.
Clarks Essay on Education.
Westleys History of the New
  Testament.
Oconomy of human Life.
Cunninghams Horace.
Considerations concerning Money.
Bibliotheca Legum.
Clarks Latn Grammar.
Geography for Children
Complete parish Officer
Tyro's Dictionary
Yoricks sentimental Journal.
Buchanans Spelling Dictionary.
Farriers compleat Guide.
Margaretta, a Sent[i]mental Novel
  2 Vol's.
Theologie portative French.
Kimbers Scotch Peerage.
Kimbers English Ditto.
McLung on Bile
Milatary Register for the years
  1770. 1771. 1772.
Westleys History of the Bible
  2 Vol's.

Joannis Barcley Argenis.
Idiotismi Verborum.
Persuis's Satires.
Cookes Hesiod.
L Apuleii de Assino Libri.
Ovids Tristia.
English Expositor.
Velleii Paterculi Historia.
Historical Companion.
Donnes Poems.
Voitures Works 2 Vol's.
Rowes Lucan 2 Vol's.
Derricks Voyage to the Moon.
Molieres Works French & English
  10 Vol's.
Hughes Works 2 Vol's.
Patersons Notes on Milton.
Miscellanous Poems 2 Vol's.
Porta Linguarum
Histoire D. Abe-lard, at D Eloise.
Puffendorf de Officiis Hominis &
  livis.
Wallers Works.
Fontenelle des Morts.
Famiani Stradae Prolusiones.
Anicii Manlii Opuscula sacra.
Grammatica Institu. Rudi.
Drydens Fables.
Steeles Miscellanies.
Miscellany Poems.
Mallets Works 3 Vol's.
Farquihars Works.
Shaftsburys Charactericstics
Rapin on Aristotles Poesy.
Musae Anglicanae 2 Vol's.
King on the Heathen Gods.
Adventures of a Guinea 2 Vol's.
Manners, from the French.
Collection of Poems. 3 Vol's.
Massons Life of Horace.
The School of Woman.
Wesleys Poems.

A Lady's Religion.
Ovids Art of Love
Whears Relectiones Hyemales.
Traps Relectiones poeticae 2 Vol's.
Compendium Historia universalis.
Menahenii Declamationes.
Blackwells Introduction to the Classics.
Present State of Polite Learning.
Zenophons Cyropedia in Greek.
Dodsleys Poems 4 Vol's.
Guide to London Trader.
Horus's Epitome of Hist. Rom.
Plurality of Words
Grotius De Veritate.
Ponds Kalender.
Memoirs de la Pompadour.
Favel of the Heavens. 2 Vol's.
Letters in Verse from an old Man to youth 2 Vol's.
Grecae Sententiae
Browns Religio Medici.
Priors Poems 3 Vol's.
Laurentii Vallae de Lingua Latinae Elegantia.
Sherlocks Sermons 3 Vol's.
Peace of King William.
Dissertatio de Atheismo.
Watts's Horae Lyricae.
A Gentlemans Religion.
Lavie de Cristofle Colombo.
Epistolae Laii Plinii.
Ladies Drawing Room
Franciscii Sancti Minerva.
Pomfrets Poems.
Eutropii Historiae Romanae.
Considerations sur le's lauses.
Les Avantures de Telamaque.
La Mechanique des Langues.
Clarks Essay on study.
Drydens Juvenal.
Cicero de Officiis.
Hist de Theadosa le Grand.

More's Utopia.
Nicols de Literis invertis.
Travels of Cyrus.
Cooks Plautus's Comedies.
Wilkies Epigoniad.
Trapps Virgil.
Free thoughts on Religion.
Wycherleys Plays
Esops Fables Greek & Latin.
Shakespears Works 8 Vol's.
Plutarch's Lives 9 Vol's.
Gil Blas 4 Vol's.
Lettres Persanes 2 Vol's.
Devil upon Crutches 2 Vol's.
Theocriti Poetae Selectae.
Prayr Book in Short Hand.
Epicteti Enchiridion 2 Vol's.
Vosii Rhetoris Libri quinque.
Poems of Sophocles Greek & Latin.
Pincieri Enigmata.
Virgilii Opera.
Polydorus de Rerum invent:
The Medley & Whig Examiner
Dominici Bavidi Epistolae.
Bonefacii Carmina.
Antoni Mureti Epistolae et Carmina.
Testament politiqe de Richlieu.
Velerii Flacii Angonautica.
Stratagems of War.
Carmina Jounnis Bonefonii.
Traduction des Ecgies D Ovide.
Famiani Stradae Decas.
Persius's Satires.
Eutropii Historiae Romanae.
Ovidii Opera 3 Vol's.
Salust Horace Hudibras.
Cicero Paterculi Historiae.
Erasmi Dialogus Ciceronianus.
Cornelius Nepos.
Plin et Caecil Panegyricus.
Castalio de Christo imitando.
Elegantiarum centum Regulae.

Erasmi Declamatio.
Annaei Senecae Tragaediae.
Account of the Death of the Persecutors.
Delitiae Poetarrum Gallorum 3 Vol's.
Corn: Tacit Annalium Libri.
Plauti Comediae.
Apologia Celesiae Anglicanae.
Monseigeneur le Marquis.
Tullii Ciceronis Epistolae.
Politiani Epistolae.
Censura Philosophia cartesiana.
Historia universalis.
Egidii Chronologia.
Atacrobius.
Blackmore's Prince Arthur.
Walkers Rhetoric.
Senecae Epistolae.
V. Paterculi Historia.
Heinsii Orationes.
Les Oevres de M. Scarron.
Quintus Curtius. Juvenal & Perseus.
Gardineri Epistolae.
Renotii Rapini Hortorum Libri.
Blackmore's Creation.
Riders British Merlin.
Millars Universal Register.
Gentlemans Kalendar 4 Vol's.
Barclaii Satiricon
Sleidani de quatuor summis Imp:
De Arte bene moriendi.
Boethii de Consolatione Philosophiae.
Medetationes Augustini.
De Sapientia Veterum.
Lucretii Claudiani Carminae.
Pia Desideria. (A Poem)
Cororna Virtutum.
Ausonius.
De conservanda Valetudine.
Hexameron Rustique.
Hobbs de Cive.

Crucii Mercurius.
Vossius de Studiorum Ratione.
Plautus's Comedies.
Terence's Comedies.
Erasmi Colloquia.
Lucani Pharsalia.
Phaedri Fabulae.
Ovids Metamorphosis 2 Vol's.
Justini Hist: Libri.
Castaings Interest Book.
Dowel on Heresy.
Morgans Book of Roads 2 Vol's.
Anacreontis et Saphonis Carmina.
Ovidii Opera.
Buchanani Poemata.
Le Berger Fidele.
Horace, Virgil., Lucian.
Grammatica Greca, a Stevenson.
Letters between Ninon & Evremond 2 Vol's.
Webb on Painting.
Almoran & Hamet 2 Vol's.
Crito 2 Vol's.
Francis's Horace 4 Vol's.
Oldhams Works 2 Vol's.
Jewish Spy 5 Vol's.
Turkish Spy 8 Vol's.
La belle Assemble 4 Vol's.
Letters from an old Man to a young Prince 3 Vol.
Molieres Works 7 Vol's.
Prince of Abyssinia 2 Vol's.
Devil turn'd Hermit. 2 Vol's.
Addisons Works 3 Vol's.
Spectator 8 Vol's.
Tatler 4 Vol's.
Guardian 4 Vol's.
Broomes Homer 5 Vol's.
Popes Iliad 6 Vol's.
Norris's Miscellanies.
Nelsons Laws of England.
Hales Descents.
Popes Odyssea 5 Vol's.

Delitiae Poetarum 2 Vol's.
Puffendorf de officio.
Janua Linguarum.
Whigs Supplication.
Cicero de officiis
Hoyles ——
Feltons Dissertations.
Petronii Satyricon:
Isocrates.
Fabulae variorum Auctorum.
French Spelling Dictionary.
Montaignes Essays.
Songe de Scipioni.
Poesies de Chaulieu.
Elements of Geometry.
Collins's Poems.
Martials Epigrams.
Rerum Scoticarum Libri.
L Maitre Italien.
Persees des Peres.
Ninii Epistolae.
Liste generale des Postes de France,
    neat in Copper-Plate.
Amusment of the Spa 2 Vol's.
The Actor.
Cockmans Tully.
King on the Heathen Gods.
Eloisa original Letters, 5 Vol's.
Hervey's Meditations 2 Vol's.
Mallets Works 3 Vol's.
Congreves Works 3 Vols.
Deism reveal'd 2 Vol's.
Dodds Beauties of Shakespear.
Collection of Poems 8 Vol's.
Rays Wisdom of God.
Vanbrughs Plays 2 Vol's.
Clark on Education.

Brachers Farriery 2 Vol's.
Trapps Virgil 3 Vol's.
Tom Jones 4 Vol's.
Connoiseur 4 Vol's.
Swifts Works 13 Vol's.
Prelectiones Poeticae 2 Vol's.
Guardian.
Newtons Ladies Phil: 2 Vol's.
Henry & Frances 4 Vol's.
Gay's Poems 2 Vol's.
School of Man.
Thompsons Works 4 Vol's.
Discourse on Toleration.
Letters from a Persian in England
    to his Friend at Home.
Shaftsburys Characteristics.
Impartial Philosopher 2 Vol's.
Paradise Lost.
Schikards Horologium Ebraium.
Trenchards Tracts 2 Vol's.
Reflections on Tar-Water.
Memoria-Tacknica.
English Grammar.
Juvenal French Translations
Observations on United Provinces.
Chronicon Carionis.
Latin Idioms.
Leonora 2 Vol's.
Cicero French Translation.
Hierionii Poemata 2 Vol's.
Janua trilinguis.
Intreciens sur les Sciences.
Tractatus, theologico Politicus.
De Obligatione Consientia.
Erasmus's Praise of Folly.
De Linguarum Artificio.

[Valentine Made by Fithian for Priscilla Carter]

To Miss *Priscilla Carter*.

Presented as a Valentine.

When *Custom* calls I must away,
She calls me now, & chides my Stay;
She asks my usual annual care,
To compliment some worthy Fair;
To hasten to *Apollo's* Shrine,
For Aid to form a *Valentine*.
    But if *Apollo* I invoke,
Gay *Fancy* I shall sure provoke
Who swears these yearly Rhimes should be,
From Order, Sense, & Learning free;
That if each line be fill'd with Stuff,
Twill please a Lady well enough
That Fancy only can inspire
A Youthful Heart with frantic Fire,
To write such inconsistent Lines,
As always please in Valentines;
That if Apollo lends his Aid,
And I address a well-bred Maid;
With Verses plain yet fill'd with sense,
The Girl would curse my Impudence;
Pedantic, earth-born Fellow! he,
A hobbling Tutor write to me!
Let him go teach his Scholars Greek,
Or learn, himself, to dance, to speak;
And learn to please, or never dare,
Disturb the Quiet of the Fair.
She spoke; but why should I obey,
What unsubstantial Phantoms say?
    Yet *Fancy* urg'd her case so well,
No human Mind could guess or tell,
What hidden Scheme she had in View,
Nor what the *Baggage* meant to do:
'Till *Pallas* Queen of wisdom came,
And told the mischief of the Dame,
For Fancy, Madam, early knew,
Twas my Desire to write to you;
She therefore whisper'd in my Ear,

That you would nought but Nonsense hear
In hopes to baffle my Design,
Or form a vulgar Valentine.
But Pallas told me what to do
If I design'd to write to you,
Make *Humour*, Truth, & Sense conspire,
With genuine poetic-Fire,
To form a Song in Taste & Ease,
Such would your Infant-Bosom please.

Now, Miss, accept in humble Lays,
My weak attempt to sing your Praise;
Nor think it rudeness when I try,
To hold your virtues up on high,
To shew their bright yet living Blaze
And make inraptured Numbers gaze;
Slander herself must disappear,
Or justify my Conduct here,
Since *Fancy*, *Wit*, & *Pallas*, too,
Are all contending, Miss, for you.

I in the common sportful Way,
With pleasure now of you might say,
That both your Eyes are glowing Darts,
Which only seen do wound our hearts;
That Venus' Son by her command
Waits always at your fair Right-Hand,
And that the *Loves* in Beauty drest,
Are always hov'ring near your Breast;
But, tho Such words appli'd to you,
In every sense should all be true;
And if you hear such pleasant Rhimes,
Sung in your Ear ten thousand Times:
Yet always doubt what makes you more,
Than ever *Mortal* was before.

When any Girl; with beauty drest,
And Innocence above the Rest,
Tho' *Fortune* has withheld her Store,
And left the blushing Maiden poor,
Yet Ladie's look with envious Eyes,
And well-born Men the *Angel* prize.

Or when the God of Wealth is kind,
Who does not *worth* nor *Beauty* mind,
And gives some sordid *Woman* Gold,
Our foolish Sex is bought & sold;

We cringe, & court, & sigh, & whine
And swear the Nymph is quite divine.
    And sometimes, tho' Examples here,
Exceeding seldom do appear,
When a good Girl of solid sense,
Who does not make the least pretence,
To what our Fancies rate so high,
A great estate & sparkling Eye;
Who knows tis only want of these,
Makes her incapable to please,
And therefore Studies hard to find,
And plant such Virtues in her Mind
As shall the place of Friends supply
With constant mirthful Company:
Sometimes these Virtues far outdo,
The power of *wealth* & *Beauty* too,
And make a low-born Virgin rise,
To seem a *Goddess* in our Eyes.
    But when we image in our Mind,
Beauty, & Wealth, & Genius join'd,
And see them all to one belong,
The Colours are so bright so strong;
None can resist the powerful Blaze
But all with *Love*, & *Rapture* gaze
    If Madam, my Presage be true,
I may apply all these to you;
And free from *Fear*, or *Interest* say,
That on some happy Future Day,
When years shall have the *worth* exprest,
Which yet lies prison'd in your Breast;
And settled more the charming Grace,
Of grave *good Humour* in your Face;
As you have been by *Fortune* blest,
And born of *Fame*, & *Wealth* possest,
Those full-blown Charms the world will see,
And with one common voice agree,
That such perfection is design'd
To be a pattern for Mankind.
Sure then I've cause with Heart sincere,
To bless the *Chance* which led me here,
And plac'd me down by *Wisdom's* Flow'r,
Which still grows lovelier every Hour;
Whose tender Branches bud & shoot

And promise early useful Fruit;
Tho' *Chance* has given me in Care,
To Nurse this plant & make it fair,
Yet generous *Nature* had before,
Been so unsparing of her Store,
That unemploy'd, with wondering Eyes,
I only stand, & see it rise!

PHILIP. V FITHIAN.

Westmorland-County
Virginia
February 2d: 1774.

NOTES

INDEX

Notes

CHAPTER I

1. Cf. Morton, Louis, *Robert Carter of Nomini Hall: A Virginia Tobacco Planter of the Eighteenth Century*, pp. 62-87.

2. In the issue of the *Virginia Gazette* for May 24, 1751, Thomas Eldridge of Prince George County advertised the sale of his "Mannor Plantation" and three other plantations. Such references to manor plantations appeared frequently in the *Gazette* and in the wills of the period.

3. Cf. Wright, Louis B., *The First Gentlemen of Virginia, passim.*

4. *William and Mary College Quarterly*, Vol. VII, series 1, p. 43.

5. Stanard, Mary Newton, *Colonial Virginia*, p. 271.

6. Hornsby, Virginia Ruth, "Higher Education of Virginians," p. 10. Typed M.A. Thesis, Library of the College of William and Mary.

7. *William and Mary College Quarterly*, Vol. XX, series 1, p. 437.

8. Cf. Wright, *First Gentlemen, passim.*

9. An Englishman visiting Virginia at the close of the eighteenth century stated, with reference to persons he met who had been educated abroad before the Revolution, that he "found men leading secluded lives in the woods of Virginia perfectly *au fait* as to the literary, dramatic, and personal gossip of London and Paris." Bernard, John, *Retrospections of America, 1797-1811*, p. 149.

10. Stanard, *Colonial Virginia*, p. 290.

11. Letter of Robert Beverley to Landon Carter, Blandfield, May 19, 1772, in possession of Mrs. William Harrison Wellford of Sabine Hall. Cf. "Extracts from Diary of Landon Carter in Richmond County, Virginia"; *William and Mary College Quarterly*, Vol. XIII, series 1, pp. 160-163.

12. *William and Mary College Quarterly*, Vol. XIX, series 1, p. 145.

13. Robert Andrews, a Pennsylvania youth educated at "the College of Phileda," served as a tutor at "Rosewell," the Page home in Gloucester County, for several years, and two young men from Princeton taught the Carter children at "Nomini Hall." Cf. letter of John Page, Jr., to John Norton. "Rosewell," September 18, 1772, in Mason, Frances Norton, *John Norton & Sons*, p. 271. See also page 160.

14. A "falling garden" consisted of a series of very broad terraces, usually connected by ramps covered with

turf, oyster shell or other surface material to prevent erosion. In some instances the successive levels were planted in elaborate patterns. In others the whole was covered with turf. The "falling garden" at "Sabine Hall" retains its eighteenth-century design intact.

15. A ha-ha is a boundary to a garden, pleasure-ground, or park of such a nature as not to interrupt the view from the mansion and may not be seen until closely approached. According to a French etymologist, the name is derived from *ha*, an exclamation of surprise, uttered by one suddenly approaching such a boundary. The ha-ha consists of a trench, the inner side of which is perpendicular and faced with a wall; the outer being sloped and turfed. The ha-ha permitted grazing cattle and sheep to appear on the landscape, and at the same time held them at a distance from the mansion. In his diary, George Washington refers, on several occasions, to the ha-has on the grounds at "Mount Vernon." Cf. Fitzpatrick, John, *The Diaries of George Washington*, Vol. II, *passim*.

16. At "Mount Vernon" the mansion and its wings together composed three sides of an open square, the main house and its wings closing the side opposite the open end. At "Stratford Hall" four dependent structures formed a square court, inside of which the great house stands. Two offices are set twenty-eight feet in advance of the main house on the land front. On the water front two others are placed in a similar relation to it. At "Shirley" the great house and four principal dependent buildings form a long rectangular court, the mansion closing the side facing the river.

17. A Huguenot Exile in Virginia, ed. and tr. by Gilbert Chinard (New York, 1934), p. 142. In writing of Maryland early in the eighteenth century, Sir John Oldmixon said: "Both here [Maryland] and there [Virginia] the *English* live at large at their several Plantations, which hinders the Increase of Towns; indeed every Plantation is a little Town of itself, and can subsist itself with Provisions and Necessaries, every considerable Planter's Warehouse being like a Shop. . . ." Oldmixon, John, *British Empire in America* (second edition, 1741), Vol. I, p. 339. Cf. Kimball, Fiske, *Domestic Architecture, passim*.

18. A historian who described the Virginia residences at the beginning of the eighteenth century stated that "All their Drudgeries of Cookery, Washing, Daries, &c. are perform'd in Offices detacht from the Dwelling-Houses, which by this means are kept more cool and Sweet." Cf. Beverley, Robert, *The History and Present State of Virginia*, Book IV, p. 53.

19. The Tidewater plantation economy had spread into the Piedmont section prior to the American Revolution. A paroled British officer writing of his situation in Albemarle County in 1779, said: "The house that we reside in is situated upon an eminence, commanding a prospect of near thirty miles around it, and the face of the country appears an immense forest, interspersed with various plantations, four or five miles distant from each other; on these there is a dwelling-house in the center, with kitchens, smoke-house, and out-houses detached, and from the various buildings, each plantation has the appearance of a small village; at some little distance from the houses, are peach and apple orchards, &c. and scattered over the plantations are the negroes huts and tobacco-houses, which are large built of wood, for the cure of that article." Cf. Anburey, Thomas, *Travels Through the Interior Parts of America*, Vol. II, p. 187.

20. A British observer reported in 1779 that ". . . before the war, the hospitality of the country was such, that travellers always stopt at a plantation when they wanted to refresh themselves and their horses, where they always met with the most courteous treatment, and were supplied with every thing gratuitously; and if any neighbouring planters heard of any gentleman being at one of these ordinaries, they would send a negroe with an invitation to their own house." Cf. Anburey, *Travels Through the Interior Parts of America*, Vol. II, p. 198. This same traveller described the hospitality shown the guests at one of the James River plantations. "I spent a few days at Colonel Randolph's, at Tuckahoe, at whose house the usual hospitality of the country prevailed," he wrote. "It is built on a rising ground, having a most beautiful and commanding prospect of James River; on one side is Tuckahoe, which being the Indian name of that creek, he named his plantation Tuckahoe after it; his house seems to be built solely to answer the purposes of hospitality, which being constructed in a different manner than in most other countries; I shall describe it to you: It is in the form of an H, and has the appearance of two houses, joined by a large saloon; each wing has two stories, and four large rooms on a floor; in one the family reside, and the other is reserved solely for visitors: the saloon that unites them, is of a considerable magnitude, and on each side are doors; the ceiling is lofty, and to these they principally retire in the Summer, being but little incommoded by the sun, and by the doors of each of the houses, and those of the saloon being open, there is a constant circulation of air; they are furnished with four sophas, two on each side, besides chairs, and in the center there is generally a chandelier; these saloons answer the two purposes of a cool retreat from the scorching and sultry heat of the climate, and of an occasional ballroom. The outhouses are detached at some distance, that the house may be open to the air on all sides." *Ibid.*, p. 208.

CHAPTER II

1. Cf. Wright, Louis B., *Letters of Robert Carter, 1720-1727* (San Marino, 1940), p. viii.

2. Cf. Jones, E. Alfred, *American Members of the Inns of Court*, p. 41.

3. Sisters of Anne Bladen Tasker and Thomas Bladen had married Daniel Dulany, Samuel Ogle, and Christopher Lowndes, all men of important political and financial connections in their world.

4. Four of the seventeen Carter children were born after Fithian had left the family.

5. Some extracts from the Journal were published in the *American Historical Review* of January, 1900.

6. Cf. Philip Fithian's *Journal*, edited by John Rogers Williams, p. xiv.

JOURNAL & LETTERS

1. Philip Vickers Fithian had left his home at Cohansie, New Jersey, in 1770, at the age of twenty-three, to enter the College of New Jersey at Princeton. Nassau Hall was the principal structure of the college, and the institution was often familiarly referred to by that name. Fithian was graduated there in September 1772. His parents had both died suddenly during the previous February. Andrew Hunter, Jr., of Cohansie, who wrote this letter, was the nephew of the Reverend Andrew Hunter, Sr., of Greenwich, New Jersey, under whom Philip was at this time studying

Hebrew in connection with his preparation for the ministry.

2. Dr. John Witherspoon (1723-1794), a Scottish Presbyterian clergyman, served as president of the College of New Jersey at Princeton intermittently from 1768 until his death in 1794. A staunch Calvinist, Witherspoon exerted a strong influence on American educational, religious, and political development. Owing largely to the labors of his former students, a number of whom went as clergymen and tutors to the Southern colonies, his influence was very extensive in that region.

3. John Debow, Oliver Reese, Samuel McCorkle and Moses Allen, and Andrew Bryan. With the exception of Andrew Bryan of Baltimore who was admitted to the bar, all of these young men were licensed as Presbyterian ministers.

4. Elizabeth Beatty, Fithian's "Laura," frequently visited in the home of her brother, Dr. John Beatty, who lived at Princeton. Fithian had known Elizabeth earlier in the home of her sister, the wife of the Reverend Enoch Green, a Presbyterian minister of Deerfield, New Jersey, under whom he had prepared for college. Cf. Williams, John, ed., *The Journals and Letters of Philip Vickers Fithian, 1767-1774*, p. 55, fn. 3.

5. The Reverend Enoch Green.

6. Mrs. Peck was the mother of Fithian's friend, John Peck of Deerfield. The two boys had studied together under the Reverend Enoch Green, and had later been classmates at Princeton. John Peck succeeded Fithian as tutor of the Carter children at Nomini Hall in 1774, and later married Anne Tasker or "Nancy" Carter, and settled in Richmond County, Virginia.

7. The Reverend Andrew Hunter.

8. The American Whig Society and the Cliosophic Society were rival literary organizations at the College of New Jersey at Princeton.

9. William R. Smith, who was one of Fithian's classmates, was afterwards ordained as a Presbyterian minister. Cf. Williams, ed., *Fithian*, p. 34, fn. 2.

10. Fithian was studying theology in Deerfield under the supervision of the Reverend Enoch Green, at the same time he was being taught Hebrew by Andrew Hunter, Sr., in nearby Greenwich.

11. William Eugene Imlay was graduated at Princeton in 1773. Cf. Williams, ed., *Fithian*, p. 41.

12. Probably Samuel Fithian, the brother of Philip's father. Philip refers to him as "Uncle Fithian" on other occasions.

13. Henry Lee (1729-1787) of "Leesylvania," in Prince William County, Virginia (known later as "Light Horse Harry" Lee) was a student at Princeton at this time. He was a brother of "Squire" Richard Lee of "Lee Hall" in Westmoreland County. Henry Lee later became the father of Robert E. Lee.

14. Dr. John Beatty had been graduated at the College of New Jersey in 1769. Cf. Williams, ed., *Fithian*, p. 90, fn. 1.

15. John McCalla, Jr., was a friend of Fithian who lived in Philadelphia.

16. Joel Fithian was the cousin of Philip Fithian, who married Elizabeth Beatty Fithian after the latter's death. Cf. Williams, ed., *Fithian*, p. xv.

17. Patapsco River.

18. Bladensburg, Maryland.

19. Georgetown, then a small town in Maryland, was later incorporated in the District of Columbia.

20. Alexandria, Virginia.

21. Colchester was a thriving shipping center on the Occoquan River, now called Occoquan Creek, in Fairfax County, Virginia, near where this creek empties into the Potomac. The town had been incorporated by an act of the Assembly in 1753 to promote "trade and navigation."

22. Dumfries, a town on Quantico Creek, had been settled by a group of Scotch merchants, who traded in the colony. Quantico Creek empties into the Potomac. Dumfries had been in-

corporated by Act of Assembly in 1749. The town had prospered owing to its advantageous position as a center of trade in the western section of the Northern Neck.

23. Aquia had originated as a Catholic settlement on Aquia Creek about the middle of the eighteenth century. A short distance from the town were located the celebrated Aquia stone quarries which had been opened as early as 1683.

24. Stafford Court House, the seat of government of Stafford County.

25. Thomas Ludwell Lee (1730-1778) of "Bellevue" in Stafford County was the fourth son of Thomas Lee of "Stratford" in Westmoreland County, who had served as president of the Council of Virginia.

26. The Chilton family owned plantations in Westmoreland and Fauquier Counties. Cf. *William and Mary College Quarterly*, second series, Vol. 10 (January 1930), pp. 56-63.

27. Benjamin Tasker Carter.

28. The Fauntleroy family owned extensive holdings and occupied a high social position in Richmond County and other sections of the Tidewater. "Mars Hill" and "Crandall" were two seats of the family on the Rappahannock River in Richmond County, and in the vicinity of the modern towns of Warsaw and Tappahannock. A third manor plantation of the Fauntleroys' was "The Cliffs," also on the Rappahannock, some miles north of the other two. The name of the family was pronounced variously as "Fantleroy," "Fantilroy" and "Fauntleroy." Aphia, Samuel and Henry or "Harry" Fauntleroy were the daughter and sons of Moore Fauntleroy (1716-1791) of "The Cliffs." Information supplied by Miss Juliet Fauntleroy of Altavista, Virginia.

29. Francis Christian held his dancing classes in rotation in a number of the manor houses of the Northern Neck at this period. After the pupils had been instructed an informal dance was usually enjoyed on such occasions.

30. Nomini Church, one of the two Anglican houses of worship in Cople Parish, stood on the bank of the Nomini River some five miles from Carter's home.

31. Isaac William Giberne, an English clergyman, thought to have been a nephew of the Bishop of Durham, was licensed to preach in Virginia in 1758. The following year he had arrived in the colony and was serving as the minister in Hanover Parish in King George County. Possessing a high tempered and somewhat contentious nature, Giberne was involved in numerous sharp controversies. An exceptionally sociable and convivial man, he spent much of his time in visiting and gambling and tippling. Admitted by his enemies at that time to be the most popular and admired preacher in the colony, he had been invited shortly after his arrival in Virginia to preach a sermon before the Burgesses. This sermon was later printed at their request. In 1760 Giberne married a wealthy widow, Mary Fauntleroy Beale of Richmond County, a daughter of Moore Fauntleroy of "Crandall." She had previously been the wife of Charles Beale. Removing to her plantation, "Belle Ville," he was two years later chosen as minister of Lunenburg Parish, and served in that capacity until 1795. He is mentioned in numerous diaries and letters of the period. Cf. Goodwin, Edward Lewis, *The Colonial Church in Virginia*, pp. 271-272; Jonathan Boucher, *Reminiscences of an American Loyalist, passim*; letter of Miss Juliet Fauntleroy of November 21, 1941 in Department of Research and Record, Colonial Williamsburg, Inc.

32. Benjamin Tasker.

33. Robert Bladen or "Bob."

34. Henry or "Harry" Willis.

35. Priscilla.

36. Ann Tasker or "Nancy."

37. Frances or "Fanny."

38. Betty Landon.

39. Harriot Lucy.

40. Benedict Pictete had first pub-

lished his *Teologia Christiana* in 1696.

41. Priscilla, "Nancy," and "Bob." This school was conducted in rotation at a number of manor plantations of the region by Francis Christian, a dancing master.

42. The banks of the Potomac River could be seen in the distance from the upper floor of "Nomini Hall."

43. Yeocomico Church, one of the two Anglican churches in Cople Parish in Westmoreland County. Built in 1706, this structure still stands.

44. Thomas Smith was the rector of Yeocomico Church at this period. Smith was a man of large means. He had been sent as a youth to be educated in the mother country. He first attended a school at Wakefield in Yorkshire and later entered Cambridge University, where he was graduated in 1763. His son, John Augustine Smith, later became president of the College of William and Mary.

45. Captain Walker was a friend of Robert Carter and often visited "Nomini Hall." Fithian frequently dined at Walker's home.

46. Stadley was a German music master who visited "Nomini Hall" regularly at this period to instruct the Carter children. He also taught in a number of other homes in the Northern Neck. Before coming to Virginia, Stadley had taught music in New York and Philadelphia. In one of Carter's account books the musician's name is entered as "Strader." Cf. Waste-Book, No. 2, September 27, 1773 to December 31, 1773, p. 45.

47. Carter was doubtless returning from attendance as a member of the General Court at this time.

48. Fithian was preparing for his examination before the Presbytery at Philadelphia at this time.

49. "Hickory Hill," the manor house of John Turberville (1737-1799) was about a mile distant from "Nomini Hall." Turberville had married his first cousin, Martha Corbin. One of their ten children, Letitia Corbin Turberville, later became the wife of Major

Catesby Jones. Their youngest son, George Richard Turberville, married his first cousin, Martha Corbin, only daughter of Gawin Corbin of "Peckatone." Their eldest son, George Lee Turberville, married Betty Tayloe Corbin. The Turbervilles were connected with the Lees of Westmoreland County in a number of ways and possessed large landed properties.

50. Jane or "Jenny" Corbin was a sister of Mrs. John Turberville of "Hickory Hill."

51. Cunningham was one of a number of young Scotch merchants who had settled in the Northern Neck. He was apparently a member of a firm referred to in the account books of Robert Carter of "Nomini Hall" as "Messrs. Fisher and Cunningham."

52. See fn. 51.

53. Lancelot Lee was the son of George Lee of "Mount Pleasant" in Westmoreland County who had died in 1761. Lancelot's brother, George Fairfax Lee, had inherited their father's manor plantation. Lancelot and George Fairfax Lee were cousins of the Lees at "Stratford," "Lee Hall," and at "Chantilly."

54. "Nomini Hall" was some ten miles distant from the seat of government in Westmoreland County, which is situated in the present town of Montross.

55. Richmond Court House, the seat of government in Richmond County, now called Warsaw, is some ten or twelve miles distant from "Nomini Hall." There were a number of enthusiastic turfmen in Richmond County during the eighteenth century.

56. Colonel John Tayloe (1721-1779) was one of the wealthiest men in the Northern Neck. His manor house, "Mount Airy," was located near Richmond Court House, and overlooked the Rappahannock River, some two miles in the distance. Tayloe was a noted fancier of fine horses.

57. Dr. William Flood lived at "Kinsail," a plantation in Westmoreland County. He frequently combined the pleasures of horse racing with the practice of his profession. Cf. Blanton, Wyndham B., *Medicine in Virginia in the Eighteenth Century* (Richmond, 1931), p. 379.

58. Since it was often difficult to secure a sufficient number of clergymen for the parishes in Virginia, young English schoolmasters and tutors were frequently induced to return to the mother country and take orders so that they might fill such vacancies.

59. Robert Carter's account books reveal that he sometimes had business transactions with one George C. Gordon of Westmoreland County.

60. See catalogue of Robert Carter's library in Appendix, pp. 221-229.

61. Hobb's Hole, the present town of Tappahannock, is situated on the Rappahannock River in Essex County. The town was a lively center of trade and shipping at this period.

62. John Warden was a young Scotsman. While a student in Edinburgh, Warden had been engaged by Dr. Walter Jones of Virginia to serve as a tutor in the family of his brother, Colonel Thomas Jones of Northumberland County. In the Jones home Warden had enjoyed exceptional advantages and he appears to have read law after coming to the colony. He later became a distinguished member of the Virginia bar.

63. Both Richard Lee (1726-1795), commonly called "Squire" Lee, and his cousin, Richard Henry Lee (1732-1794), who was known as "Colonel" Lee, lived on estates on the Potomac River in Westmoreland County. "Squire" Richard Lee's manor plantation was called "Lee Hall." The home of Colonel Richard Henry Lee was known as "Chantilly." A second Richard Lee, also known as "Squire Lee," and a cousin of the above mentioned persons, lived on the Potomac in Charles County, Maryland.

64. This schooner had been named for Carter's daughter, Harriot Lucy.

65. Carter described the harmonica as "the musical glasses without water,

framed into a complete instrument, capable of through bass and never out of tune." Quoted in Williams, ed., *Fithian*, p. 59, fn. 1.

66. The Yeocomico River.

67. Yeocomico Church.

68. Grigg, the captain of an English vessel, often mingled with the plantation families of the Northern Neck when he was in the colony.

69. Letitia Corbin Turberville.

70. William Booth, who was a planter of considerable means in Westmoreland County at this time, was probably the father of this youth.

71. "County-dances" were English dances of rural or native origin, especially those in which an indefinite number of couples stood face to face in two long lines. Country dances had been popular on greens and at fairs in England long before they were introduced into polite society. When the country dance was imported into France the name became *contre-dance*, and it has been erroneously assumed that "country-dance" is a corruption of the French term.

72. Goodlet was apparently a tutor in the Fauntleroy family of "The Cliffs."

73. Philip Ludwell Lee (1727-1775) was the eldest son of Thomas Lee, who had served as president of the Council. He had inherited his father's manor plantation, "Stratford," on the Potomac River in Westmoreland County. Like Robert Carter, Philip Ludwell Lee was now a member of the Council.

74. Probably Elizabeth Lee, daughter of John Lee of Essex County, a nephew of Thomas Lee of "Stratford."

75. Matilda Lee was the daughter of Philip Ludwell Lee of "Stratford." She later married "Light Horse Harry" Lee.

76. One Joseph Lane was a prominent planter in Westmoreland County at this time.

77. This song occurs in an opera, *Artaxerxes*, by Thomas Augustine Arne, which was first performed in

London in 1762. The libretto of Arne was an adaptation of an Italian drama, *Artaserse,* by Metastasio (Pietro Antonia Domenico Bonaventura). Metastasio was born in 1698 and died in 1782.

78. Dr. Walter Jones of "Hayfield" in Lancaster County, was known as "the luminary of the Northern Neck." He was the son of Colonel Thomas Jones, a planter-businessman of Williamsburg and Hanover County. His mother, Elizabeth Cocke, was a niece of Mark Catesby, the well-known English naturalist. Dr. Jones had been educated at the College of William and Mary and he studied medicine at the University of Edinburgh. At the former institution he became a fast friend of Thomas Jefferson and of Bathurst Skelton, whose widow Jefferson later married. Jones achieved distinction both in the field of medicine and in politics. In 1777 he was appointed physician-general of the Middle Department, but declined the office, which was later filled by Dr. Benjamin Rush of Philadelphia. Jones was made a member of the American Philosophical Society in 1774. He served as a member of Congress for a number of years. Dr. Jones' wife was Alice Flood, the daughter of William Flood, the well-known physician and turfman of Richmond County.

79. The custom of firing powder during the Christmas season is one that persists in the South today in various forms.

80. John Lowe (1750-1798), a Scotsman, was the tutor of the children of Colonel John Augustine Washington, a brother of George Washington, at this period. John Augustine Washington's manor plantation, "Bushfield," was located on the Potomac River in Westmoreland County, a short distance from "Nomini Hall" and "Hickory Hill." Lowe was the author of a number of ballads which are still popular in Scotland today. After serving for some time as a tutor and conduct-

ing an academy at Fredericksburg, he was ordained an Anglican clergyman, and appears to have served as minister in both St. George's and Hanover Parishes. An unhappy marriage is believed to have led to a dissipation which resulted in his early death. Cf. Meade, *Old Churches, Ministers and Families of Virginia,* Vol. II, p. 185; *Virginia Magazine of History,* Vol. 29 (January 1921), pp. 102-105.

81. Dr. Henry Francks of Westmoreland County.

82. Dr. Moore Fauntleroy (1743-1802) was the son of William Fauntleroy of Naylor's Hole in Richmond County. Fauntleroy, who had studied medicine in Aberdeen and Edinburgh, practiced in Essex County after his return to Virginia in 1770.

83. Richard Lee of "Lee Hall."

84. The account books of Robert Carter show that William Taylor was at this period overseer of three of Carter's plantations or "quarters," called Dicks, Morgans and Rutters.

85. Thomas Thompson was a well known physician of Westmoreland County. Robert Carter retained the services of Thompson for the blacks on his plantations for a number of years.

86. Probably James Balendine of the firm referred to in the Carter account books as "Messrs. James Balendine & Co."

87. "Dotterell" was an English blooded horse that had been bred by Sir John Pennington. He was regarded as the swiftest in that country with the exception of one, called "Eclipse." Dotterell had been imported into the colony in 1766 by Philip Ludwell Lee of "Stratford" in Westmoreland County.

88. Miss Sarah Stanhope was the housekeeper at "Nomini Hall."

89. Colonel Henry Lee of "Leesylvania."

90. Apparently George Fairfax Lee of "Mount Pleasant."

91. Parson Giberne was not so fortunate in escaping criticism on other occasions. Fithian, himself, notes his gambling several times, and the Reverend Jonathan Boucher, Landon Carter and Robert Wormeley Carter all comment upon it in their journals.

92. See this valentine in Appendix, pp. 230-233.

93. Francis Lightfoot Lee (1734-1797) of "Menokin" in Richmond County was the fourth son of President Thomas Lee of "Stratford." His wife was Rebecca Tayloe, a daughter of Colonel John Tayloe of "Mount Airy." Lee served as a member of the House of Burgesses from Loudoun County and later from Richmond County.

94. Frances Ann Tasker Carter died in 1787 and was buried in the family graveyard at "Nomini Hall." Her husband, who died seventeen years later, was buried in Baltimore.

95. Samuel Griffin Fauntleroy (1759-1826) was the son of Moore Fauntleroy of "The Cliffs" in Richmond County.

96. Leedstown was a thriving center of trade and shipping. It had been incorporated in 1742.

97. John Murray, Earl of Dunmore, served as Governor of the colony from 1771 to 1775. Lady Dunmore did not arrive in Virginia to join him until the latter part of February of 1774.

98. The *Virginia Gazette* was founded by William Parks at Williamsburg in 1736. This journal continued to issue until 1778. In 1766 a rival sheet bearing the same name was established and was published in Williamsburg until 1776. In 1775 a third *Virginia Gazette* had been established which continued to issue until 1780.

99. John Bracken served as minister of Bruton Parish Church at Williamsburg from 1773 to 1818. He also served for a period as master of the grammar school at the College of William and Mary, and for two years as president of the college. At this time Bracken

had just incurred the bitter enmity of Samuel Henley, professor of divinity and moral philosophy at the college, who had hoped to secure the appointment given his rival. The two men aired their grievances in a long and acrimonious controversy carried on in the columns of the *Virginia Gazette*. Henley, a Tory, left the colony for England in 1775 and never returned. He later became principal of the East India College at Hertford.

100. At "Bushfield" on the Potomac River.

101. James Gregory was employed at various seasons to assist and instruct the colored gardeners at "Nomini Hall."

102. Probably Colonel John Tayloe of "Mount Airy."

103. Joseph F. Lane of Loudoun County, Virginia.

104. Phillis Wheatley had been brought from Africa to Boston as a slave in 1761. Educated by the daughters of her owner, John Wheatley, Phillis manifested remarkable acquisitive powers and soon attracted attention by the excellent character of her verse. Her first bound volume, *Poems on Various Subjects, Religious and Moral*, was published in 1773.

105. James Waddell (1739-1805) was an outstanding Presbyterian minister in the colony. His gentle manner and forceful sermons did much to advance the cause of his church. At this period he was the pastor of a congregation in the Northern Neck, composed of families of Northumberland and Lancaster Counties. He later exerted a strong influence in the Shenandoah Valley and Piedmont sections. After 1787 he was blind for a number of years and was later celebrated as "The Blind Preacher" in William Wirt's *The Letters of the British Spy*.

106. An American juniper or "red cedar."

107. William Felton (1713-1769), an English clergyman, was well known in the eighteenth century as a composer, and performer on the harpsichord and organ. "Felton's Gavot," which was long highly popular, had been introduced into Legrenzio Vincenzo Ciampi's opera "Bertoldo in Corte" in 1762. The music was written for the gavot, a lively dance of French peasant origin, in which the feet were raised in the step instead of being slidden.

108. Oliver Reese.

109. Middleton.

110. Mundy's Point is located on the Yeocomico River near the mouth of that stream.

111. Colonel John Tayloe of "Mount Airy."

112. Mrs. John Tayloe of "Mount Airy" was the former Rebecca Plater, daughter of Governor George Plater of Maryland.

113. Mrs. Tayloe.

114. This manor plantation has remained in the possession of Carter's descendants to the present time. The original manor house was destroyed by fire in 1850. A wooden structure erected shortly after that time still stands. Carter's daughter, Harriot Lucy, married a well-known lawyer, John James Maund. A daughter of Harriot Lucy and John James Maund became the wife of Dr. John Arnest. "Nomini Hall" is today the residence of Dr. Arnest's grandson, Mr. T. M. Arnest, who is the great-great-grandson of Councillor Robert Carter. The only known representation of the original manor house is a crude watercolor sketch done by an amateur artist "E. Maund," a relative, who visited the family and made the sketch shortly before the house burned in 1850. One obtains a clearer understanding of the imposing character of this manor house from Fithian's comments regarding it. This is especially true of his observation made when spending an evening once at "Mount Airy," the "elegant seat" of Colonel John Tayloe in Richmond County. "The House," he said,

referring to "Mount Airy," "is about the size of Mr. Carter's. . . ."

115. A merchant mill was a mill in which flour was manufactured and packed for sale. The owner of such a mill customarily purchased wheat for manufacture. In Virginia it was a common practice for the owner of the mill to pay for the wheat in flour. A mill used exclusively for grinding grain for local consumption was called a grist or custom mill. A portion of the grist was usually allowed the owner for his services.

116. The Heale family was a well-known one in Lancaster County where they lived on "Peach Hill" and other manor plantations. The name was apparently pronounced Hale all through the eighteenth century. Priscilla Heale was the daughter of George Heale of Lancaster County. Heale had served as a Burgess from that county.

117. Dr. George Steptoe of "Windsor" in Westmoreland County had been graduated in medicine at Edinburgh in 1767.

118. Miss Sally Panton.

119. Lowe was apparently not licensed as a Presbyterian minister at this time for he shortly afterwards appears as an Anglican clergyman in St. George's and Hanover Parishes in Virginia.

120. Thomas Willing (1731-1821) was associated with Robert Morris in the house of Willing and Morris. He was later president of the Bank of North America and the Bank of the United States.

121. Mrs. Charlotte Belson Thornton was the widow of Colonel Presley Thornton (1722-1769) of Northumberland County. Mrs. Thornton had been born in England and she returned to the mother country with her children just prior to the outbreak of the Revolution. Her three sons served in the British forces during the War. At the conclusion of hostilities two of them, Presley and John Tayloe Thornton, returned to Virginia.

122. Perhaps a member of the Corbin family. Elizabeth Tayloe, sister of Colonel John Tayloe, had married Richard Corbin of "Laneville," in King and Queen County.

123. Dr. John Morgan was one of the founders and most eminent professors of the medical school at Philadelphia which is now a part of the University of Pennsylvania. Morgan later served as director-general of hospitals and physician-in-chief of the American army from 1775-1777.

124. Samuel Leake, Jr., of Cohansie, New Jersey, was at this time a student at Princeton. Leake apparently did not accept the position in Mrs. Thornton's home.

125. Mattox Bridge was some eighteen miles from Westmoreland Court House, and twenty-eight from "Nomini Hall."

126. Round Hill Church was the "upper church of Washington Parish" and stood at the site of what is now the town of Tetotum.

127. Tyler's Ferry in Westmoreland County, Virginia, was opposite Cedar Point on the Maryland side of the Potomac River.

128. Port Tobacco, Maryland.

129. Piscataway, Maryland.

130. Upper Marlborough, Maryland.

131. The Digges family was a well known one in both Maryland and Virginia.

132. Marlborough, Maryland.

133. Alexandria, Virginia.

134. Patuxent River.

135. Rock Hall, Maryland.

136. Chestertown, Maryland.

137. Wall gave a lecture on electricity in Williamsburg, Virginia, the following year. He is doubtless identical with the comedian and "Mental Physician," Dr. Llewellyn Lechmere Wall, who was described as "of Orange County," North Carolina in 1797. He appeared in numerous comedies in Newbern that year. Cf. *Virginia Gazette* (Pinckney, ed.), January 5, 1775; original playbill in Department of Re-

search, Colonial Williamsburg, Inc., Williamsburg, Virginia.

138. Frederick, Maryland.

139. Stockton.

140. Port Penn, Delaware.

141. Warwick, Maryland.

142. A brother of Elizabeth Beatty.

143. James Lyon, a graduate of the College of New Jersey, had compiled and published a large collection of church music, *Urania, or a choice collection of Psalm-Tunes, Anthems and Hymns.*

144. Colonel John Tayloe.

145. "All-fours," derived its name from the four chances involved, for each of which a point was scored. The game was later renamed "seven-up."

146. A brother of Elizabeth Beatty.

147. Israel Evans had been graduated at Princeton in 1772, and had afterwards studied theology under Dr. Witherspoon there.

148. Middleton, Delaware.

149. New Town, Maryland.

150. Stephen Reeve was a Philadelphia silversmith.

151. Tyler's Ferry.

152. See this catalogue of Carter's library in Appendix, pp. 221-229.

153. Mrs. Tayloe.

154. John Dunlap had established the *Pennsylvania Packet* in 1771.

155. Colonel Richard Henry Lee of "Chantilly."

156. This Betsey Lee was perhaps Elizabeth, the daughter of John Lee of Essex County, a nephew of President Thomas Lee.

157. This Elizabeth Lee was the daughter of the late George Lee of "Mount Pleasant" and his first wife Judith Wormeley of "Rosegill" in Middlesex County. She died unmarried.

158. A trill, or rapid reiteration of two notes comprehending an interval not greater than one whole tone, nor less than a semitone.

159. James Marshall, Fithian's predecessor as tutor of the Carter children, had formerly been an usher at the College of William and Mary. Marshall had inherited a plantation in Orange County. The *Virginia Gazette* of April 18, 1773 had announced the death of Marshall, at "Nomini Hall" and had corrected the error in its next issue.

160. The Gaskins family lived in Northumberland County. Elizabeth Gaskins, daughter of Colonel Thomas Gaskins of that County married Edward Digges of "Bellfield" in York County in 1775.

161. The Taliaferro family was a prominent one in Tidewater Virginia. While the name is pronounced "Tolliver," it is believed to be of Italian origin.

162. Richard Parker (1729-1813) of "Lawfield" was a distinguished lawyer in Westmoreland County at this time.

163. Colonel John Tayloe.

164. The Beales were a prominent family in Richmond and Westmoreland counties. Several members of this family had intermarried with the Carters. Robert Carter's uncle, Landon Carter of "Sabine Hall," had taken Elizabeth Beale as his third wife in 1746. Landon's son, Robert Wormeley Carter, married Winifred Beale, and Robert Wormeley's sister, Judith, married Reuben Beale.

165. Colonel John Tayloe.

166. Archibald Ritchie was a prominent merchant of Hobb's Hole.

167. The Edmundsons were a prominent family in Essex County. Thomas Edmundson, whose will was proved in 1759, had a daughter named Dorothy Edmundson.

168. The Brockenbrough family had been a well-known one in Richmond County since the beginning of the eighteenth century. William Brockenbrough (1715-c.1778) had married Elizabeth Fauntleroy, whose sister Mary was the wife of Parson Giberne.

169. Richard Henry Lee of "Chantilly."

170. Richmond County.

171. Richard Buckner (1730-1792) of "Albany" in Westmoreland County was a planter who sometimes had business dealings with Robert Carter. Members of the Buckner family had been prominent planter-merchants in Tidewater Virginia since John Buckner had emigrated from England and settled in Gloucester County shortly after the middle of the seventeenth century. John Buckner had imported the first printing press into the colony.

172. John Duffield was graduated at Princeton in 1773. He served as a tutor there during the next two years.

173. Dr. William Shippen (1736-1806) was a distinguished physician of Philadelphia. He was at this time professor of surgery and anatomy at the medical school of the College of Philadelphia. Shippen had married Alice Lee, a sister of Richard Henry, Arthur, Frances Lightfoot, and William Lee.

174. Thomas Sorrel owned a plantation near "Nomini Hall" in Westmoreland County.

175. Gawin Corbin of "Yew Spring" in Caroline County.

176. Apparently Randolph Carter's clerk.

177. There were frequent references in the *Virginia Gazette* during the previous year to the arrival in Williamsburg of "Dr. Graham, the celebrated oculist and aurist, at Philadelphia."

178. Probably Benjamin Harrison of "Berkeley" in Charles City County, who attended the Congress in Philadelphia in 1774.

179. In 1771 William Rigmaiden was the master of a free school in Richmond County that was supported by Landon Carter. *William and Mary College Quarterly*, Vol. XIII, series 1, p. 158.

180. Colonel John Tayloe.

181. "Chantilly."

182. Kent Islands, Maryland.

183. Queenstown, Queen Anne County, Maryland.

Index